Understanding
I R A N

BOOKS BY WILLIAM R. POLK

Backdrop to Tragedy: The Struggle for Palestine
(with David Stamler and Edmund Asfour)

The Opening of South Lebanon 1788–1840:
A Study of the Impact of the West on the Middle East

The United States and the Arab World

The Arab World

The Arab World Today

Beginnings of Modernization in the Middle East
(editor with Richard Chambers)

The Elusive Peace: The Middle East in the Twentieth Century

The Golden Ode
(translator)

Passing Brave
(with William Mares)

Neighbors and Strangers: The Fundamentals of Foreign Affairs

Understanding Iraq

Out of Iraq: A Practical Plan for Withdrawal Now
(with George McGovern)

Polk's Folly: An American Family History

Personal History: Living in Interesting Times

The Birth of America

The Diary of President James K. Polk
(editor)

Understanding
IRAN

EVERYTHING YOU NEED TO KNOW,
FROM PERSIA TO
THE ISLAMIC REPUBLIC,
FROM CYRUS TO AHMADINEJAD

WILLIAM R. POLK

palgrave
macmillan

First published in hardcover in 2009 by PALGRAVE MACMILLAN® in the
US—a division of St. Martin's Press LLC, 175 Fifth Avenue, New York, NY
10010.

Where this book is distributed in the UK, Europe and the rest of the world,
this is by Palgrave Macmillan, a division of Macmillan Publishers Limited,
registered in England, company number 785998, of Houndmills,
Basingstoke, Hampshire RG21 6XS.

Palgrave Macmillan is the global academic imprint of the above companies
and has companies and representatives throughout the world.

Palgrave® and Macmillan® are registered trademarks in the United States,
the United Kingdom, Europe and other countries.

ISBN: 978-0-230-10343-6

Library of Congress Cataloging-in-Publication Data

Polk, William Roe, 1929–
    Understanding Iran : everything you need to know, from Persia to the
Islamic Republic, from Cyrus to Ahmadinejad / William R. Polk.
        p. cm.
    Includes bibliographical references and index.
    ISBN 0-230-61678-X
    (paperback ISBN 978-0-230-10343-6)
    1. Iran—History. I. Title.
DS272.P65   2009
955—dc22

                                                            2009035743

A catalogue record of the book is available from the British Library.

Design by Letra Libre

First PALGRAVE MACMILLAN paperback edition: January 2011

10 9 8 7 6 5 4 3 2 1

Printed in the United States of America.

For Monique and Raja

Ann and Brican   ✝

Bibi and Gabriel

Liv and Donald

Jane and Hugh

Mary and David   ✝

Nahed and Amr

Beloved friends all.

CONTENTS

ACKNOWLEDGMENTS

*I*n the more than half a century during which I have visited, read about, and relished Iran, I have incurred debts to scores of people. My first visit to Iran was in 1956 with Khodadad Farmanfarmaian, who made me an honorary brother of his large family and gave me my first taste of Persian culture. Later, as head of the Plan Organization, he did much to shape modern Iran. Cyrus Ghani, also a friend since the 1950s, when he was Iran's greatest bibliophile, kindly read sections of this book. My State Department colleague, William Miller, slated to be ambassador to Iran if the hostage crisis was solved, and Kenneth Hansen, a fellow member of the "Iran Task Force," were constantly stimulating. Roy Mottahadeh, briefly my student and later professor of history at Harvard, wrote the best book on Iranian Shiism, *The Mantle of the Prophet*. From Peter Avery, Laurence Lockhart, John Bulliet, Charles Issawi, Nikki Keddie, Joseph Upton, Leonard Binder, John Woods, Marvin Zonis, Donald Wilber, Jahangir Amuzegar, and Richard Frye, each of whom has been a colleague at various times, conferences, and organizations over the many years, I have profited greatly. Juni Farmanfarmaian Ardelan and Farhad Diba checked my transliterations from the Farsi. Finally, I cannot fail to mention Sion Soleimany, my teacher in the fine art of Persian carpets. I have been fortunate to be able to visit Iran frequently, to travel extensively throughout the country, and to discuss and negotiate with many of the major figures of modern Iran. I end by seeking refuge, to paraphrase the common Muslim remark, in a statement by that great scholar on Iran, Edward G. Browne: "that he who would write a flawless book writes nothing [but] even the most imperfect book, [may] prepare the way for a better."

William R. Polk

A FEW WORDS
ON WORDS

During the two thousand years covered in this book, the Iranians spoke, wrote, and read a number of languages and dialects from four of the great "families." The first literate inhabitants in Elam used a language from the Dravidian family; then came the Indo-European peoples from Central Asia whom Herodotus knew as the Medes and the Persians; next a people speaking a Semitic language, the Arabs, invaded and occupied Iran; and finally, over the last thousand years, another Central Asian people, the Turks, brought into Iran a language of the family linguists call East Asian or Ural-Altaic.[1] Dravidian almost completely died out, at least in Iran, but the other languages interacted, borrowing from one another, changing intonation, re-defining concepts, and becoming specialized. This diversity and change offer fascinating insights into culture and history, but make difficult the attainment of clarity in writing.

There is no easy way to overcome this problem. What I have done here is not a perfect solution, but it is the best I could devise. For the early period, I have used the method of transliterating words from ancient languages that is standard in *The Cambridge History of Iran*. The few Turkish or Azari words I have kept I have written in the modern Turkish spellings. It is Arabic and Persian (Farsi) that present the challenge.

In the Middle Ages, Iranian scholars often wrote in Arabic, and Arabic has remained the liturgical language of Islam. As the language in which the Quran was written, it was at the medium of Iranian intellectual exchange over the last thousand years. To thoroughly understand the Quran, scholars, jurists, and moralists believed that they had not only to master its text but also to probe into the vast corpus of pre-Islamic literature. (A parallel attempt to understand more fully the Old Testament, incidentally, was what motivated eighteenth-century European scholars to study Arabic, which they thought to be a "primitive" form of Hebrew.)

Among the members of the Iranian Shia religious establishment, the *ulama,* Arabic also came to be the preferred language of communication. So when I refer to religious matters, I use a simplified transliteration—that is, I omit the diacritical marks that stand for letters that do not occur in English but write the words as they sound in Arabic.

Modern Persian, Farsi, contains a large number of Arabic words and is written in a modified form of the Arabic script. But many of the words are differently pronounced so that several Arabic letters take on modified sounds. For example, the Arabic *q* is pronounced "gh" so that an underground irrigation canal, which is written in the Arabic/Persian script as *Qanat,* becomes in the spoken form *Ghanat;* the Arabic *u* becomes the Persian *o* so that Muharram, the first month of the Islamic lunar year, becomes Moharram; and the Arabic *i* becomes the Persian *e* so that the spiritual guide, the Arabic *Murshid,* is pronounced *Morshed.*

When the words are distinctively Iranian, for figures such as the *molla* (a low-ranking religious figure), concepts such as *moghaled* ("to be required to accept the judgment or ruling of a senior religious figure"), or offices such as the *Marja-e Taghlid* (the ultimate religious authority), I use the standard form of Farsi transliteration. And for names and offices that have been "Englished," I write as they appear in the media, so the former Iranian prime minister is Muhammad Mossadegh.

But this is a book on history and not on language. So, while linguists may argue over the niceties of transliteration, they need not disturb the readers for whom I am writing. I mention them here only so that readers will not be confused if they see Farsi words spelled differently in other books. The spelling differences are minor and can easily be spotted.

FOREWORD

*D*uring the Cold War, mathematicians and economists at the Massachusetts Institute of Technology (MIT) were searching for a means to understand and evaluate trends and events in the conflict. Borrowing from the German army, they hit on the "war game," the *kriegspiel*. What the German General Staff used for essentially tactical military simulations, they elaborated to deal with politics as well as military confrontations. Their "politico-military" version of the war game became a popular tool in university courses on world affairs as well as in the government.

The assumption behind the "game" was that it would enable one to predict reactions to events in an evolving series of "moves"—for example, how "Blue Team" should react to a threatened attack by "Red Team," followed by how "Red Team" would then respond, and so on. War games were used to analyze the 1962 Cuban Missile Crisis, in which I played a small role; they have been repeatedly used since that great event and have been employed to predict reactions in the current conflict between the American-led coalition and Iran. Dozens, perhaps even hundreds, of war games have been "played" by the U.S. Department of Defense and the Central Command (the combined army, air, and naval forces assigned the military role on the frontiers of Iran) to ascertain how much pressure or threat would be required to force Iran to give up its nuclear program and to otherwise not challenge American hegemony in the Middle East.

I find many faults in war gaming, but for my purposes here, two are particularly important. First, implicit in each "scenario" was that conflict was the norm: It was threat, followed by attack and either surrender or counterattack, that was assumed to constitute relations among nations. Second, war gaming assumed that the logic of actions and reactions was so clear that, regardless of whom the opposing teams were presumed to represent, they would always react "logically," guided by a balance sheet of potential profit and loss. Gaming thus views the foreigner as a sort of accountant—culturally disembodied, mathematically precise, and governed by logic. If he does not *add them up accurately* (as the mathematicians taught us to say), then he has "miscalculated." In short, the game posits in him precisely those qualities that do *not* shape our actions.

All other considerations—culture, religion, and memory of historical experience—were essentially irrelevant. So when we apply the lessons of war games to "grand strategy" in our culturally diverse world, the results of the war game are nearly always misleading. It is, in part, my belief that war gaming as a means to understand foreign affairs is fatally flawed that led me to write this book. My aim has been to bring forward what war games omit: in short, what it means when we speak of Iran and Iranians.

I begin in Chapter One, "Becoming Iranian," with how the people we know today as Iranians became a distinct cultural group. Since these people are sometimes called Persians, I must clarify what is meant by the words *Iranian* and *Persian*. To simplify, I call the people who live in Iran "Iranians," just as I would say that those who live in the United States are "Americans." But just as American society is composed of subsets of different groups—Native Americans, African Americans, Latinos, Catholics, Protestants of many varieties, Jews, and Muslims—so Iran is inhabited by peoples who think of themselves as Persians, Turkmens, Arabs, Kurds, Lurs, and various others; followers of different faiths—Shiis, Sunnis, Jews, Christians, Bahais, and Zoroastrians; and people who earn their livelihood in different ways—peasants, nomads, and city people. However, as in America and also in Iran, one cultural group has, so far at least, stamped the whole society with its culture. The early American colonists were mainly English and thus stamped the evolving society with their language and their culture; in Iran, the first dominant group was the ancient people we call Persians, whose Farsi is the dominant language of Iran.

In America, the English-Protestant basis of culture has been transformed over time. The early Americans had to make way for new groups and their ideas. This was also true for Iran: group after group, mainly Arabs and Turks, followed the Indo-European peoples into Iran. Recognizing their diverse background but also anxious to overcome ethnic divisions, today's inhabitants prefer to use as the neutral term Iranian. Indeed, they were ordered to do so by their then king, Reza Shah, in 1935.

𝒥ran has had one of the world's richest and most fascinating historical experiences. One should ask, How much of it is pertinent today? Do Iranians today really remember their past over the last two thousand or so years? Or is this book just a historian's contrived assemblage of events?

My answer is twofold: Much of even the remote past *is* directly remembered by modern Iranians because it is being constantly reinforced—to a degree and with an intensity alien to the Western experience—by the repetition of poetry, folktales, and ceremony. Moreover, national history is studied everywhere and often in Iranian schools, colleges, and universities. Additionally, much is encapsulated in the pervasive and passionate religious observance of the Iranians' Shia sect of Islam.

That is the easy part of my answer; I illustrate it in the following pages. The harder part is what Carl Jung called "the collective unconscious"—the real but hidden memory of what a society accepts as its heritage and the guide to what is "normal." It is this shared substratum of heritage that makes a society distinct. We are guided by it in our choice of what is right and proper, but it is so common that we normally pay no attention to it unless we lose it. What it amounts to is, of course, much harder to document, but we may take it as the summation of the historical experience. I attempt to bring it out by using the historical events as building blocks for my interpretation of Iran.

Related to the collective unconscious—indeed, evolving from it—is what political philosophers have sometimes referred to as the "social contract." That is a crucial but often elusive concept. To put it simply, the social contract is the implicit relationship of a people to one another, to their institutions, and to their leaders. Such an understanding usually evolves over a long period of time as changing circumstances cause shifts in the internal relationships. Sometimes such a contract is made explicit. In the American experience, the social contract was made explicit in the Pilgrims' first document, the Mayflower Compact, and, later, when America's Founding Fathers wrote the Constitution.

Underlying these documents was an implicit agreement on what was "right." If this agreement is overthrown, as occasionally happens in revolutions and wars, then military or police power becomes a paltry force. Put in more familiar circumstances, if the implicit social contract of, say, the inhabitants of Dallas were to be overturned, the whole American army could not keep the peace there. That is exactly what happened in Iran in the months preceding the 1979 revolution: The huge army and security apparatus of Muhammad Reza Shah could no longer control even Tehran. I mention this here to point out that underneath the events we can document in history are other, more intangible mores, conventions, and habits that are real, effective, and pervasive. Thus, for reasons I make clear in this book, I am certain that the inhabitants of Iran today are largely governed by their past regardless of whether they consciously remember it. Because Americans and the British are not part of that heritage, I attempt to make explicit what to Iranians is largely implicit. Thus, I have offered you in this book what might be termed a historical portrait rather than a chronology or a fully spelled-out history.

*W*hy is this worth considering? The humane reason is that we live in a world whose manifest diversity both challenges our understanding and enriches our lives. It would be boring if everyone in the world actually was, as the war gamers profess, interchangeable. A great civilization, Iran is special. The great English scholar of things Persian, Edward G. Browne, at the beginning of the last century compared Iran to a "beautiful garden filled with flowers of innumerable kinds" and remarked that nothing could "compensate the world, spiritually and intellectually, for the loss of Persia."

I agree with him—enjoyment of diversity is enriching to life—but in these difficult times in which we live, I would urge that there is also a practical purpose in figuring out how to get along with people whose cultural guides are different. To put it in crass terms, what will be the reaction of the Iranians, who are governed by a cultural code that is not that of America or Britain, to the threat of force? Fifty years ago, answering that question was a challenge to British strategists who sought to hang on to their oil fields in Iran. They failed. Today, understanding what the Iranians will do in response to threats and incentives, particularly on the nuclear issue, is the challenge that the American government is attempting to meet, so far unsuccessfully. The war gamers would have us believe that Iranian beliefs, mores, and memories are irrelevant, or nearly so. Such a view could mislead us into disaster. But the danger is certainly clear and present today—we can see by current events that Iranians have not reacted as we assumed they would. Perversely, they refuse to act like Americans or the British, and their reactions often appear to us not to be governed by "logic." They are people, not "players."

Thus, as I write, American and British strategists debate whether the application of threats, imposition of more severe sanctions, or actual employment of force will convince the Iranian government to abstain from attempts to acquire a nuclear weapon. They assume that if threats do not work, sanctions might. If relatively mild sanctions do not work, then more severe measures might. That line of action leads next to a blockade, which is, in itself, an act of war. Ultimately, if none of these measures work, bombardment and invasion will.

Let's leave aside moral and legal considerations and focus just on the issue of effectiveness. As stage after stage in the growing and extremely dangerous—indeed potentially catastrophic—confrontation has been reached, Iran has moved steadily forward with its own plan. So it seems reasonable and useful to ask, Why is its reaction to this pressure what we see it to be? I seek to answer that question in terms of the Iranian experience. Because both the answer and the experience are complex, I use history to construct what the intelligence analysts call an "appreciation" of Iran.

J propose, therefore, that you both enjoy the Iranians for the many fascinating experiences embodied in their past and also move toward a world in which we can all live in a greater degree of peace and security. Please join me in both of these quests.

William R. Polk
March 7, 2009

Understanding
IRAN

One

BECOMING IRANIAN

*W*ho were the ancestors of today's Iranians? How did they get to what we today call Iran? How did the first of them become "Persian"?

Answering these queries is the first mission of this book. I start as close to the "beginning" as is possible in order to establish a base from which we can examine the complex evolution of the modern Iranians.

*F*or thousands of years before human events were recorded, Central Asia functioned as a giant heart, pumping periodic jets of nomadic tribesmen into Europe, the Middle East, and South Asia. Why they left their original homelands is unknown and the sagas of their migrations are obscured by "the mists of time," so we see them only once they have arrived at their destinations.

The earliest of the peoples about whom we have at least some information spoke languages in the family we know as Dravidian. The Central Asian heart pulsated along arteries that led south and west. As they pushed outward, tribesmen established themselves on a broad arc of territory ranging from the Indus River in what is today Pakistan, where in the centuries around 2500 BC they founded a flourishing urban culture composed of hundreds of cities and towns, through Iran, further across Anatolia, and perhaps all the way to Italy, where they may have been the people we know as Rome's teachers and rivals, the Etruscans. In these various places, they created what were the first great civilizations. They laid the foundation stones of history.

Following on the heels of the Dravidian speakers were the first groups of another great wave. These nomadic peoples spoke languages from the family of which both English and Persian are members; we call them Indo-Europeans.[1]

What particularly distinguished the Indo-Europeans from the Dravidians was that, sometime around four thousand years ago, they managed to domesticate the horse. That accomplishment enabled them to move rapidly over vast distances and gave them overwhelming military superiority over more sedentary peoples. Mounted on or pulled by horses, they fanned out over much of Asia and Europe beginning about 2000 BC. We can follow their movements today by the telltale markers of DNA inherited by their descendants.

As they moved, they interacted with already resident peoples so that, over centuries, they gradually became Greeks, Romans, Germans, Slavs, Indians, and Persians. Much later, as other waves followed, they would become the ancestors of the French, Spaniards, Scandinavians, and English. So they are part of the bloodline from which most of us are also descended.

The Indo-European–speaking nomads shared veneration for the animal that had made their migrations possible, the horse. It became their "magical animal," or totem. One of the great nomadic groups that invaded Europe, the Goths, took their name from their word for "horses." Another group, ancestors of the Persians, used personal names derived from their word for "horses." Around the horse, Romans, Greeks, Indians, and Persians, among others, elaborated rituals that exemplified religion, defined politics, and even governed foreign relations. The first great Persian king was commemorated by the sacrifice of a horse each month at his tomb, and Indian kings regulated their frontiers periodically by allowing a horse to run wild among them. Horses even gave our ancestors their distinctive drink—one that Central Asian nomads still relish—*khumiss*, fermented mare's milk.

As important as it was, the horse was just one of a trio of developments that enabled the Indo-Europeans to shape world history. The second of the three great innovations was the light two- or four-wheeled chariot, which came into use sometime around 1800 BC. In fact, the oldest written document in an Indo-European language is a manual on training chariot horses. Riding on a chariot, even a few warriors could achieve tactical superiority over a much more numerous but immobile infantry force. Like the modern tank, the horse-drawn carriage was widely adopted by friend and foe. Horse-drawn chariots became both the symbols and reality of military victory. The charioteers, known as *rathaeshtars,* soon formed a new social class similar in status and function to medieval European knights.

The third of the revolutionary changes was the weapon that would dominate warfare for nearly three thousand years—the bow. Possibly because they did not have suitable wood in sufficient quantities, the Central Asian nomads invented the most powerful variety, the compound bow, which got its strength from the use of bone and sinew in the shaft. Homer makes managing to pull it the arbiter among Odysseus' rivals for Penelope, and the Egyptian pharaoh Amen-hotep II brags that there was no one among his soldiers who could draw his bow. Its later adaptation, the crossbow, was regarded as so lethal a weapon that when it was introduced into Europe in the twelfth century AD, the Church banned it for warfare among Christians. The bow was the original weapon of mass destruction.

What the Indo-Europeans first brought to Iran from Central Asia in those dim early times set the theme for much of later history. Everywhere they went, they overwhelmed existing societies. Because of the horse, the chariot, and the compound bow, we and the modern Iranians are distant cousins.

It was not only weapons of war that the Indo-Europeans brought to the West: They also brought religious ideas that, as I later elaborate, deeply influenced Judaism, Christianity, and Islam.

The original religion of the Indo-Europeans focused on the great forces of nature, which—as nomadic herdsmen, exposed as they were to rain, lightning, thunder, and wind—their shamans personified as gods. We know them best from the Greek and Norse myths and legends as Zeus (the sky god), Apollo (the sun god), and Poseidon (the earthquake god).

The nomads merged their religion, as they did their language and their "magic animal," into the cults and practices of the people among whom they settled—the local, agricultural peoples. The religions of the settled peoples they encountered in Iran, India, Greece, and elsewhere were more closely tied to the earth because the people were so bound to it. What mattered most to them was what they believed controlled the production of crops. Thus, while the nomadic religion had no permanent holy sites but was drawn from the ever-changing forces of nature, the religion of the settled people was fixed in sanctuaries of sacred groves, rivers, caves, and mountains. Over time, the two schemes—the "sky" and the "earth" religions—merged in new and diverse patterns and gave birth to new visions of the spirit world.

As they became more sophisticated, the Indo-Europeans and their new kinsmen underwent a major change in their religion. How it happened, we do not know, but the primitive Central Asian "sky religion" and its modification with the addition of "earth religions" began to be recast or reinterpreted, presumably first by tribal shamans. A whole range of new questions began to be posed. How had life begun? What was man's relationship to the unseen powers? How could people protect themselves in the dangerous world? How could they ward off or prepare for death? The general answer of the shamans was that the gods must be appeased by ritual, prayer, and sacrifice. From this beginning, what gradually took shape among the people who would become Persians was an urbane, complex, and sophisticated cultural pattern that would underlie the actions of successive Iranian rulers and their societies for centuries and, in broad outline, still exists today as the Zoroastrian religion. It would also contribute to shaping the Shia Islamic religion that today molds Iranian life. The religion that the great Persian prophet Zoroaster began to codify was the first coherent cosmology and theology.[2]

Although there are many myths and legends about Zoroaster, we know almost nothing about him, not even when he lived. Scholars have put forward guesses that are a thousand years apart—anywhere between roughly 1500 and 500 BC. What he said was memorized and repeated until written down long after his life; those writings contain thoughts and descriptions suggesting that he lived when the Indo-European invasions had begun but before the Medes and Persians arrived in Iran (i.e., perhaps around 1200 BC). So completely, however, was he to encapsulate the yearnings, beliefs, and fears of the Persians that his doctrine, finally set forth in the *Avesta,* became the Iranian "church" for hundreds of years—and it is still extant in Iran and India (where its followers are called Parsees)—and it deeply influenced Judaism, Christianity, and Islam. So to understand the Persians and today's Iranians, we need to understand Zoroastrianism.

Zoroaster proclaimed that there was a single god, Ahura Mazda (also called Ohrmazd), who was the creator of both the physical world (*getig*) and the spiritual world (*menog*). The fundamental question that Zoroaster confronted—the question that prophets and theologians of all religions must attempt to answer—was: If there is a supreme being who is beneficent, why do we experience evil, sickness, and death?

What we all seek, health, happiness, eternal life, what Zoroaster called "The Truth" (*asha*) obviously had not prevailed on earth; the "Lie," or Evil remained. Because people suffered and died, it was clear, he believed, that there were two forces at work: The Good comes directly from the supreme god, Ahura Mazda, who dwells in the "Abode of Light." Opposed to the supreme god, but also created by him, was disorder, untruth, and evil, known as *drug*. *Drug* was the preserve of Ahriman, the Devil, whose abode is darkness. Ahriman and his henchmen, the *daevas,* oppose humanity's well-being and seek to corrupt the *ashavan,* those the King James version of the Old Testament calls "the Righteous." Ahriman and his devils and fiends employed magic and greed to entice the *drugvant,* the human wicked, or, as the Quran calls them, the "corrupters of the Earth" (*al-fasiduna ʿala'l-ard*) to tempt the Righteous.

Human life is thus a struggle between good and evil, *asha* and *drug*. In this struggle, humankind is not passive; each living person has a role to play. Indeed, man was created precisely to play this role, and, willing or not, he must do so. Some humans will be *drugvant,* and the *ashavan* must struggle against them. The outcome of their contest is ultimately predestined: Ahura Mazda will prevail. But this final victory in the far-distant future does not relieve the living from their tasks. They can take heart from the belief that, on "the Last Day" (the *rasho-keretfi* or *frashegird*), a world savior or messiah, the *Soshyant,* will return to earth to raise the dead and judge them, passing them through holy fire to burn away their sins.

What Zoroaster taught was that, although originally all creation was at rest, it was set in motion in a sort of "big bang" to create the physical world as we know it. At that point, the cycle of life and death, the daily motion of the sun across the sky, and the parade of seasons were begun. That first day, although the original meaning is now forgotten, is known in Persian as *No Ruz,* and it is still celebrated as a feast of joy with the coming of spring on March 21 each year.

Many incidental notions that figure in later religious thought first occur in the *Avesta*. The notion of a "poor man of good will," the *dregush,* seems to have been a sort of forerunner of the later Muslim *dervish*. The concept of ritual cleanliness and ritual cleaning carries over into Hinduism and Islam and is particularly strong in Judaism. The belief that God has ordained a code of life, the Law, incumbent on every living person is particularly strong in Islam.

The idea of the Last Day is echoed in the Bible and is believed by religious fundamentalists throughout the Western world today. Fire (*atakhsh*), particularly central to Zoroastrianism and present in its temples as an emanation of the divinity, will, on the Last Day, cleanse or punish the newly arisen dead. Raising, healing, or punishing the dead is, of course, a belief common among Jews, Christians, and Muslims. On the Last Day, the newly purified and arisen dead will be given the gift of eternal life (*anosh*). Also strongly asserted in Judaism, Christianity, and Islam is the role on that Last Day of God's agent— the Hebrew and Christian messiah, the Muslim *mahdi*, and the Zoroastrian *Soshyant*—who will "return" to earth to perform God's final work with humankind. Finally, and even more important, is the concept of a single, supreme God, which is fundamental to Judaism, Christianity, and Islam. Thus, at a minimum, we can say that Zoroastrianism prepared Iran for the advent of Islam.

The land of today's Iran is different in several respects from the lands of the ancient inhabitants. The peoples we know as the Persians called their land Parsa, but Parsa was just a small part of the country that was known in history as Persia. Persia was officially renamed Iran in 1935, and after the 1979 revolution it became known as the Islamic Republic of Iran. Today's Iran is about the size of a combination of the American states Texas, New Mexico, Colorado, Oklahoma, Kansas, and Arkansas, or the United Kingdom, Ireland, France, Germany, Switzerland, Holland, Belgium, and Denmark.

The modern state of Iran is situated in an extraordinarily complicated neighborhood, sharing about 4,400 kilometers (approximately 2,734 miles) of frontiers with Iraq, Turkey, Armenia, Azerbaijan, Turkmenistan, Afghanistan, and Pakistan and a long coast fronting the Caspian Sea, the Persian Gulf, and the Indian Ocean. At various periods in its history, it was far larger, comprising much of what we now call the Middle East (i.e., additional territories in what today is divided among Turkey, Syria, Lebanon, Palestine, Israel, Egypt, Yemen, Oman, Saudi Arabia, Bahrain, Kuwait, and Iraq to the west and south, and Azerbaijan, Turkmenistan, Afghanistan, and Pakistan to the east). (See map.)

Most of modern Iran is made up of a high desert with less than the eight inches of rainfall needed to sustain agriculture. In the mountains, the Zagros on the western frontier and the Elbruz in the north, rainfall is heavier than

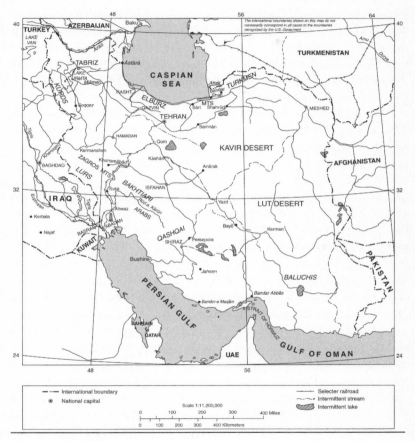

Sketch map of modern Iran

on the plains, but it falls mainly during the winter months when it is less beneficial to agriculture. Consequently, agriculture has been largely concentrated
in oases or in their extensions through irrigation. Long before pipes and
pumps were available, the early Persians invented a remarkable system of underground canals, known as *ghanats,* that took water long distances from
sources to where crops could be grown. Some of these channels required the
digging of vertical shafts as much as a hundred meters (328 feet) to excavate
the earth and keep the water flowing. Where agriculture could not be practiced, the population existed by nomadism based on herding animals, often
trekking hundreds of miles over great mountain barriers from the lowland
pastures in the winter to upland meadows in the summer.[3]

The eastern expanses of Iran are composed of a mainly salt desert about
a thousand meters (over 3,200 feet) above sea level with virtually no rainfall; in
contrast, one-sixth of Iran is about twice as high with often heavy rainfall. Tem-
peratures vary greatly from the northern highlands' mean monthly average of
−10° C to 20° C (14° F to 68° F) along the Persian Gulf. The summer temperature on the coastal lands of the Gulf sometimes reaches 53° C (127.5° F) with
high humidity, whereas the lush, tropical coastal strip along the Caspian Sea in
the north is adjacent to Iran's ski resorts. So there are extreme contrasts from
high to low, cold to hot, wet to dry, and lush to barren.

A notable feature of Iran today is that in 1909 an oil field was brought
into production near the Persian Gulf. Large gas reserves were subsequently
found and developed nearby. Plentiful and usually cheap Iranian energy has
played a major role in the industrialization of the European developed world
ever since and today turns the wheels of Asia. Currently, Iran produces about
8 percent of the world's energy supply. The way these resources were developed, as we shall see, was often skewed to fit the world market rather than the
needs of the country and often was a cause of disruption and discontent
rather than support and security for Iran.

The land that the ancient Persians thought of as their *original* homeland is
also different from modern Iran. Their ancestors thought they had "origi-
nated" in an area situated in what is now northern Afghanistan, Uzbekistan,
and Tajikistan, which they called *Aryana Vaejah* (the homeland of the
Aryans). When they were driven out or launched themselves from that area
sometime around 800 BC, the Indo-European peoples who would become

Persian moved south of the Caspian Sea along the Elbruz mountain chain. As they reached the northern part of what is today Iraq, they ran into one of the most powerful empires ever known, Assyria. The Assyrians stopped them in their tracks, massacring some and enslaving others. Pushed back toward the east, one group of them, known as the Mada or Medes, settled in what is now northern Iran, where they became agriculturalists and formed a number of small village "kingdoms." Then sometime in the seventh century BC, most of these separate kingdoms merged into a more or less unified state.

Other tribes of Indo-Europeans slowly made their way south to the hinterland of the Persian Gulf, where both they and their area were known to the ancient Greeks as *Persis* and to themselves as *Parsa*. It is from *Parsa* that the word *Persia* is derived. What little we know of them comes mainly from the observations of the man Cicero called "the Father of History," the great Greek traveler, gossip, and observer Herodotus. Herodotus was not a casual observer. Curious he was, but his curiosity had a practical, even hard, edge. The Medes and the Persians had merged into Iran's first empire in around 553 BC. It was expanding and already ruled Herodotus's home city. It seemed poised to take over the whole Western world, which in his time was made up of scores of small Greek-speaking *poleis* (city-states). He wanted to understand how the Persian Empire arose, how it was organized, who lived in it, how strong it was, and what its intentions were. It is this search for information that drove him to write what today we could think of as a "national intelligence survey" of the kind produced by the Central Intelligence Agency. That is what makes his quest seem so "modern" and so relevant to us today. But there was much more in Herodotus than just observations on the Persians. His was an open and hungry mind, and he sought a deeper understanding of all the peoples of the "East" who made up the then vast Persian Empire. Although he was culturally Greek, Herodotus was a Persian subject. Born about 485 BC on the west coast of Asia Minor in the little Greek city-state of Halicarnassus (now the Turkish city of Bodrum), he was uniquely qualified to try to understand both political systems. He listened to the Persians as carefully as he listened to his own people and meticulously reported even what must have affronted his Greek pride.

Remarkably, Herodotus details the Greek violations of what were then regarded as sacred preserves of diplomatic usage. They included a contemporary parallel to the Iranian seizure of the American embassy in Tehran in November 1979 and the imprisonment of the American diplomats. In

Herodotus' time, when Persian envoys were sent to Sparta and Athens to negotiate a ceasefire, the Spartans and Athenians threw them "into a pit like criminals." To try to make amends, the Spartans sent two volunteers to the Persian Shah to atone with their lives for what Sparta had done. Xerxes, says Herodotus, "with truly noble generosity replied that he would not behave like the Spartans, who by murdering the ambassadors of a foreign power had broken the law which all the world holds sacred."

Much of what Herodotus wrote, like much that is written on Iran today, was based on hearsay, and some of it was wrong. For his mistakes, he apologized in advance, writing, "My business is to record what people say, but I am by no means bound to believe it." So generations of scholars have dissected his work, correcting, reinterpreting, and augmenting it, as no doubt future scholars will do to the flood of works on contemporary Iran by modern observers. Herodotus traveled widely and talked to an astonishing range of both Greeks and Persians; he was a humane, observant, and open-minded student of the way people of his time—not only the Persians but also his own people, the Greeks—lived and thought. It is the search for a similar understanding of the issues and peoples of our times that motivated me to write this book.

Shortly before Herodotus' time, in the middle of the sixth century BC, a man of the Parsa peoples of the south, Cyrus, who was a vassal of the Median ruler of the north, had achieved dominance over the Medes in what was apparently a sort of coup d'état. Merging the Medes and the Parsa, he laid the basis for the superpower of his time, the Achaemenid Empire. It was the first great Iranian empire.

Surprisingly, we know little of Cyrus, although he became the archetype of the Persian ruler and perhaps the most famous man in Persian history. He conquered most of western Asia, but, judged by the standards of his time, he was both humane and tolerant. Unlike earlier and later rulers, both Eastern and Western, he did not massacre the people he conquered and did not try to suppress local cults. While in Babylon, he gave the resident Jews, whom the Assyrians had exiled to the "Babylonian Captivity," permission to return to Jerusalem and restored to them the temple utensils that Nebuchadnezzar had confiscated. In appreciation, the Jews referred to him as "the anointed of the Lord," and Isaiah said of him, "He is my shepherd." Jews even used the word *messiah* for him. To his own people, not only the Parsa but also the Medes, he was a father figure. The Greeks also sang his praises. The Greek mercenary soldier and historian Xenophon thought of him as the ideal of monarchy, and Alexander the Great is said to have tried to model his imperial persona on Cyrus.

Cyrus had great virtues, but his faults too were monumental. He was vain, headstrong, and avaricious. He often chose war rather than diplomacy to gain his objectives, and when he warred, he did so in a remarkably sophisticated fashion. In fact, some of the innovations of Cyrus and his immediate successors were not duplicated by other countries' armies for centuries.

Sophisticated propaganda was another hallmark of the Persian regime. When three Greek spies were caught snooping on the Persian army, the Persian military commanders condemned them to death, but the Persian king, Cyrus' successor Xerxes, had them brought to him and escorted around his encampment

> to see the whole army, infantry and cavalry, and then, when they were satisfied that they had seen everything, let them go . . . pointing out [to his military commanders] that, if the spies had been executed, the Greeks would not have been able to learn in good time how incalculably great the Persian strength was—and the killing of three men would not have done the enemy much harm; but if, on the other hand, the spies returned home, he was confident that their report on the magnitude of the Persian power would induce the Greeks to surrender their liberty before the actual invasion took place, so that there would be no need to go to the trouble of fighting a war at all.

As Herodotus tells us, the empire established by Cyrus and enlarged by his followers stretched eastward from the Mediterranean (i.e., from western Anatolia, some of the Greek islands, Phoenicia, Palestine, and Egypt) right across the Middle East to the lands north of modern Afghanistan and down into modern Pakistan. The problem for the Persians, as for all ancient peoples, was to hold together such a vast space with primitive means of transport and communication. The Persian answer was a road system that would be unmatched until the time of the Roman Empire centuries later. As Herodotus recounts, on the "Royal Road" from the main city in western Anatolia, Sardis (near modern Izmir), to the capital Susa in western Iran, a distance of about 2,500 kilometers (1,600 miles), travelers were served by some 111 "recognized stations, with excellent inns, and the road itself is safe to travel. . . . [A] man will take just ninety days to make the journey." But urgent messages could be sent by relays of post riders in just nine days. "There is nothing in the world which travels faster than these Persian couriers," Herodotus wrote.

Although an intelligent and open-minded man, Cyrus, like some modern rulers, failed to appreciate the fundamental fact of political life. Herodotus clearly identified it: "Everyone without exception believes his own native customs, and the religion he was brought up in, to be the best; and that being so, it is unlikely that anyone but a madman would mock at such things. There is abundant evidence that this is the universal feeling about the ancient customs of one's country." People everywhere resist when they are invaded by foreigners, even if they come with benign intent.

As we too have painfully learned, even with overwhelming force, war is always uncertain. Cyrus' insatiable quest for glory and his belief that he was God's instrument for imposing order on the fragmented and dangerous world were to lead to his destruction at the hands of the greatest unknown woman ruler of all time, the queen of the Scyth peoples, Tomyris.

Queen Tomyris confronted Cyrus at the end of his triumphal march through western Asia. The queen sent a message saying, "Glutton as you are for blood . . . get out of my country with your forces intact. . . . If you refuse, I swear by the sun our master to give you more blood than you can drink, for all your gluttony." Indeed she did. When Cyrus was killed in the ensuing battle, one of Tomyris' soldiers cut off his head and delivered it to the queen. His fate fitted her warning. As Herodotus tells us, Tomyris "pushed his head into a skin which she had filled with human blood."

Cyrus' bloody end did not, of course, stop the military machine he had created, nor did it daunt his successors. Once created, military machines are hard to stop, and those who stand at their head are pushed as often as they lead. The great wars lay ahead. Huge as it was, the superpower of its age, the Persian Empire impacted on events far beyond its frontiers, even in peace. This process worked both by expulsion—some of its subject peoples migrated and formed new cities in what is today Italy—and by attraction. Its enormous army incorporated detachments from virtually all the peoples of North Africa, the Middle East, and Central Asia. Its "security policy" caused it to transfer whole populations from their ancestral areas to distant places and thus mingle languages and peoples. In its quest for power, Cyrus' dynasty reformed virtually the whole of the Middle East. It was a policy some modern rulers would like to follow.

Coming against Persian power, the Greeks developed for the first time, temporary and incomplete as it proved to be, a contemporary sense of Greek nationhood and the more enduring idea of Hellenic civilization and liberty against "Oriental" barbarism and tyranny. Indeed, our concept of "East versus West"—or, as it has been called, "the clash of civilizations"—arises from Greek opposition to Persia. As we listen to Greek propaganda, we envisage just this theme—which is strikingly apposite today—but it is largely a myth. In their own time, the Greeks deeply admired the Persians. The "nation" for each person was his own city-state, his *polis*—the Greek word from which the English word *politics* derives. Greece was bitterly divided into hundreds of these little societies. Many people—even kings who were driven in exile from their city-states, as was one Spartan king—went to live at the Persian court. When Cyrus' successors invaded Greece, many, indeed probably most, of the Greek city-states sided with the Persians. Even the Delphic Oracle famously advised the Greeks to make offerings of earth and water, which symbolized Persian hegemony.

Why did the Persians invade Greece? After all, there was little in Greece that would have enriched Persia and much that would have drained its resources. At the time, many of the Greek city-states were hovering on the brink of famine. The answer, I believe, must be the same that drove Cyrus to his death in Central Asia—vanity and avariciousness. But perhaps there is a lesson in the event that even we could heed. Arguably, Cyrus' successor Darius can be regarded as the first of the neoconservatives: He was convinced that he had a mission, even a divine mission, and that, by defeating Greece, he could restructure the world because, he believed, all the lands of the Mediterranean would follow Greece into the Iranian world empire. Moreover, the Persians deprecated the Greeks, whom they regarded as a little people for their violence, intolerance, and division. After a show of force, they would surely see the light and welcome the Persians with open arms, even with flowers in their hands. This would happen, the Persians were sure, because the Greeks needed the Persians. Left to themselves, the Greeks would destroy one another. They were too uncivilized to live in an ordered world—as they showed when the Spartans and Athenians violated the sacred rules of diplomacy. They were just an unruly nation of shopkeepers, petty people mired in materialism, with no lofty aspiration or saving grace. Shortly after the disastrous Peloponnesian War, when they nearly destroyed one another, the Greek states were appealing to the Persian Empire for protection from one another and willingly surrendered to the Persians that liberty that they have told us was the essence of their legacy.

*O*ne effect of the long series of conflicts in Greece was that the balance of power among the Greek states, unstable as it always was, completely shattered. This opened an opportunity for the near-barbarian state on the edges of the Greek world, Macedonia. There, for years, an ambitious and shrewd ruler had been preparing a powerful army. As would later be said of Prussia, Macedonia had made warfare into the state industry. So when King Philip died in 336 BC, his son, Alexander, inherited a military force that no Greek city could counter. Alexander's Macedonia had been a Persian ally during the great invasions, and when they withdrew he quickly subdued the Greek states. But for him they were merely stepping-stones; the Persian Empire was the great prize. Three years after becoming king of Macedonia, he attacked Persia.

In a series of battles, Alexander crashed through the Persian Empire: From Egypt, through Syria to Iraq, on to Central Asia and Afghanistan, and down to India, he chased the Persian ruler and destroyed his armies. As he moved east, he killed off the royal family, disrupted the bureaucracy, and suppressed the "church" that had held the Persian Empire together, razing Zoroastrian temples, massacring the Zoroastrian priests, the *magi,* and trashing their holy books. We have no record of the Persian reaction to the invasion, yet as one of the foremost scholars of the period has written,[4] we can

> guess at the bewilderment and profound distress that the rout of the Persian army, the fall of the royal house, and the emergence of the Greeks as masters must have caused in the heartland of Iran. A faint echo of the people's dismay and the priests' outrage is found in the Zoroastrian Pahlavi literature, which remembers the "accursed" (*gijastag*) Alexander as the destroyer of fire-temples, the burner of the holy scriptures, and the murderer of the magi; the early Sasanian propaganda portrayed him as the annihilator of Iran's unity and power. . . .

Alexander was oblivious to the Persian attitude toward him, unsatisfied with his victories, and thoughtless about the damage and pain he was causing. Paradoxically, in the course of his attack, or perhaps in part from what he knew of Persia before his invasion, he developed a sort of love affair with the

Persian culture, people, and what he clearly saw as its world image. As he moved eastward toward India, he tasted the delights of a culture far richer than that of primitive Macedonia, and he began to copy Persian dress, court ritual, and etiquette. After a brief incursion into India, where his exhausted army revolted, he began his return toward the west. When, after what must have been a soul-searing march (to which, from knowing the area, I personally can attest) through the scorching and nearly waterless deserts of southern Iran, he reached Susa, the then capital, he decided on one of the most dramatic and bizarre exhibitions ever enacted: Dressed as a Persian, he performed the Persian marriage ceremony, taking Roshanak, the daughter of the defeated Persian emperor, as his wife and marrying out to 80 of his senior officers captive young women of the noblest Persian families. Then to cap the occasion, he arranged that ten thousand of his soldiers marry their mainly Persian camp followers: East was to meet West on the bridal bed. Alexander then enrolled into what had been the Macedonian army some thirty thousand Persian youths, dressed in the Persian army battle uniform. All this, said Arrian, a Greco-Roman historian and military commander, "was a cause of deep resentment to the Macedonians, who could not but feel that Alexander's whole outlook was becoming tainted with orientalism, and that he no longer cared a rap for his own people or his own native ways." Indeed, we now know that Alexander planned to go still further: His dream was that the Persian capital, Susa, would become the capital of the world and that from the ruins of the Persian Empire, stiffened by Macedonian troops, would emerge a new world state. Alexander proclaimed his wish in the form of a prayer, "that Persians and Macedonians might rule together in harmony as an imperial power."

For Alexander, the prayer was not answered. He died in 323 BC in Babylon. His generals then fought over his legacy; his dream of a world empire split into warring states. What had been the eastern part of the Persian Empire was seized by his general Seleucus, who solidified his claim to empire by capturing the old capital of Babylon in 312 BC and building a new capital near Ctesiphon on the Tigris River. He and his half-Persian son and their successors were able to keep at least a part of their empire for nearly three centuries.

Not only in the east but also in the central Persian world, during the centuries after Alexander's death, there was a sort of replay of early Indo-European history: A new group of Central Asian "Persian" or at least

Indo-European nomads swept into the northeastern part of what had been Cyrus', Alexander's, and Seleucus' empire. In fact, throughout the centuries since Cyrus, nomads in small groups and even whole tribes were periodically arriving in Iran. We do not know the individual tribal names; most are referred to as *Scyths* or *Sakas,* words that probably simply meant "nomads." Already at the battle of Marathon, some of these peoples served in the invading Persian army. There must have been dozens of others in the following years. But in the third century BC, a group large enough and significant enough to be remembered began to arrive from Central Asia. Known as the Parmi, they were or became Persian-speaking and founded the second great Persian empire, the Parthian.

At first, the Parthians, like the other nomadic invaders, served the ruling power in Iran as governors of one of the eastern Iranian *satraps* (provinces), but they soon aspired to take Persia for themselves. Around 230 BC, their then chief declared his independence from the Seleucid Empire and made himself king of the Parthians as Arsaces I. Emphasizing a return to the Zoroastrian religion, whose priests, the *magis,* had come to be regarded as the guardians of Persian culture during the "foreign" domination, the Parthians restored the symbols of "Persia," its original alphabet and calendar, and brought to the fore what Iran had never before had, a sort of national church, *Mazdaism,* based on the teachings of Zoroaster. Thus, Arsaces and his successors gradually unified the Persians enough to drive the Seleucids out of Iran. In 141 BC, they completed the task when they captured Babylon.

Having reclaimed "Iran," they found themselves almost too successful. Although they won all the major battles, they needed help to win the peace. So like Asian and African colonies in our own times, they turned to their former European overlords for help, in this case, the Greeks. Strikingly, their leader did something difficult to imagine a nationalist leader in Asia or Africa doing in our times: The Parthian conqueror of Babylon took as his reign title "Lover of the Greeks" (*Philhellene*). He then set about promoting a new form of the melding of Persian and Greek culture: The religion was Zoroastrian, the language both Greek and Persian, the national myth drawn less from Cyrus than from Alexander,[5] but the military power remained Central Asian. Initially, at least, this coalition of ideas and practices was overwhelmingly powerful. But the Parthians soon ran into an opponent against which, over the longer term, no contemporary could resist—Rome.

Rome was drawn into Iran as it was drawn into Spain, Gaul, Switzerland, Germany, and England: because of the ambitions of its rulers. The first
to move was Pompey, who from 69 to 63 BC threatened the Parthian state.
Pompey did not get very far because he was too involved in Rome's other
wars. However, a decade later, the Roman general Crassus followed up Pompey's earlier foray. Apparently, he believed, as have some later commanders,
that the Persians would greet him with flowers. But he was prepared to ensure that they would do so not merely from love, but also from fear. So he led
into Iran what he thought was an overwhelming force of about thirty-six
thousand troops; for the times, the invading army was indeed a massive armada. Some twenty-eight thousand of these men were the elite of the Roman
military establishment, its disciplined legionnaires. Another ten thousand
were battle-trained Gaulish veterans of the wars in areas that became France,
Switzerland, and Germany, lent to the coalition by Julius Caesar. The Romans
and Gauls outnumbered the Persian force by nearly four to one. But the Persian force was made up of cavalry. About a thousand of them, the *cataphracti*,
resembled medieval Western knights encased in heavy armor; riding not the
small ponies of the nomads but huge destriers, they were the Persian shock
troops. Another seven thousand or so were light cavalry armed with the Central Asian compound bow. The Persians ensured a supply of missiles by following their forces with a train of camels bearing vast numbers of arrows.
The ensuing encounter—Roman infantry against Persian cavalry—was not
so much a battle as a massacre: The Persian horsemen circled out of range of
the Roman infantry's swords and javelins and deluged them with arrows. The
result was that nearly twenty-eight thousand Romans were killed and ten
thousand marched off as prisoners. The battle of Carrhae in 53 BC was the
greatest military disaster the Roman Republic ever suffered. The Parthian
Empire had established itself as the other power in a bipolar world.

When he was assassinated, Julius Caesar was readying his armies to attack Iran; then, fearing Antony's vengeance for Caesar's death, Brutus and
Cassius turned to the Iranians to save themselves. The Iranians could not save
them but took the opportunity to invade the Roman Levant, where they allied themselves with the Jews. It was to divide them that Antony made Herod
the king of Judea. In an interlude of his affair with Cleopatra in Egypt, Antony
went on to attack Iran, and under him Rome lost another army to the dash-
ing Iranian horse-borne bowmen.

The Roman-Parthian war was one in which both sides lost. The Romans were quicker to recover, given their vast resources, population policy, and aggressive leadership. Determined to make up for their humiliating defeats, time after time they invaded Parthian territory. Nero stopped his indulgences long enough in AD 59 to order an invasion, Trajan followed a generation later in AD 86, Verus attacked Iran in AD 164, and Septimus Severus led his armies in a devastating raid in AD 198. The Romans not only intermittently harassed the frontiers but even destroyed the Parthian capital at Ctesiphon on the Tigris. Because they had no means to duplicate the Roman ability to convert aliens into members of their society, the Parthians were always outnumbered by the Romans. Worse, over the succeeding generations, members of the Parthian royal family fell out among themselves time after time. As they proved unable to prevent Roman raids, their subjects judged that they had lost their right to rule.

Worse than these military engagements was the first of the great epidemics that were to change the course of history: Smallpox appeared among the people of the Persian-Indian Kushan kingdom in what is now Pakistan and southern Afghanistan and spread to the West. Because no one had immunity against it, the onslaught of the disease was lethal: In some areas, one in four people perished. A sort of peace of the graveyard descended on both the Parthians and the Romans. As one modern historian has written, "this disaster was the greatest single cause of the decline of Roman civilization."[6] The effects on the Parthians are undocumented, but they must have been similar to those on Rome: disastrous.

So it was that around AD 224, the governor of the central province of Pars broke away to establish a new order that became the Sasanian Empire. The Sasanian was to be the third of the great Persian empires. Its task, it must have seemed to its rulers, was to restore the concept of Iran. Central to this task was the role of religion. So it is to the Sasanian period that the codification of Zoroastrianism into the state religion and the state "church" of Mazdaism can be attributed.

The great figure of this movement was the Zoroastrian religious leader Kartir, known in Persian as the *magupat,* or chief of the *Magi.* Kartir was honored as an *ehrpat*—"a master of knowledge"—a Zoroastrian title comparable to the modern Shia Muslim title *Ayatollah.* Indeed, remarkably resembling Ayatollah Ruhollah Khomeini in his stature and policies, Kartir set out to purge and unify Iran, employing all the coercive power of the state to do so. Although the record is far from complete, it appears that Kartir was able to organize the *magi* or *mobads* (roughly equivalent to the later Muslim *mullas*) into a hierarchy at the head of which he became the high "priest" (*mobadan mobad*) with wide powers to control public education and the administration of law. Unlike Khomeini in our time, however, he did not seek to supplant the state but rather to guide its actions. Although Kartir did not set out a program, it is clear that what he attempted was to embody in the "church" the essence of the Persian traditional way of thought and custom. He used his position to purge or at least contain a variety of movements, including Judaism, Christianity, Buddhism, and Hinduism, that were then active in Iran. He attacked them all, but came down the hardest on the heresy begun within Zoroastrianism and led by a rival prophet, Mani.

Not only in religious matters but generally, at least in the urban society, Iran was strikingly cosmopolitan. Unlike Byzantium, which could draw little cultural inspiration from the primitive tribal peoples of the Balkans and western Europe, who were falling into "the Dark Age," the Sasanians enjoyed the already sophisticated culture and literature of their Indian "cousins." From Parthian times, they had also been in touch with the rich and vibrant society of Han China. Relations with Byzantium, although occasionally hostile, were normally relaxed and open. People and goods traveled relatively freely, and ambassadors and trade missions were regularly exchanged.

Even more striking, there was a fairly steady and often quite sizable movement of peoples. In addition to the forcible transfer of peoples from the frontier provinces, there was then, as ever since, casual movement across the shifting frontiers by nomads and semi-nomads. When opportunities closed in one state, as they did, for example, when Byzantium monopolized the silk industry, workers sought them in the other, as the silk workers did in Iran. Scholars moved as well. When the Byzantine emperor Justinian closed the Platonic Academy in Athens, its dismissed philosophers were welcomed in Iran. These philosophers were non-Christians, but Iran was also hospitable to Nestorian Christians, who were discriminated against in Constantinople. As we shall see, this is a recurrent theme in history—the seeking of sanctuary and the quest for education, in our times, have brought tens of thousands of Iraqis into Iran. Most of the current leaders of Iran have spent years studying in the seminaries there, and under the tyranny of Saddam Hussein, a large part of the Shia Muslim population of Iraq's south fled or was driven there.

Ideas traveled even faster and more easily: The Sasanians were avid consumers of foreign literature. Khusrau I (AD 531–579) became a great patron of translation not only from Greek but also from Sanskrit. His efforts were culturally enriching, but in the eyes of later Persians, the most interesting cultural contribution of the Sasanians was that they gathered the myths and legends that had grown up all over Iran and brought them together in a collection known as *Khwaday-namag,* which formed the basis for what is recognized as the national epic of the Iranian people, the poet Firdowsi's *Shahnameh.* The influence of that great epic, comparable to Homer's *Iliad* and *Odyssey,* Virgil's *Aeneid,* and the Indian *Mahabharata,* would come later. At the time, the Sasanians—even without a Herodotus to guide them—studied the way the Byzantine state worked, minutely examined the elaborate ceremony of the court, where protocol became the essence of politics, borrowed Byzantine military technology, and even, when possible, coopted Byzantine personnel.

Meanwhile, the Iranian rulers were grappling with more obvious military challenges. Their response varied over the years and generations. When Iran was strong, it attempted to expand. The Sasanians became serious and dedicated practitioners of warfare and even captured the Roman Emperor Valerian in battle in AD 259. But when weak, they would retreat into Iran's central core. Over the centuries, Iran's military history can be described in these terms: advance, retreat, regroup, and advance again. But in the Sasanian era, the Iranians increasingly found themselves faced with war on two fronts: On the western frontier, Rome, as the Parthians had known it, had become Byzantium and was often in alliance with Armenia against Iran, whereas on the eastern frontier, a newly arrived and aggressive people, the Hephthalites (White Huns), were making inroads, and tribes of Turks were also beginning the incursions that they would carry forward for the next thousand years.

To counter these threats to the stability of the then bipolar world, the Sasanian ruler Khusrau II tried a novel approach. Instead of attempting to destroy Byzantium, which had proved as impossible as it had been for the Romans/Byzantines to destroy Iran—the Roman writer from Syria, Herodian, famously remarked that the Roman infantry and the Persian cavalry were both invincible—Khusrau decided that they should jointly undertake to bring order into the world. In this move, Khusrau was proclaiming the Zoroastrian ideal—to heal the suffering of humankind. It was a dramatic, indeed an unprecedented, venture and was broached in a novel form: Khusrau wrote a remarkable letter to "my brother," the Byzantine emperor Maurice, arguing that the two powers had not profited from "Hot War" or from their version of Cold War. Rather, each had served its own interests best when it acted to control the "restless and warlike nations." In Zoroastrian terms, these "rogue states" were the agents of Ahriman, the Devil, who brought disorder and evil (*drug*). The *drugvant,* the human wicked, were more or less those we today would think of as terrorists. The role of a wise ruler was to create conditions in which "the lives of men are ordered and ruled." That should become the policy of both states, Khusrau wrote. They should give up destroying one another's frontier cities and abandon attempts at "regime change." He lectured the Byzantine ambassador : "It is impossible for a single empire to take upon itself the innumerable concerns for the order of the world and to succeed in ruling all the peoples upon whom the sun looks down with the single oar of its wisdom."[7] Alas, this wise move toward a peaceful and respectful world was dashed when the Byzantine emperor was murdered.

Iran also faced another group of nomads, Arabs, on its southwestern frontier. In the sixth and early seventh centuries, they did not appear to be a regime-threatening foe but already were causing considerable damage in the rich agricultural lands between the Tigris and Euphrates rivers. So the Iranians hit on the solution adopted by the Romans, the Byzantines, and the Chinese Han dynasty: use barbarians to control barbarians. As practiced by Iran, this policy was accomplished by creating and subsidizing a subordinate Arab city-state at Hirah on the desert frontier. Hirah was to act as a buffer, and its rulers were to use their kinship ties, expertise, and Iranian money to divert or suborn the wild tribesmen. Although not a perfect solution to the "Arab problem," it worked satisfactorily until, partly as a measure of economy, Hirah's quasi-autonomy was quashed and its rulers were replaced by a Persian governor. The true cost of this economy measure would become evident in the great Arab-Muslim invasion of 651.

For a while, the Sasanian Empire brought together diverse cultural elements that were enjoyed by a rich and refined society in security and peace. So astonishing was this feat to later generations living in a world of danger and turmoil that they looked back upon the Sasanian Empire as a sort of Persian Camelot, a golden epoch when the world was at peace and humans were happy. Alas, it did not last long. The Byzantines and the Sasanians fought one another to mutual exhaustion in the early seventh century. By then, both Byzantium and Sasanian Iran were bankrupt and without ideas on how to end their wasting conflict. The end was in sight.

After the death of the Prophet Muhammad in 632, many of the previously pagan tribes of Arabia ended their allegiance to Islam. In their eyes, they had submitted to Muhammad personally and had no binding ties to whatever tribe, confederation, state, or religious fraternity had come into existence in Madinah. As the Arabic words precisely differentiate and as the Quran specifies, the bedouin tribes had *salamat* (submitted), becoming *Muslims* ("those who submit") rather than *amanu,* becoming *mu'minuna* ("believers"). So, as the Arabic phrase has it, when Muhammad died, they "turned back on their heels," *irtaddu ʿala ʿaqibihim.* That is, as later theologians would put it, they apostated. Across Arabia's vast steppe and desert, Muhammad's "empire" vanished like a mirage. To bring the tribes back into the fold, the new Islamic state began the "war of the *ridda,*" against the "going back" to paganism. That war was the most vicious ever experienced in Arabia, but Muhammad's immediate successors quickly realized that to succeed they must use a carrot as well as a stick. The carrot was a raid, already suggested by Muhammad, into Byzantine territory in what is now Jordan and Syria. The raid was successful. Seeing the Muslims return loaded with booty, the chastened "apostates" flocked to join what they thought would be profitable and exciting raiding parties. Thus was formed a supratribal or at least multitribal army.

In 633, this new force, under a brilliant practitioner of desert warfare, the leader of the war of the *ridda* Khalid ibn al-Walid, feinted an attack on the Iranian capital, then at Ctesiphon on the Tigris River near the modern city of Baghdad. Then he led his nomadic warriors across the Great Syrian Desert, where he surprised the Byzantine garrison and seized Damascus. In 636, Khalid's forces, by then multiplied by new war parties of tribesmen hungry for loot and glory, destroyed a Byzantine army at the battle of Yarmuk. Thus, what had started as a punitive expedition became a raid, and the raid became a war of conquest. In 635, after a desperate battle in which one in three of the Arabs was said to have been killed, Arab tribesmen defeated the Sasanian regular army near the later city of Kufa in what is today Iraq.

Following the initial shock of the invasion, the Arab conquest of Iran took seven years. The Sasanian shah rallied support from all over Iran, but piece by piece, town by town, he was defeated. As Zoroastrians would have explained, he had lost what they called *xvarenah,* which comes close to the Chinese "Mandate of Heaven." Having lost *xvarenah,* Yazdgard was doomed. But in his struggle against fate, he even sought assistance from the T'ang dynasty in faraway China. As Yazdgard retreated toward the east, Arab armies chased after him, ultimately right up to the Chinese frontier.

Historians have long puzzled over the stunning collapse of this mighty empire under the attack of a previously disorganized and mutually hostile collection of nomadic tribes. Seeking understanding, we should start, where this book does, with the fact that Iran was always susceptible to nomadic invasion; indeed, as we have seen, Iran was the creation of nomadic invasions. But there are other important causes. The Sasanian regime was exhausted and bankrupt; its Zoroastrian "clergy" was blamed for some of its ills, particularly by the large numbers of Persians who in the previous century had converted to Christianity; and the governing elite appear to have been disaffected.

The Arabs, however, were apprehensive. They were adrift in an enormous country whose language and geography they did not know, whose people had a strong sense of identity and were known to be valiant fighters. Some parts of it were not "pacified" for years; indeed, the northern province along the Caspian, the original territory of the Medes, held out for nearly 70 years. The new Arab/Muslim regime, the caliphate, was militarily successful but had no illusions about its still tribal army. Having recently survived the war of the *ridda,* Muhammad's inner group was determined not to allow their vacillating followers to scatter among the Iranian population. They wanted them to keep together to be ready for action, so they created garrison towns, Basra, Kufa, Qom, and other places, where they settled their tribesmen. This is, of course, the pattern followed by invaders throughout history—to create safe redoubts from which to sally in case of danger. But in Iran, creation of these garrisons had a second and unintended result. Because they quickly became prosperous towns, they attracted large numbers of Persian merchants, craftsmen, and laborers. This development brought to the fore the issue of how the Arabs should relate to the Persians and, even more important, how the Persians should relate to the Arabs and their religion. The way this dilemma began to be addressed would shape much of Iranian society and political life down to our own times.

Three aspects of this encounter became evident almost immediately: The first arose from the fact that Islam is a monotheistic religion. Because Judaism, Christianity, and Zoroastrianism are also monotheistic—and so met the absolute requirement of Islam, which is belief in one god—Islam could accommodate their followers in a status that was already traditional among bedouin tribes as tolerated and protected outsiders, *dhimmis*. The protected communities did not have to perform either military service or compulsory labor, and the taxes they were required to pay were assessed on them individually by the leaders of their own communities and were only slightly more than the taxes levied on Muslims. Moreover, women, children, religious men, and the crippled were exempt. Provided they did not revolt, members of these "tolerated" religions—the so-called "Peoples of the Book" (i.e., the Bible)—were accorded more freedom to practice their faiths than before. By extension, this tolerance also was accorded to the Zoroastrians of the *Avesta*. Thus, it appears that much of the population passively accepted the victors.

However, the problem became more complex when Persians chose to convert to Islam. The Quran had proclaimed that, although Islam was the same religion as Judaism and Christianity, it was specially aimed at the Arabs in their language, Arabic. So when the Muslims spoke of Islam, they meant the Arab religion. There was no provision for the conversion of non-Arabs. Far from trying to convert them "with the sword," the Arabs wanted the Persians to follow their own religions but to behave *like* the Arab Muslims—that is, not to violate their version of God's will, but to do so in their own ways and in their own communities. So it came as something of a shock when, as defeated people commonly do, the Iranians began to convert to the religion of the dominant community. Perhaps the Arabs could have prevented this by some sort of apartheid, but they did not, nor could the Arabs prevent the procreation of children in mixed marriages. So a new sort of Iranian came into being, usually called a *mawla* (Arabic plural: *muwali*). Soon, the *muwali* sought to regularize their status in Islam by proclaiming themselves Muslim but to keep their national identity by becoming Muslim in a particularly Iranian way. This tendency began early and was ultimately to produce the Shia sect of Islam.

The second aspect of the encounter was that there was much in Islam that would have been familiar to Zoroastrians. The most obvious custom was that both faiths required five prayers a day, and a number of beliefs were shared by both: the dualism of God (Allah, Ahura Mazda) and the Devil (Iblis, Ahriman); the primacy of law to regulate social behavior; and the belief in the Last Day (the Zoroastrian *rasho-keretfi* or *frashegird* and the Quranic *al-Yaumu'l-akhir* or *yaumu'l-qiyamah*) when a messiah, *mahdi* or *Soshyant*, will return to earth and God will resurrect the dead, judge them, give the righteous everlasting life, and condemn the evil to Hell. Both religions assert that God created humankind for a purpose—to pursue the good and struggle against evil—but also that mankind is weak and needs the help of a text (*Avesta*, Quran) and men of religion (*magi* or *mobad*, *mullas* or *mujtahids*) to regulate their lives. These similarities eased the path to conversion of Zoroastrians.

The third aspect of the encounter of Arabs and Persians was more contentious: The Persians, even those whose wealth was undiminished by the invasion, were intensely nationalistic, as Persians had been since the time of Cyrus the Great and as Iranians remain down to our times. Like all peoples, as Herodotus long before had pointed out, they resented the intrusion of foreigners into their country. Even when they opposed aspects of the Sasanian regime, most Persians probably felt at least a pride in it. Moreover, from long pre-Islamic contacts, they had come to dislike the Arabs. Some had suffered from bedouin raids, but even of those who had not, many had adopted a racial stereotype of the Arabs as primitive, dangerous, lesser beings. In Persian literature, particularly in the great epic the *Shahnameh*, they are commonly associated with the Devil, Ahriman. As we shall see, these attitudes remained strong for centuries after the invasion and indeed still do. So it came as a shock when these same *untermenschen* became their rulers. In the aftermath of battle, many had seized Persian women, appropriated Persian property, and treated Persians as second class. Persians were not allowed to marry Muslim (i.e., Arab) women, but Arabs could marry Persian women. Persians were forbidden to try to convert Muslims to other religions, to carry weapons, to ride horses, or to build new churches or temples. Resentment may have begun early, but it was some years before grievances burst into revolt. One of the most striking revolts occurred in AD 655 under the fourth caliph, Muhammad's son-in-law and cousin, Ali. The issue was nonpayment of taxes, and Ali, who was by then the father-in-law of a Persian woman (his son had married a daughter of the family of the last Shah), ordered a savage suppression of the rebels. This is particularly ironic because it is Ali who was to become a virtual saint to Iranian converts to Islam.

After the death of Ali, who was murdered in 661 by an Arab Muslim extremist, the old oligarchs of Mecca took over the leadership of the Islamic caliphate and established themselves as the Umayyad dynasty in Damascus. Two of Ali's grandsons tried to rebel and were killed. That event formed the subject of the great passion play (later known as the *Taziyeh,* which I discuss later) that became one of the defining events of Iranian culture. Inflamed by a sense of injustice, shamed at not having prevented Ali's murder, and hating the regime for a variety of reasons, a covert revolutionary movement began in the far east of Iran. Spread mainly by propaganda, it rapidly gained adherents there and in Central Asia. A secret movement that had to hide to survive, it is still veiled from full analysis. What we now know is that it drew on disaffected Arabs, newly converted Persians, and even Zoroastrians and that it was fired by a mystical belief drawn from both Islam and Zoroastrianism: that the world was nearing the Last Day and that a *mahdi* or *Soshyant* was about to return to judge humankind. This figure was concealed but would be revealed, the leaders of the movement claimed, when the existing regime collapsed.

Nearly as hidden as God's agent was the movement's leader, a man known as Abu Muslim. It is now generally believed that he was a Persian convert to Islam: a *mawla.* Like the growing number of *muwali,* he staked out a political position against the "usurpers," as they and Muhammad's closest associates regarded the Umayyads. As Muslims, they began to explain their beliefs and politics by proclaiming themselves to be *Shiis* (Partisans) of Ali. Although still amorphous, the sect they were beginning to formulate was to incorporate more of the Zoroastrian tradition than would be acceptable or even understandable to the orthodox, or *Sunni,* Arab Muslims. Centuries later, the Shiis would grow into the second-largest division of Islam. Though there are many differences, for convenience we can think of the Shiis and Sunnis as comparable to the Protestants and the Catholics (I have more to say about Sunnis later). At this time, however, the Shiis had not yet formalized their beliefs into a coherent canon; as nearly as we can now see it, what Abu Muslim led was a movement of political and social protest, using as its symbols and ideology the eschatological beliefs of both Islam and Zoroastrianism.

Abu Muslim was a master propagandist, and he addressed a receptive audience. So having proclaimed his mission, known as the *Hashimiyyah,* in AD 747, and donning what would become the distinctive sign of his forces, a black gown, an echo of which could be seen in the black-clad protesters in the March 2009 riots in Tehran, he quickly gathered together a motley band of peasants, tradesmen, and craftsmen. Misjudging them and the intensity of their *jihad,* the Umayyad governor sent only a small force to crush them. When that counterinsurgence force was defeated, still more partisans joined the revolt. As these insurgents won their first battles, Abu Muslim was able to explain their victories in mystical terms so that new adherents flocked to the movement's black banners, which signaled the imminent arrival on earth of the agent of God, the mahdi. Area by area, Abu Muslim's forces defeated the Umayyads in eastern Iran and then launched attacks on the Umayyad forces in the western parts of Iran, Iraq, and Syria. Little more than a year after the revolt began, the final defeat of the Umayyads came in a battle near Mosul in what is now Iraq.

Then a strange event or series of events happened. Somehow, and it is still far from clear how, the movement was "hijacked" by its titular leaders, the branch of Muhammad's family known as the Abbasids. As soon as they could, just eight years after Abu Muslim gave them the Umayyad empire, the Abbasids executed Abu Muslim. Instead of returning to the pristine purity of early Islam or bringing to some sort of fruition the mystical impulses of the revolution, they created a regime patterned on an entirely different mix of Arab and Persian ideas and practices. From the Arabs, they adopted the language and more or less what had come to be the "orthodox" form of Islam, Sunnism, whereas from Iran, they adopted a traditional model of imperial administration. Despite, or perhaps because of, the revolutionary past, they turned away from the relatively open Arab style of the Umayyads toward the more monarchal court ritual of Cyrus the Great. This was the Abbasid caliphate.

Only a century passed before the Abbasid hold on Iran weakened. One province after another broke away, and one—the area along the Caspian Sea where the Medes had once held sway—gave rise to an Iranian dynasty known as the Buyids, who became in AD 946, effectively if not in name, the real rulers of the Abbasid caliphate and the first Iranian group to reunite Iran since the Arab invasion. Often the plaything of Buyid generals and Turkish mercenaries, the caliphs became largely symbolic figures. But, in name and in symbolism, the Abbasid caliphate was to linger for five hundred years.

The decline of the Abbasid dynasty ushered in a period of chaos and destruction, but paradoxically the period was also one of cultural flowering. The Persian Buyids in the west and another dynasty known as the Samanids in the East laid the foundation by collecting into their libraries the literary survivors of the years since the Arab invasion. Military dictators though they were, the Buyids were both curious and ecumenical. They drew works from all the languages they encountered. Even more creative were the Samanids in what is now Afghanistan. Under their patronage, Iranian authors, particularly poets to whose works Persians have always been addicted, prospered.

During this time, a new medium of expression came into vogue. In the early centuries after the Arab conquest, Iranians had tended to write in Arabic; then sometime around AD 900, a few began to write in the mixture of Arabic and what is known as "middle" Persian or Pahlavi, which would form the new Persian language (Farsi). In this new language, which was and still is written in a modified Arabic script or in Arabic itself, Iranians composed books on Arabic grammar and syntax, wrote the basic and still most influential commentaries on the Quran, and became notable connoisseurs of classical Arabic poetry. One of them, the Iranian Shia scholar Abu'l-Faraj al-Isfahani, edited the most famous collection of works on Arabic culture, *The Book of Songs* (*Kitab al-Aghani*). Not content with collecting and editing, Iranians also began to compose notable works on their own. If they were not quite up to Herodotus, the scholars Muhammad ibn Jarir al-Tabari from the far northern province of Iran, Tabaristan, which had been the land of the ancient Medes, and the Neo-Platonist Abu Ali Ibn Miskawaih from the ancient city of Ray near modern Tehran produced two notable histories, *The Chronicles* and *The Experiences of the Nations*. The Persian philosopher Abu Ali Husain Ibn Sina became the guide for generations of medieval Europeans as "Avicenna." Also from Bukhara came Abu Nasr Muhammad al-Farabi, a scientist, logician, musicologist, and a spur to the European Renaissance.

Above all, it was at this time that the national epic of Iran, the *Shah-nameh*, a vast poem of sixty thousand verses, was partly composed and partly collected over half a lifetime by the great poet Abol Qasem Firdowsi, who was born in the far east of Iran, Khorasan, in AD 935.[8] More famous in the West, Omar Khayyam was born a century later, probably in the then Persian city of Nishapur, and spent most of his life in Samarqand and Bukhara. He thought of himself as a mathematician and an astronomer, but his lasting fame rests on his *Rubaiyat.*[9]

Collectively, their works would catapult the new Persian into the language of diplomacy, culture, and refinement not only for the next great Persian empire, the Safavid, but also for the Indian Mughal and the Turkish Ottoman Empires and even for the Central Asian Turkish and Mongol kingdoms. Persian was widely used even in faraway T'ang China and was the lingua franca of the "Great Southern" (Indian and Pacific) Ocean.

Language at least was impervious to arrows and spears, but men, libraries, and whole cities were not. So it was that this period of cultural growth was virtually swept away in one of the greatest onslaughts recorded by history—the invasions of the Turks and Mongols.

*F*ar to the east, across Asia in China, a Turkish general overthrew the T'ang dynasty in AD 907 and set in motion the first ripples of what would become the tidal wave that swept across most of the world. When the Chinese regrouped and formed a strong new government, the Song dynasty, they sought to end the "Turkish threat" by closing their frontiers to the Turks. Blocked to the east and attacked by the warlike Mongol Ch'i-tan, the Turks turned west. Their first major incursion was by a group of tribes known for their early leader as Seljuk; the Seljuks conquered eastern Iran in 1040 and plunged into Baghdad 15 years later. In 1071, their then sultan Alp Arslan defeated and captured the emperor of Byzantium and thus upset the balance of power in the Middle East as completely as had the Arabs four hundred years earlier.

Most of the Seljuk actions fall outside of Iran, but there and elsewhere in the Middle East they briefly stimulated a sort of mini-renaissance. The Seljuk prime minister, a Persian by the name of Nizam ul-Mulk, created the most impressive educational systems in the world of his time. He aimed to establish a college of higher learning in every significant city in the Seljuk Empire to train a competent civil service. Events overwhelmed his efforts, but he planted in the minds of successive rulers down to our own times an ideal of government that could be measured by its dedication to education.

Following on the heels of the Seljuks, in 1215, Genghis Khan put together the greatest military force the world had ever experienced. His armies captured the Chinese capital (later known as Peking or Beijing), and in 1221 they made their first raids into Russia. At the same time, they invaded Iran for the first time. After Genghis Khan's death, Mongol armies conquered Russia, and Genghis Khan's grandson, Hulagu Khan, smashed across Iran in 1258 to capture the still-partly Persian Baghdad, killing perhaps 800,000 people and ending the Abbasid caliphate. At that time, many of the cities of Iran were far larger than Paris, London, or Venice; thus, they had much to lose by the Mongol invasion. Descriptions by eyewitnesses are horrifying. Everywhere they went, the Mongols razed cities, carried away or killed the craftsmen who had enriched them, and destroyed irrigation works so that both cities and the countryside were virtually depopulated. Their policy aimed to convert the agricultural lands to the open pasture the nomads wanted, and they carried it out by genocide. Most of the famous old cities of Iran were virtually annihilated by attack after attack—Herat, for example, was sacked six times between 1270 and 1319—and in the wake of the armies came famine and pestilence. Cities shrank into towns, and towns shrank into villages. Many villages simply disappeared. The well-informed Persian (and probably Jewish) historian Rashid al-Din reported that half of the houses in Iran's cities were abandoned, and "[i]n some areas . . . the native population was either completely annihilated or had fled, leaving their land waste. . . ." Those who survived clung precariously and miserably to niches in the old societies and economies, as we would imagine the survivors of a nuclear war might in our time.

Then, tenaciously, the survivors began to pile bricks on top of one another, plow neglected fields, and fashion the necessities of life. No sooner had they begun to do so than they were struck by the second wave of the tsunami: In the last years of the fourteenth century, another member of the dynasty, Timur (known in the West as Tamerlane), led his armies back and forth across Iran to ravage its cities. When the people of Isfahan defied him, Timur built pyramids of seventy thousand of their skulls. The medieval culture that had slowly, partly, and painfully recovered from the first wave was devastated.[10] Even a century later, Marco Polo and the great Arab traveler, Ibn Battutu, found in Iran just decaying ruins. Those who had survived must have wondered whether survival was worthwhile and whether Iran could possibly recover. It was surely this horrifying experience, repeated as it was over a century and virtually everywhere throughout Iran, that planted in the collective memory of Iranians an abiding fear of foreign invasion. The effects linger to this day.

*J*n this attempt to get at what it means to "become Persian," I have recounted a number of the events and streams of thought—pride and fear, belief and conflict, foreign intervention and domestic reaction, unification and division, and aggression and defeat—that together constitute the country's "collective unconscious": the sum of influences that have shaped this people into Iranians.

Two

BEING IRANIAN

*I*n the dreary years following the century of devastation caused by the Mongol armies of Genghis Khan, Hulagu Khan, and Timur Khan, Iranians—like the descendants of the Mongols' other victims in Russia, India, Iraq, Syria, Turkey, and China—hunkered down in the ruins. True, there were oases of relative prosperity in the otherwise bleak desert of razed cities and shattered irrigation works, but they were few. So, all over Iran, people turned inward from what remained of their real estate toward their "unreal estate": If life on this earth had become intolerable and rescuing the old life from the smoldering ruins seemed impossible, they concluded that they must find salvation elsewhere. The macabre pyramids of skulls left behind by the rampaging armies pointed away from earth toward Heaven. Men's minds followed their trajectory.

While they destroyed the physical structure of the Middle East, the Mongol invaders also destroyed governmental and religious institutions. Foremost among them was, at least theoretically, the unifying force of Islam—the caliphate in Baghdad. This act loosened the bonds of theology so that divisive tendencies that had long been present were given a freer rein. Those theologians who had survived lost much of the authority they had derived from the caliphate, and they also lost touch with the common man: He was less interested in their arguments over dogma than in acquiring solace amid misery and poverty. In this climate of despair, the weakening of ecclesiastical guidance thus allowed the growth of otherworldliness and the belief in mysticism, miracles, and magic, and it focused hopes on holy men who they believed offered a path toward salvation from earthly horror.

Among those men who offered guidance, in which Islamic society has always been particularly rich,[1] was a wealthy merchant in the then important provincial city of Ardabil, northeast of Tabriz. Shaikh Safi ad-Din Ishaq was born in AD 1252 during the rule of the descendants of the Mongol conquerors. In two ways, he echoed the career of the Prophet Muhammad: He was both a man of profound spiritual conviction and a practical leader. Whereas six centuries earlier, Muhammad had founded the religious community of Islam in the little town of Mecca, Shaikh Safi set out to found a religious order, the Safaviya, in the little city of Ardabil.

The Safaviya was a "brotherhood" of dedicated believers known as Sufis. The word *sufi* derives from the word shared by Arabic, Persian, and Turkish for "wool" (*suf*) because the brothers were known for their simple woolen gowns. In affecting the clothing of the poor, the Sufis resembled the European followers of Saint Francis of Assisi. Like the Franciscans, the Sufis turned aside from the richer things of life toward the austere. Also like the followers of Saint Francis, the followers of Shaikh Safi struck a note of compassion that led to fellowship with the destitute, inspiring loyalty and even love.

In the lifetime of Shaikh Safi, the destitute were legion. With so little physically remaining intact, men valued the more emotional sense of brotherhood with fellow sufferers and fellow seekers of solace. Shaikh Safi offered them a transcendental "way." His way (*tariqa*), he claimed, was marked out by the "spirit" (*ruh*) of God, which, he asserted, had been passed down to him through the Prophet Muhammad. He was believed both because, in their misery, people wanted to believe and because of his personal piety. These two attributes—divine recognition and personal piety—placed him apart from and above the feared and often hated military figures whose actions had created mass misery. His contemporaries believed that his life, his message, and his lineage were literally of a different order. So his Sufi brotherhood soon spread all over Iran and across the rest of the Middle East.

Shaikh Safi did not trouble his followers with theological pronouncements on orthodoxy and heresy but spoke to them in simple terms of their yearning for surcease from misery and their beliefs in the coming of a divine savior. He made the convents (*ribat*) he founded the retreats of the downtrodden, passing out among them food bought by the donations he received from his followers. Succor combined with belief was a winning formula—one that has often been followed by religious movements down to and in-

cluding the Palestinian Hamas and the Afghan Taliban in our own times—
and it made him a power that no secular ruler could ignore.

Reversing the career of Saint Francis, who began as a soldier before shifting to pacificism, Shaikh Safi only gradually became a militant. But inherent
in his movement from the beginning was *jihad*, "striving" or, when necessary, "fighting" for the faith. Also implicit was the absolute rule over the dis-
ciples (*muridun*) by the master (Persian: *pir*) or "the rightly guided one"
(Arabic: *murshidu'l-kamil*). These concepts, although called by Arabic and
Persian Islamic terms, recall older Zoroastrian concepts. The Zoroastrians
named the assertion of divine wisdom *ehrpat* and named the leader of their
holy men a *magupat*. Disregarding the change of names, the continuity of
concept and functions is striking.

Unquestionably, Shaikh Safi was a remarkable man. He would have been
remembered for his piety and his benefactions, but what gave his movement,
the Safaviya, its historic opportunity was not only the Iranians' quest for some
escape from misery but yet another great migration of peoples—the Turks—
into Iran.

Turks, both individually and in small groups, had begun to arrive in the
Middle East in the Abbasid caliphate, and their numbers increased in the
eleventh century. Most passed from what are today Turkmenistan and other
parts of Central and East Asia along the narrow corridor of relatively wet and
flat lands that divides Iran's northern Albruz Mountains from the vast southern desert. That was the route taken by the original Medes and Persians. The
Turks who founded the Seljuk Empire followed in their footsteps; then, as
they migrated farther to the west, they were followed by a number of other
Turkish fighting bands (Turkish: *ahis*), among whom the Ottomans were the
most successful and became the most famous. Other groups remained in
Central Asia, where they made up large portions of the armies of the Mongol conquerors and the descendants of Timur Khan. Still others found their
way into territories that are today divided among India, Pakistan,
Afghanistan, Turkey, and Iran so that, at the present time, about one in three
Iranians is of Turkish descent.

In the time of Shaikh Safi, Iran was ruled by descendants and followers
of Timur. None of them had the power, grim determination, or martial skill
of Timur, so as they struggled against one another for dominion, they split

Iran apart into petty states. Those conditions favored the spread of the Safaviya order because none of the secular rulers was able to provide the security the people wanted.

Then the descendants of Timur began to be replaced by clans and tribes of Turkmen, one of the many subdivisions of the Turkish people. The Turkmens gathered into two large confederations, known as the "Black Sheep" (*Qara Quyunlu*), which ranged over what are today northern Iran and the southern Caucasus while the "White Sheep" (*Aq Quyunlu*) controlled eastern Anatolia. As sheepherding nomads they were natural warriors but, constantly shifting in location and allegiance, and balanced against one another, neither confederation was able to form a coherent and lasting state. Then in 1467, the leader of the White Sheep, a man by the name of Uzun Hassan, overwhelmed the leader of the Black Sheep and began to build what became virtually a nomadic empire covering large parts of the Middle East, including Iran.

To the Europeans at the time, Uzun Hassan seemed a gift from God. Attacked by the rising power of the Ottoman Empire, which in 1452 had conquered the greatest city of Christendom, Constantinople, and was moving inexorably into the lands of the Mediterranean and the Balkans, Europe was looking for a way to stop the invasion. They cherished the myth of a great anti-Muslim, presumably Christian, leader whom they called "Prester John," living somewhere east of the Muslims they knew. The myth was born out of fear and was undisturbed by the passage of centuries. Uzun Hassan was the latest incarnation of Prester John. Overlooking the fact that he also was a Muslim, the then superpower of the Mediterranean, Venice, sent the first diplomatic mission to the East and shrewdly formed an alliance with him in 1464.

The first alliance of its kind, it was notable for its key feature: the western power, Venice, would provide its eastern partner with military equipment. That program has set the style of relations down to our own times. The Venentians carried it out with great skill. Caterino Zeno, the ambassador they dispatched to Tabriz, the Turkmen capital of what the Venetians saw as "Persia," knew the country, was said to be fluent in Persian or Turkish, and even was related by marriage to Uzun Hassan. Few of the Western ambassadors to Iran in later centuries had even one of these attributes, which is one of the reasons that an understanding of Iran has proven so elusive in our times. Moreover, the transfer of technology was slower than agreement on strategy. Uzun Hassan did not have the time to learn to effectively use the arms he got from Venice while the Ottomans had been using firearms for a century and were among the leaders in the new art of casting cannons. Having already integrated artillery into their superb standing army, the janissaries, in the summer of 1473 the Ottomans were able to gun down the traditional cavalry of the Turkmens. For this disparity in modernization Iran would pay a heavy price in the years to come.

But what was really important for the long run in Iran was that during the years of Uzun Hassan's rule, the religious brotherhood of the Safaviya not only had spread across the Middle East but also had become increasingly militant. Perhaps it would be more accurate to say that it had, from the beginning, thought of itself as a military embodiment of Islam, a movement of warriors for the faith, people we now call *jihadis* and who were then called *ghazis* (Turkish: "warriors of the faith"). Thus, it attracted, either as members of the order or as associates, many Turkmen tribesmen. While Uzun Hassan was alive, the brotherhood cooperated with the White Sheep Turkmen, but, at first covertly and after his death openly, it began to create its own military force. What set it apart from dozens of informal tribal armies was that the then leader of the Safavi order realized that he could increase the cohesion and power of the Turkmens who joined him, and also tighten the bond between them and himself, by weaning them away from their own tribes. This he did by distinguishing them, as modern armies are set apart, with a uniform. The distinctive mark of the uniform he ordained was a red turban—so they became known as the "Red Heads" (Turkish: *Qizilbashlar*).[2] Accustomed to living by fighting and plundering, all the *Qizilbashlar* needed was direction. So, as the successors of Muhammad raided Byzantine Syria, Haidar directed them to raids on the Circassian villages in the Caucasus. Success in gathering booty encouraged recruitment then as it had in the early days of Islam, but as guerrilla armies often do, they moved too fast; they suffered a major defeat and their leader was killed. Luckily for them, a new grand master of the order stood in line.

*J*smail was born in 1487, just 12 years after the death of his maternal grandfather, Uzun Hassan, and just one year after his father was killed. He then spent his childhood as a virtual prisoner of one of the aspirants to the Turkmen throne. Still only a child, he managed to escape captivity and was only

12 years old when he made his bid for power. Thereafter, by skillful policy and great personal bravery, he reconstituted Iran as a powerful state after centuries of destruction and alien rule; as the founder of the fourth great empire of Iran, the Safavid dynasty, he "led Iran back on to the stage of world history."[3]

A remarkable man in his own right, Ismail was empowered by his inheritance. From his father, he got what, with skill and determination, he could turn into a new style army, the *Qizilbashlar*. From his paternal grandfather, he acquired his position as leader of the ideological force, the Safavia, behind this new fighting force. And, from his maternal grandfather, Uzun Hassan, he gained the recognition of his claim to kingship. I will examine these in detail because they are the keys to understanding what was recognized to be the greatest of the Iranian dynasties, the Safavids.

Even at the age of 12, Ismail was apparently so absolutely sure of himself and his divine right to rule that he could chance a sweeping revolution. He proclaimed that he had inherited the spirit of God and that he was either the long-awaited messiah, the *mahdi*, or at least the earthly champion who was preparing his way. His followers accepted this assertion as manifest truth. As a contemporary visitor, the Englishman Lionel Plumtree, observed, he "is loved and reverenced by his people as a God."[4] In their eyes, he occupied a position not unlike that taken by Ayatollah Ruhollah Khomeini in our times—divinely authorized to exercise both religious and political power. But more than Khomeini, Ismail claimed direct descent both physically and, more important, spiritually from the Prophet Muhammad through his cousin and son-in-law Ali and from Ali through an unbroken line of *imams*. I will now examine what contemporaries thought that meant.

At the beginning of the sixteenth century, Shiism had not yet become the fully articulated religion we see today. Indeed, there is evidence that it was not fully distinguished from Sunnism even in the minds of many of the religious leaders and certainly was not by the general public. But there is also evidence that Shiism had already come to be recognized as an Iranian manifestation of Islam. There are, undoubtedly, various reasons for this, but I find one reason particularly striking: To judge by the popular literature, festivals, and other habits, the ancient religion of Iran, Zoroastrianism, still deeply colored Iranian culture. It was to have little, if any, impact on Sunni

Islam, but, as I have described earlier, it certainly had an important impact on Shia Islam. In effect, what it did was to allow the Iranians to proclaim themselves true Muslims but to do so in a way that retained their traditional distinction from the Arabs and their more recent distinction from the Ottoman Turks. It was perceived in these terms in the great national epic of Iran, the *Shahnameh*. Although the *Shahnameh* cannot be treated as history and made no attempt to provide us with a poll of public opinion, I think we must assume that had it not encapsulated the general belief, it would not have been so universally adopted as the heart of Iran. It was recited, read, and even partly memorized by generation after generation of Iranians. What was then and remains today important about this cultural portrait is that it encapsulated the pre-Arab past and underwrote the national identity of Iran, shaping its dominant religion as distinctively Iranian. The rise of Protestantism in northern Europe, although not shaped in the same way, had a comparable result.

So it was that in the summer of 1501, when Ismail conquered the Turkmen capital, Tabriz, where he crowned himself Shah, he decided to force the people of Tabriz, who were Sunnis, to adopt Shiism. How stunning a change this was we can hear from the report of one of the English merchants even more than half a century later, in the time of Ismail's son, Shah Tahmasp. As the Englishman reported even in the traditional center of the Safaviya brotherhood, the city of Ardabil, "The difference of religion [Sunni versus Shii] bred great broiles [quarrels or fights] in this towne whiles they [the English merchants] remained there: for the brother sought the destruction of the brother, and the neerest kinsmen rose up one against another, insomuch that one of their company Lionel Plumtree hath seene in one day sometimes 14. slaine in a garboile [riot]."[5]

Why did Ismail adopt this disruptive and dangerous policy? Perhaps personal conviction played a role, but statecraft cannot be denied. Ismail needed to distinguish his new state. He could not do it on the basis of tribal loyalty; nor could he do it on the basis of ethnicity as he and all of his rivals were Turkish; nor could he do it with religion if his sect of Islam was Sunni. The obvious answer was Shiism which offered the scope for a "national" religion that, if adopted by the Iranians, might solidify his dynasty. In short, Shiism was the best available distinguishing characteristic. Whether he thought his decision through in these terms, we don't know. But the people were certainly immediately receptive and, henceforth, Shiism would be the distinctive characteristic of the Safavid state. We know today the depth of the emotional commitment Iranians have to their beliefs. We can date this loyalty to the Safaviya movement. Their devotion and dedication deeply impressed the only outside observer who has left us his account, a Venetian merchant who wrote, in words that might have been used to describe Iranian soldiers in the war with Iraq in the 1980s, that soldiers "enter into battle without armor," so sure they were of their faith.[6] Then as later, they believed that death on the battlefield would be followed immediately by rebirth in Heaven. Ismail's Iranian warriors marched to the attack chanting, "I sacrifice myself for my spiritual master."[7]

In the quest for uniformity, which above all had to be manifested in religion, Ismail acted in ways comparable to Henry VIII of England but with far greater severity. Many highly respected and popular leaders, especially religious leaders, but also even poets, on whom Iranians have always lavished praise, refused to convert to Shiism, and were driven into exile or even executed. But Ismail recognized that "victory" on the religious battleground could not be won only with violence, so he also invoked an Iranian form of civic propaganda that long predated Islam.

We do not know much about the ancient rites, but we know that at least as early as Iran's second great empire, Parthia, over a thousand years before, the Zoroastrian priesthood guided mass public demonstrations designed to enforce religious beliefs with mourning songs, public demonstrations, and the *Geristan-i Mughan,* "the weeping of [their priesthood,] the Magi." By Ismail's time, the original figures in the Zoroastrian drama were largely forgotten. But similar roles were taken up and elaborated by Muslims while the underlying goal of the drama remained the same. In summary, the "guides" or storytellers gathered around themselves listeners whom they aimed to transform from audience members into vicarious participants. Listeners were to be overwhelmed by a sense of inadequacy, even personal guilt, for the murder of the Imam Husain, just as the earlier Zoroastrians had reacted to the recitation of the fate of Zare.

As in the Zoroastrian passion play—and similar Christian passion plays enacted in Europe and America—the Iranian Shia Muslim audience was led to a stunning outburst of emotion, a deep sense of personal guilt, weeping, and even mutilation in their attempts to expiate the sin they had inherited from the forefathers.

Probably the transformation of the Zoroastrian ceremony into the Muslim recitation long predated Ismail's time, but Ismail must have seen it as a means to energize his followers, attract new adherents, and build a popular consensus among his people for his new religious policy. So he organized what had been private storytellers (*rowzeh-khani*), who drew on a collection of stories known as *The Garden of Martyrs,* into a sort of corps of preachers (*naqqal*). As the Japanese American scholar Kumiko Yamamoto found,[8] Ismail gathered the *naqqal* into some 17 groups and commissioned each one to carry his Shia-based message to a different sector of Iranian society. As she wrote, "Development of the *naqqali* [the story they told] thus proceeded along with the penetration of Shiism into the society." What Ismail began, his successors carried to a new dimension; his grandson, Shah Abbas, even built coffee shops in all the major cities to give the storytellers places to assemble their audiences.

From private houses and public theaters, demonstrators also took to the streets, chanting the tragedy of Husain, evincing the most profound grief, whipping and gashing their bodies. Such demonstrations remain even today the most stunning events of Shia society, but over the years, from the time of Ismail, his son Tahmasp, and his great-grandson Abbas, the older traditions gave birth to a new form. As it evolved, the Shia saga became a true theatrical production, a passion play known as the *Taaziyeh.* The general theme remained the same, but the battle and martyrdom of Husain was reenacted with both actors and audiences literally reliving the tragic events. So important and so popular were these performances that they gave birth to specially constructed theaters (*takiyehs*) in all the major cities. They may be said to have been the most popular assemblies of Iranian society.

As I have mentioned, religion was not the only factor that shaped the rise of the new empire Ismail had begun to form. He also drew upon the recognition of his claim to monarchy from his maternal grandfather, Uzun Hassan. The Persian tradition of kingship was already ancient. From the time of Cyrus the Great, the concept of kingship, often regarded as divine or semi-divine, had dominated Iranian political thought. Tales of Iran's monarchy were constantly repeated by the same itinerant storytellers (*naqqals*) who related the tragedy of the Imam Husain. Firdowsi's *History of Kings,* the *Shah-nameh,* was the greatest and most popular, and was often partly memorized by illiterate audiences who had heard it time after time. It was popular in a time of little public entertainment, but it also "fit" with what was accepted in

Iranian society. How the kings acted and how they were regarded was echoed down each layer of the social order: Landlords were kings to the peasants, and within his house each father was a king to his wife and children. So the monarchy was not an abstract establishment, alive only at a distant court or in a fable, but a living institution embodied in the ritual of daily life.

Taking his place in this national tradition, Ismail had both an ancient and a modern claim on kingship. Like Muhammad Reza Shah in our times, he cast himself in the image of Cyrus the Great and the long parade of monarchs through each of the three preceding Iranian empires. To those who had not placed him in the long parade of royal stories related by the *naqqals*, he could point out that he was also a grandson of Uzun Hassan, the last great monarch then known in Iran. From him Ismail could claim to have inherited a semidivine attribute almost as powerful as the mystical spirit of God that came down to him through the Prophet. That second attribute was of even more remote Iranian ancestry and was specifically associated with kingship. It was the notion of divine favor, *farr*. Ismail demonstrated that he had *farr* in his first battle when, outnumbered, young, and untried, he managed to defeat the enemy who had killed his father. Ismail had no need to explain himself; he was accepted for what he claimed to be, the ideal of the Iranian ruler and the anointed of God.

Riding on the wave of popular support and moving to reconquer territories lost after the death of his grandfather, Uzun Hassan, Ismail was able at least initially to put aside the problems of ethnic, tribal, and economic diversity. (They have remained debilitating for Iranian governments down to today.) So powerful were the emotional forces that Ismail released that they drove him and his followers into what was virtual state suicide: war with what was probably the most powerful state in the contemporary world, the Ottoman Empire. The Ottoman sultan, who was a Sunni Muslim, obviously regarded the Shia Islam that Ismail was encouraging both in Iran and in Ottoman Anatolia as an aggressive, subversive movement. One religious fanatic, presumably a Shii, had tried to murder the Ottoman Sultan Bayezid II in the time of Ismail's father in 1492, and Safaviya missionaries were roaming through Anatolia stirring the populace against the Ottoman government. Not content with this "proxy" war, Ismail allowed his troops to invade Ottoman territory. That move was the making of a disaster. When Sultan Bayezid proved to be "soft" on the Shia challenge, his high command forced him to retire and replaced him with his son, Selim, whose policies were to earn him the *nom de guerre* "Selim the Grim." As soon as he could, Selim in 1514 hurled his armies into Iran to destroy Ismail's new regime and to suppress its Shia religion. He nearly succeeded in both objectives.

Outnumbered, Ismail retreated and left behind a scorched earth. Had he kept on retreating—the analogy of the Russian defense against Napoleon is not far-fetched—he might have saved his army. However, Ismail was so sure of his *farr* and the divine spirit he embodied that he actually welcomed battle. Battle came at Chaldiran near the modern frontier of Iran and Turkey in the middle of the summer of 1514. Despite the inhuman bravery of the *Qizilbashlar,* the steady discipline of the janissaries did not crack. *Qizilbash* warriors' swords were stopped short of their ranks by janissaries' firearms while the Ottoman artillery, perhaps the best in the world at that time, decimated the Turkmen cavalry. Chaldiran was more a massacre than a battle. So complete was the defeat that the Turks only just missed taking Ismail and did capture his harem. Even more important than the Iranian casualties, which were enormous, was that the central elements in Ismail's claim to rule were themselves refuted: He had lost *farr.* Chaldiran showed that he was *bad qadam* (ill-omened), and even his claim to be anointed of God was called into question. As they would have often heard in a celebrated chapter of the *Shahnameh,* "See that you do not swerve aside from God's way. . . . After I have died, an army of Turks will come and they will decide who sits on Persia's throne and who wears her crown." The ruler in the *Shahnameh* did not follow God's way and "the royal *farr* departed from him."[9]

The message for Ismail was clear and after the battle of Chaldiran, Ismail suffered a sort of moral collapse. He never again attempted battle to restore the fortunes of Iran or introduced administrative reforms to bring order into the provinces he still held, but instead he gave himself up to the pleasures of his court. So profound was the impression his lethargy made on his own son, Tahmasp, who was just ten when Ismail died in 1524, that Tahmasp was reputed after some years of active life to have similarly holed himself up in his compound in the city of Qazvin. As Geffrey Ducket, one of the first English agents sent to Iran toward the end of his reign, wrote,

> The king hath not come out of the compasse of his owne house in 33. or 34. yeeres, whereof the cause is not knowen, but as they say, it is upon a superstition of certaine prophesies to which they are greatly addicted: he is now about 80. yeeres of age, and very lusty. And to keepe him the more lusty, he

hath 4. wives alwayes, and about 300. concubines, and once in the yeere he
hath all the faire maidens and wives that may be found a great way about
brought unto him, whom he diligently persueth, feeling them in all parts,
taking such as he liketh, and putting away some of them which he hath kept
before. . . . [10]

The enticements of the harem would continue to plague the government
in Iran. Sex, opium, and liquor were the bane of the imperial families of the
Ottoman Empire, Safavid Iran, and Mughal India. In each of them, the sovereign was the keystone of the arch of government. If he lost his place, the
whole structure was soon in danger of collapsing. Indeed, even while he was
in office, his place was often so insecure that he had to spend much of his
time stifling real or potential revolts. Shah Tahmasp exemplified the process
and its effect.

Tahmasp feared, with good reason, the forces that had put him in
power—the Turkmen warriors. He had no sooner become Shah than the various tribes and clans of the Turkmens began to fight among themselves for
wealth, prestige, and power. They turned the young Shah into a virtual plaything. He would hear the accounts of one party, turn on its rivals, and then
lose faith in the original source. So disturbed did he become that when he
reached 13 or 14 years of age, he famously shot an arrow at his guardian and
would-be tutor (*atabeg*). This was his first entry into the politics of the realm.
But all he accomplished was to become the pawn of another set of Turkmen
leaders. Not until he was about 20 years old had he acquired the skill and resources to take effective control of the state. Like his forbears, he consolidated
his power by launching a series of raids and foreign wars. But this policy inevitably involved him in wars with Sultan Sulaiman the Magnificent, whose
troops invaded Iran and occupied Tahmasp's capital of Tabriz, forcing him to
relocate deeper into Iran to the city of Qazvin, where he was visited by Geffrey Ducket. Never during his reign was he free from intrigues and attempts
to overthrow his government and replace him with his brother or sons.

In addition to the intrigues among the Turkmen factions, the Shah had
to contend with the intrigues of the women in his harem. They sought pref-
erence for their sons or brothers and were prepared to murder to achieve
their goals. In 1576, when he thwarted one of them, Tahmasp was poisoned
after a reign of 52 years. His imprisoned son Ismail was freed to become the
Shah. He was the candidate of one of the strong women in Tahmasp's harem,

his own sister, and her Turkmen allies. Having taken power, he immediately set out to murder all possible rivals, including his brothers. When he died, of either poison or drugs, the only adult member of the family left alive was his nearly blind brother. His brother's wife, in turn, became the power behind the throne and had Ismail's sister murdered. A period of near chaos followed until 1587, when the surviving heir, the 16-year-old Abbas, took the throne from his father.

What each of the four Shahs who ruled before Abbas was trying to accomplish was what the Ottomans had already done in the fifteenth century and what contemporary European monarchs were also then doing—centralizing the state. To do this, the reigning Shah had both to create an independent military force owing loyalty only to the state—that is, to him—and to abolish or weaken the feudal lords who, always in the past, had provided military force and were paid to do so with estates or whole provinces as fiefs.

Abbas moved on both of these aspects of previous regimes. First, he arrested and killed the most troublesome group of the Turkmen leaders and then turned on and eliminated their rivals. Having seen his mother and brother murdered by the Turkmens, he struck without pity at the men and their families. But he knew this could be only a temporary measure. He had to move to counterbalance the Turkmens as a whole with another group. That was what he could observe the Ottoman state had done, importing non-Turkish slaves, converting them to Islam, and employing them to administer and fight for the states. For such a group, there was no credible candidate in Iran. So Abbas, like the Ottomans, drew from abroad—that is, outside the Turkmen tribal groups that had been the fist of the monarchy and now threatened to hold a dagger to its heart.

Importing foreign slaves was an old and widely practiced tradition from ancient times in the Middle East, Africa, and Europe. Slaves were drawn from many sources, but in the medieval Middle East, the peoples of the Caucasus, Greeks, and Slavs were favored. In Muslim Spain, the word for slave was *saqalaba,* or Slav; in Egypt, they were called *mamluks* (Arabic: "the owned"); and in the Ottoman Empire, the term was "slaves of the Porte" (Turkish: *qapi qullari*). Slavery was not necessarily a demeaning status. Upon conversion to Islam, the slave became free and, if skilled, could become rich and powerful.

In Egypt, former slaves became the military aristocracy from whom the rulers were drawn; in the Ottoman Empire, they became the elite infantry and artillery, the janissaries (Turkish: *yeni cheri,* or "new troops"), who were the first standing army in Europe.

The path Abbas followed was well-trod. And the materials were at hand: He had at his disposal large numbers of Georgians and other foreigners. What he did then was precisely what the Egyptian Mamluks and Ottoman sultans did: He converted them to Islam and formed them into military units. Because they did not hold estates, they had to be paid by the central treasury. This virtually forced the Shah to take the next step and gave him the means to do so. No longer dependent on the goodwill of the feudal lords to supply him with soldiers, he used his new power to begin to replace them with state officials. In this way, as we might say, he cut out the middlemen. His officials went straight to the source of wealth—the peasant farmers, craftsmen, and merchants—levied predetermined taxes on them, and remitted it directly to the central treasury. Therefore, at this point it is useful to consider just what Iran had become and what it largely has remained down to our times.

As we have seen, the dramatic events of Iranian history—similar to what would happen in early European history—were largely punctuated by great tribal invasions. The Medes and the Persians were followed by a sequence of other peoples who spoke related languages, Kurds, Lurs, and Bakhtiari, who settled along the Zagros Mountains. A Semitic people, the Arabs occupied a territory along the Persian Gulf from ancient times and began to arrive as conquerors in the seventh century AD. They were to fan out across the whole extent of what is today Iran and far beyond into Central Asia. But unlike the other nomads, they quickly gave up that way of life and, merging into the existing Persian society, settled mainly into an urban life. Next, in the tenth and eleventh centuries, new waves of Turks and Mongols began to arrive. The nomadic Turkmens who stayed mainly in the northern parts of Iran and eastern Anatolia, as we have seen, formed the basis of the Safavid Empire, but they were not alone. Along the southwestern and southern areas of Iran were various other Turkish-speaking peoples, such as the Qashghai, Khamseh, and Afshar. Many of their descendants remained nomadic because large areas of Iran were suitable only for nomadism.

Western observers and most Iranian governments have viewed these mainly nomadic peoples with a jaundiced eye. As long as they remained nomads, they were seen as unruly and occasionally destructive. Worse, they were thought to contribute little to the nation. So, when central government was strong enough to do so, it often attempted to beat them down, drive them away, or force them to settle. These have been policies of Iranian governments from ancient times. Thus, it is difficult but useful to get a more balanced view of the nomads' role in Iranian society.

Like nomads everywhere, the various Iranian tribes were shaped by climate and geography: Water was the key determinant of their lives. In periods of ample rainfall, they spread out over vast and otherwise empty landscapes, and then they posed no serious problems for settled government. In times of drought, in contrast, they hovered close to whatever sources of water they could find. These were desperate times when they clashed with or raided settled peoples. Between these extremes, their lives were governed by the seasons. They had to go where pastures for their animals existed. Hence, most of them migrated between winter and summer areas.

Two central facts emerge about them. The first is that there were never very many because the land and rainfall would not support dense populations. Probably a reasonable guess is that they never aggregated much more than a million people. The second fact is that they alone could tap the resources of most of the land area of the country. Only by moving with the seasons could animals, and therefore people, draw sustenance from semi-desert lands.

Unlike the more familiar Arab bedouins, who always were split into small clans of only 50 or so people and had no effective chiefs, the Qashghai and Bakhtiari congregated into large-scale tribes and developed hierarchical governments. At the apex of the tribe, which might number as many as twenty thousand people, was a kinglike figure, the *khan.* Beneath him were subordinate chiefs, *kalantars,* and still lesser leaders known as *kadkhudas* or *kikhas.* Of course, such numbers and positions varied from time to time, but the imperative of fixing the time and route of migrations (*il rah*) tended to mimic the structure of the state.

The wealth of tribes derived from their animals, mainly sheep, and their weakness lay in the vagaries of the weather. But life was rarely far from the edge of hunger. Thus, when they could, the nomads resisted attempts by government to confiscate their flocks, and when driven by starvation, they stole what they could from villagers. But in general, they traded with settled peoples on more or less equitable and mutually beneficial terms: They offered animal products in exchange for the farmers' agricultural produce.

*F*ar more numerous than the nomads were Iran's peasant farmers. The proportions varied over time. As nearly as I can deduce, in times of relative peace, there were about 10 to 15 villagers for each nomad, but as towns and cities suffered earthquakes, famines, or invasions, the proportion of settled urban dwellers fell far lower. Towns grew quite large, but few villages would have included more than a hundred or so families. Most were far smaller. Over the years, some villages contracted or even disappeared entirely. In times of desperation, villagers might flee to towns. They had no other refuge because the nomadic life, far from being as primitive as outsiders are wont to think, required a high level of skill, and tribal groups tended to be homogenous and exclusive.

The villagers planted food grains (wheat, barley, and rice). Because they did not "own" the land, but had only customary or usufruct rights on it, they usually had to give up a third to a half of their production to the agent (*mustajir*) of the absentee owner. What they had left, they mostly ate, usually baking the wheat into bread on the sides of earthenware pots or over fires made of dung cakes. For them, meat was a rare delicacy. Almost inevitably it would be chicken because larger animals were far too expensive to be eaten. Indeed, animals became members of the household, usually living in or under the dwelling.

Farming was done by human and animal power with light wooden plows. Threshing was effected as in medieval Europe by cattle walking in circles or pulling a sort of sled over piled-up stalks of grain. With wooden forks, men and boys threw the grain into the wind to separate the chaff. Fodder was then gathered, bundled, and stored on the rooftops while grain was protected against wet and rats in clay pots. Few villages managed to market even a part of their crops, but virtually all contributed to the food supply of cities by payment in kind as taxes. It followed that the villages imported virtually nothing from outside. Autarkic, they passed down, generation after generation, their tools and even their clothing. Women wove simple fabrics and rugs from the wool of their sheep or that acquired from passing nomads. They had essentially no luxuries. The occasional piece of jewelry a woman might have was more a "bank account" than an ornament.

Houses were made of unbaked mud brick. Roofs were usually flat, supported by beams where wood was available or formed into cones where it was not. The village was fortunate if a water channel could be directed through or alongside it both to supply fresh water for humans and animals and to dispose of waste.

Society was narrow and inward-looking. Marriage to first cousins, contracted at birth and consummated at puberty, was common. If the village was large enough, it would have some sort of religious establishment, often just a room, in which the inhabitants could gather to hear one of their members or an itinerant *mulla* read or recite the Quran. Also there, the village children, when not needed to work in the fields, might be taught the rudiments of reading by a *mirza*. Because this man was of meager education, the villagers would welcome infrequent traveling entertainers (*taziehkhans*), who would regale them with the tale of the martyrdom of the sons of Ali, or, if their village was situated on a route between cities, occasional storytellers (*nuqqals*), who would recite parts of the *Shahnameh*. Fear of the evil eye was almost universal in rural Iran, and talismans or scraps of the Quran were regarded as the only possible remedies against it or other wounds and disease. Village religion, in the broad sense of the word, was thus an amalgam of Islam, traditional tales, and magic.

Other than the mosque, the communal property of the village would have been a bath. There, as elsewhere, the social hierarchy of the village was evident, but the bath offered a sort of clubhouse in which men and women gathered, separately, and where village consensus on common issues might be reached.

Inevitably, the richer members of the village also acted as moneylenders to the poor so that the village, like the tribe, developed a hierarchy going down from the headman through the more or less independent landowners to the landless workers. If the village depended on water brought from a remote source by an aqueduct, its owner, who usually was also a landowner, acted like the *khan* of a tribe, except that he was likely to be an absentee, living in a city, with several villages under his command.

How to squeeze revenue out of tens of thousands of small and poor villages was the perennial problem of Iranian governments (Iran had about forty-five thousand villages in the 1960s). Over the centuries, governments hit on three solutions. The first was to recognize the existing provincial grandees, the *dihqans,* who imposed on the people in their areas more or less traditional duties and taxes and sent a portion of what they got to the central government. This was the solution generally followed by the Arab invaders. The second solution was to turn over the collection of revenue to merchants, moneylenders, or army officers, who, by paying an agreed fee, were given the rights of *daman* or *muqataa* to "farm" the taxes—that is, to "squeeze" whatever they could get from the people of a given area for a year or so. The third solution, introduced by Shah Abbas, was to appoint central government officials to levy, collect, and transmit taxes to the treasury.

Whichever approach the government took, the villagers were horribly, often viciously, oppressed. When warned that tax collectors were coming, whole villages would empty as the inhabitants fled. If any were caught, they could expect to be tortured to reveal the hiding places of the rest. Yet the life of the peasant everywhere was hungry, anguished, and brief, and many European observers found the Iranian peasantry better off than their counterparts in Italy, France, Spain, and Ireland.

Most villages were small because, like the nomadic tribes, they depended on limited sources of water. Only in the north, along the Albruz Mountains, could peasants raise crops by rainfall alone. In the center and south of Iran, they congregated in or around oases on rare wells or in the lee of hills from which they could draw water by underground aqueducts. Usually, construction of such an aqueduct was too expensive for even a group of villages, but it was a common feature of cities.

*I*n its long historical experience, Iran has gloried in its cities. Time after time, they have been newly founded and have waxed, declined, or been obliterated by invasion and raid, by massive earthquakes to which Iran is particularly susceptible, or by pestilence, but the urban tradition has remained vigorous. By the early years of the nineteenth century, probably about one in seven or eight Iranians lived in a city. Today, the proportion is about seven in ten.

As with nomads and villages, so in cities water was the determinant. What differed in the cities was that their larger congregations of people made it possible for them to force nature to work for them. They learned very early that they could build cities if some source of water could be found—often as much as 30 or even 50 kilometers (20 or 30 miles) away. Not having metal to make pipes, they learned how to dig underground aqueducts from a source so that water would flow down toward the site of the dwellings. These aqueducts, known in Arabic as *qanat* and in Farsi as *Kariz,* required the skilled traditional engineers, the *muqanni,* to dig shafts, many as much as 100 meters (roughly 330 feet) deep, every 30 or 40 meters (about 100 to 130 feet), down to the tunnel to evacuate the earth. This technique dates back at least to the earliest recorded times.[11] All over Iran, one can see small mounds where the earth was brought up, making a pattern that from the air appears to be strings of dots leading to towns and cities from distant hills. I watched one being dug in 1958 just outside Tehran.

Where the climate was almost insufferably hot, as, for example, in the great interior desert at Kerman, the people invented a passive form of air-conditioning. They built towers, known as *bad-girs,* to catch drafts of wind and channel them down into their houses. Because the houses would heat up during the day, they—like people throughout the hot lands of India, Iran, and Iraq—adapted their habits and architecture to the daily temperature routine. In the cool of evening, they slept on the flat roofs; when hit by the first searing rays of the morning sun, they retreated to the half cellars they had dug under their houses.

Theirs was an old habit. When one of the first English visitors came to Iran in June 1628, he followed the local habit. Sir Thomas Herbert wrote,

> The house where we lodged overtopped all the rest; from whose high terrace, early one morning, I took a prospect both of city and country. I could perceive thence that most of the masters of families slept nightly with their seraglios upon the tops of their houses, which were spread with carpets; some (I easily perceived) had three, some six women about them, wrapped in cambolines or fine linen. . . .[12]

Herbert must have observed rather more closely than it was considered polite to do as he found "the women lovely." He admits that "this curiosity (or rashness rather) had like to have cost me dearly, the penalty being an arrow in his brains that dares to do it. . . ."

The flat roofs were composed of thick layers of earth supported by wooden beams. The layer of earth provided some insulation for the houses below but had to be rolled after each (infrequent) rain. They were also dangerous because, in the (frequent) earthquakes, the beams would come apart and dump tons of earth on the rooms below. Earthquakes in Iran often caused—and still cause—huge loss of life.

When I lived in Baghdad in the days before air conditioning, everyone still slept on the roofs. I followed their habit. By night, like Herbert, I escaped the still-hot house below for the relatively cool roof. When the sun rose, I could see hundreds of my neighbors scurry below. I followed. Down I went to a sort of half cellar that in Arabic was called a *sirdab* and to the Persian speakers was known as a *zir-i zamin*.

Dealing with the heat of the day also imposed an urban plan on the Iranians, as it did on many of the other Middle Eastern and North African peoples. Streets or alleys (*kucheh*) were narrow so that each house partly shaded its neighbors. Often the houses almost touched one another as balconies arched across the lane below. Like the slit trenches dug by soldiers, the alleyways turned and twisted so that none of the houses had to suffer the full blast of the sun throughout the day. Many ended in culs-de-sac (*bumbast*), which were often determined by the accidents of inheritance or purchase. To the visitor from colder climates, the traditional Iranian cities thus appeared chaotic, a labyrinth, the nightmare of a city planner. But when considered in the context of climate and economy, they evinced a fundamental rationale.

Where climate and economy allowed, Iranian houses developed a different style. Then the traditional house was built around a walled garden. The walled garden is the origin of the English word *paradise*.[13] At the center of the garden, where water was plentiful enough and the house owner rich enough, was a fountain. So important was the garden that it became, in folk literature, religion, and poetry, the symbol and description of Heaven. Indeed, the Quranic description of Heaven is "a garden beneath which rivers flow." In Zoroastrianism and later in Islam, "the redeemed soul is [compared to] a radiant and ever-verdant garden." In "The poetic gardens of medieval Persia share an important and unifying feature: they are paradises of love."[14]

Inside the garden, behind the walls that fronted on the street, a house was generally divided into two sections. The family lived in the inner (*birun*) part, where outsiders were not welcome and where the sleeping quarters and kitchen were located; the adult males spent much of their time in the outer (*anderun*) section, where guests were received.

Beyond the individual houses were the civic buildings and institutions that made the city more than the sum of its parts. A city was usually divided into quarters (*mahalleh*) that often were walled—they were the original "gated communities"—and often focused on a religious meeting place. The mosque, temple, or church—usually all the inhabitants of a given quarter were of the same faith[15]—was both a community meeting place and an informal school where the children of the quarter would be taught to read. Inevitably, the quarter also had one or more public baths.

Linking the quarters together would be a *bazar* (the word comes from the Middle Persian or Pahlavi word *vajar*). Although the function of the bazaar (as we spell the Persian word) was essentially to exchange goods, it was the fundamental urban institution. Its merchants formed a distinct social group, indeed a pressure group, that almost uniquely, if only occasionally, counterbalanced the ruling institution. It was the place where the craft guilds (*asnaf*) operated, and in its hotels (*caravanserais* or *timchehs*) foreigners could safely sleep and store their goods. Thus, it was the link among cities and even foreign countries. Also in the bazaars would be coffeehouses (*qawahhanehs*) or teahouses (*chaihanehs*), which served drinks and acted as impromptu theaters for storytellers and other entertainers.

Because Iran was a large country in which travel was often difficult and always expensive, its cities developed distinctive local cultures. Many were ancient or were built on the ruins of ancient cities. Over the centuries, names sometimes changed, but often the old name will reveal its original function. Hamadan in western Iran, originally known as Ecbatana, probably was founded by the Medes before their unification with the Persians in the eighth century BC. In old Persian, its name meant "the meeting place" because it was on the junction of trade routes. Founded in the time of Cyrus the Great, Isfahan's ancient name meant "soldiers' assembly ground." Newer cities sometimes replaced more ancient neighbors as Mashad replaced Tus, which was destroyed by the son of the Mongol invader, Timur, in 1389. Mashad, where the tomb of the Imam Ali Reza is located, derives its name from its function as a center of pilgrimage and means "Place of the Martyr." Shiraz, which supplied laborers to build the great palace of Darius at Persepolis, may be dated to at least 517 BC. It came to be known as the "poetic capital of Iran" because of the fame of Saadi and Hafiz, among many other poets. A number of other famous cities, including Qazvin, Nishapur, and Kermanshah, were founded by Sasanian monarchs.

European visitors were sometimes charmed, and often infuriated, by the Iranians they met. Although most of what they wrote down concerned the Shahs and the factions fighting power as these concerned their ability to trade, they sometimes found time to describe Iranian society. For example, the English agent Lionel Plumtree reported that

> Cassan [Kashan] is a towne that consisteth altogether of merchandise, and the best trade of all the land is there, being greatly frequented by the merchants of India. . . . The towne is much to be commended for the civil and good government that is there used. An idel person is not suffered to live amongst them. The child that is but five yeeres old is set to some labour. No il rule, disorder or riots by gaming or otherwise, is there permitted. Playing at Dice or Cards is by the law present death.[16]

Foreigners found the Iranians exotic and bizarre, but sometimes enchanting. The English merchant Anthony Jenkinson in 1561 judged them to be "comely and of good complexion, proude and of good courage, esteeming themsleves to bee best of all nations, both for their religion and houlinesse, which is most erroreous, and also for all other their fashions. They be martial, delighting in faire horses and good harnesse, soone angrie, craftie and hard people."[17]

The visitors were also intrigued by the cities. What little we know of the cities' histories makes tragic reading but testifies to the indomitable spirit of their citizens. Time after time, the cities were razed by foreign invaders, sacked by marauding nomads, or leveled by earthquakes. The lovely old medieval city of Nishapur, the home of Omar Khayyam, has probably been destroyed and rebuilt more times than any other city in the world. Almost every half century, Tabriz, which was probably founded by the first Indo-European immigrants in the ninth century BC, was knocked down by earthquakes. The earthquakes on which records exist hit the population with the intensity of nuclear bombs, each killing tens of thousands of people.

The most famous and beautiful of all the cities was Isfahan, to which Shah Abbas transferred his capital in 1598. Western visitors were stunned by its size—at nearly a million people, larger than contemporary London—and the majesty of its architecture. As Tsar Peter did to St. Petersburg, so Shah Abbas did to Isfahan, bringing in the foremost architects, master builders, and artisans from Europe, particularly from Italy. Abbas went Peter two better, also bringing skilled men from both India and China. Tsar and Shah personally supervised their work, and both laid out their playgrounds on a vast scale. An Anglo-French visitor reported that Isfahan contained 162 mosques,

48 colleges, 273 public baths, and nearly 2,000 caravansarais. As one of the foremost historians of his period has written, he added "a new array of jewels . . . to the rich treasury of brilliant architectural achievements left by the earlier dynasties in Persia, and such as represented a culmination of the aesthetic standard of a whole epoch."[18]

Most impressive of all, everyone agreed, was the enormous central square, the *Maidan-i Shah*, which is about six times as large as Venice's Piazza San Marco. So grand an area, it was used as a polo field (with Shah Abbas sometimes taking part), a mounted archery ground, an arena for gladiatorial combats and fights among wild animals, as well as the strolling ground of the inhabitants moving from one coffeehouse to the next, tasting the caramel cakes for which the city was famous and being entertained by storytellers, jugglers, acrobats, and poets. Overhead in the gallery of the high palace gatehouse was a balcony for the orchestra (the *naqqarkhane*) that played when the Shah was in residence. Musical performances were a Zoroastrian tradition. On occasion, Abbas would cause the buildings around the square to be lit by oil lamps, said to number upward of fifty thousand. European visitors found the sights unforgettable.

Situated at the head of the great square, the *Masjid-i Shah*, the Shah's Mosque, is surely one of the most imposing of the world's religious monuments. Building it is said to have consumed some eighteen million bricks and half a million polychrome tiles. It was begun in 1611 and was not finished when Abbas died in 1629.

The bazaar leads off from the *Maidan-i Shah*. It spreads over an enormous area, a virtual city in itself with shops, small factories, houses, restaurants, mosques, baths, caravansarais, and warehouses. Each walled and gated area of the bazaar was maintained by a craft guild—brass workers, silver workers, silk weavers, carpet makers, potters, leather workers, carpenters, and tailors—whose members provided all necessary social services for their separate areas, from police and firemen through schools and clinics. The leaders of the guilds (*reshsafedan-e asnaf*) were potent figures in the politics of the city because they could close the bazaar in protest against government actions. Each guild was collectively responsible for a tax (the *bunicha*), which the guild's leader apportioned among the members. He also ensured the payment of rent because the bazaars were the property of the reigning Shah.

The popular Iranian slogan sums it up: "Isfahan is half the world" (*Isfahan nisf-i jahan*).

Alas, there was a dark side to the Iranian state: It was the monarch himself, the capstone of the arch of power. If he was weak, as many Shahs were, the state fell apart and was subject to invasion or civil war; if he was strong, it was almost worse. Abbas, for all his love of beauty, his promotion of the well-being of his subjects through public works projects, his endowment of the cities, and his tolerance of other religions and other ways of life, was not restrained by any institutional mechanisms or by custom. Living with the fear engendered by the fragility of his power, he often used his control savagely in what he thought was self-defense. He was sure that the hand of every man actually or potentially held a dagger. In this fear and its bloody consequences, he was not unlike his Russian near contemporary, Tsar Ivan the Terrible. As had Ivan's, Abbas' fear had tragic consequences for both his family and his country.

Abbas thus prepared the way for the decline of his dynasty. Having come to the throne in a coup against his father, he had his surviving brothers blinded so that they were ineligible for the throne. He so mistrusted his sons that he restricted them to the harem, refusing to let them learn anything about political or military affairs. Then, fearing that his eldest son the crown prince might still have managed to learn enough about statecraft to become a potential rival, he had him stabbed to death, and he followed this act by having his other sons blinded. By the time he died in 1629, the only surviving heir was a grandson. That man, who actually did become his successor, carried on his grandfather's tradition of mayhem and added to it his addiction to opium and wine. Unbridled cruelty and instability were inherent in the institution of the monarchy and Iran's lack of balancing institutions. Abbas would not be the last Shah to prove the adage of the great English historian Lord Action that power corrupts and absolute power corrupts absolutely.

Three

SHAHS, *ULAMA*, AND WESTERN POWERS

In this chapter, I take up six themes that permeate Iranian history and are essential to understanding Iran: (a) the nature and justification of kingship, (b) the turmoil caused by the conflict between the monarchy and the powerful tribes, (c) the way kingship was affected by Shia Islam and traditional Iranian beliefs, (d) the growth of the Shia religious establishment, (e) the growing role of foreigners in the economy and government of the country, and (f) the Iranian response to foreign intrusion. I turn first to kingship.

From their earliest recorded history, Iranians assumed that society was organized in a pyramid, with an ascending order of rulers beginning with the head of a family and rising through various stages to a monarch. The authority of a father over his children seemed self-evident, and the power of a village headman could be explained by his ownership of water rights or land, while a clan of nomads was usually led by their father or grandfather, who performed the necessary functions of organizing migration. But the claims to leadership beyond these basic orders were more abstract and are more difficult to analyze. How did a man become the leader of a large tribe that rarely, if ever, assembled as a whole and was composed of clans, each of which had its own leader? How did several tribes that were often enemies and always "foreign" to one another, that sometimes spoke different languages, were shaped by different cultural traditions, and even followed different sects or re-ligions, combine to support a single leader? Finally, how did all these some-times conflicting needs and ambitions coalesce behind the supreme ruler?

Power, however necessary, was not, in itself, sufficient to justify monar-chy. From early times, monarchs sought to validate their positions by claim-ing a tie, however remote, to previous royal figures. The early Iranians termed this *farr*. The concept of *farr*, as pointed out in Chapter Two, is dif-ficult to translate, but, approximately, it means "divine favor." Divine favor could be measured by worldly success; a ruler who had divine favor won his battles.

I have described how the founder of the Safavid dynasty, Shah Ismail, began with such a surge of unlikely military success that those around him—and he himself—became sure that he enjoyed divine favor; many apparently even believed that he was a god incarnate. Then when he was defeated by the Ottoman Empire in the great battle of Chaldiran and lost his army, his harem, and nearly his life, his followers and even he came to believe that he was *bad qadam,* or ill-omened. Loss of *farr* is a recurrent theme in the great epic of the Iranian monarchy, the *Shahnameh*. When a ruler loses it, he is doomed. This is not just a recondite bit of ancient history. It shaped the Iranian revolution against the Shah in our times.

Thus, to understand Iran and the Iranians, it is necessary to probe the nature of power, and particularly the justification for the possession of power. To gain insights into the Iranian form of social organization and attitudes toward it, so different from the one with which Westerners are familiar, I turn briefly to the writing of the man who has been recognized as the earliest and perhaps still the most perceptive student of Islamic tribal societies, the great fourteenth-century historian Ibn Khaldun.[1]

Ibn Khaldun learned about tribal societies primarily in his own neigh-borhood, North Africa. There, he observed that tribesmen were often driven by fear of one another and by hunger or greed. Many observers have noticed these motivations, but what Ibn Khaldun raised was a more penetrating ques-tion: Why are tribesmen who are divided by geography, are in competition for scarce resources, and, as he wrote, are virtually wild animals sometimes able to overcome their divisions and organize themselves in such a way as to suc-cessfully project power?

The simple answer, he believed, arose naturally among men who belong to a single lineage "since the absolute attachment to one's immediate group of relatives is the most important of the emotions that God put into the hearts of His creatures." This attachment weakens in conditions of affluence, and particularly in cities, but in the harsh conditions of the desert, men need one another to survive. They are thus motivated by a force he called *asabiyah.* The word is particularly evocative. In its basic sense, used with a rope, it means "twisted tightly," and used as a metaphor, it means "to draw a folk close together" (*asaba'l-qawm*). For Ibn Khaldun, *asabiyah* meant "that emotional attachment to a group which causes men to overcome their selfish aims to act in the collective interest." Without this force, nomads are mutually destructive, weak, and easily beaten, but by "turning their faces in the same direction," *asabiyah* makes them politically and militarily effective.

Ibn Khaldun did not visit Iran, but had he done so, he would have found two characteristics of its experience understandable. He observed that in a country with many tribes, it is rare that a dynasty can establish itself because each separate group is internally tightly bound and each seeks its own aggrandizement. Each group is motivated by the fact that "rule is a noble function whose gratifications include access to all earthly good things, bodily desires and personal delights," so in their quest for these things, each group is in conflict with others.

The second motivation that Ibn Khaldun would have stressed is that men seek order and stability. It was inherent, if often only theoretically, in the social structure of Iran. That social structure was—from the top tier to the individual family—a hierarchy of commanding individuals: Beginning with the Shah, the grandees of the state, the tribal chiefs (khans), the village headmen (*kadkhudas*), down to the lord and master of the most humble hut, each man claimed absolute obedience from those below him and gave nearly complete, if opportunistic and sometimes grudging, obedience to those above him. Thus, time after time, it was possible for leaders to raise armies that, although usually small in actual numbers (rarely more than a few thousand), were, when evaluated in terms of the population, overwhelmingly powerful.

Why should such autonomous groups, particularly the tribes, each hungry for plunder and driven, as Ibn Khaldun wrote, by "the tyranny and aggressiveness in [man's] animal nature," subordinate themselves to a leader? Even if tribesmen sensed the danger of destroying themselves by fighting over the spoils of their victims and decided to be governed by a strongman, how did they decide on a particular strongman when, as often is the case, he was not an immediate kinsman?

The answer is that what Ibn Khaldun observed rests on a perception common among tribal societies: that there is a certain group that has inherited over generations the aura of rule so that its members are, as he rather poetically writes, marked by "the dye of leadership" (*As-subghah ar-riyasah*). The aspiring ruler must establish his position on the basis of what those he seeks to lead accept as his right to do so. Among tribal peoples, Ibn Khaldun found that this right arose from a belief in noble lineage. That is to say, tribal peoples accept that the current aspirant to rule has inherited from past rulers a legitimate claim on their loyalty. Only then will they agree to support and fight for him.

Finally, in Islamic societies, another force that Ibn Khaldun calls "the dye of religion" (*as-subghah ad-diniyah*) tends to dispel individualism and envy and lifts the tribesmen's faces toward a higher goal.

If we apply Ibn Khaldun's analysis to the rise of the Safavid dynasty, the fit is suggestive: Aspiring to kingship, the first Safavid Shah, Ismail, gathered to himself the Turkmen tribesmen whom his father had already reformed into a sort of artificial tribe, known as the *Qizilbashlar* for their distinctive red headdress. Ismail bound them closely to him and to one another by leading them in successful military actions. At the same time, he convinced them of his right to leadership by asserting that he was of royal descent—marked with "the dye of leadership"—from his grandfather, Uzun Hassan, who had ruled the Turkmen Empire, and also that, through him and other ancestors, he was heir to an even longer lineage of Iranian kings. Finally, he asserted his claim on the tribesmen's loyalty by emphasizing his leadership of the Sufi religious order founded by his ancestor Shaikh Safi, from whom he was colored by the dye of religion. So strong was this combination of military power, royal lineage, and religious inheritance that it enabled him to survive the shocking defeat he suffered at the battle of Chaldiran and enabled his heirs, despite their frequent incompetence and habitual cruelty, to continue the Safavid dynasty through what were occasionally nearly disastrous events for another two centuries.

Toward the end of the second century of the Safavid dynasty, Iran fell into a period of chaos. The history of this period reads like a nightmare of pillaging raids, massacres, and destruction of whole towns and even cities, including the forced migration or flight of tens of thousands of people. With a change of names and dates, the record of those years seems to be a replay of the horror of the Mongol invasions, complete even with pyramids of skulls outside town gates. Indeed, Iran had less a "history" than a funeral dirge. According to such records as we have, all sense of rule and order collapsed. Could it be that the records are simply exaggerations? Medieval statistics are notoriously inflated. But even if we apply a sizable discount to what we read, the results are still almost genocidal. So what can we make of them?

It seems to me that we cannot discount the violence by ascribing it to just armed militants oppressing a downtrodden mass of villagers and the urban poor. As the records make clear, the armed militants were also casualties, and the downtrodden masses were rallied into armies. After all, the "armies" about which we read were mainly collections of peasants, herdsmen, and the urban poor. So why, after appalling defeats, did they pick themselves up and again fling themselves into the fray? Why did they so often rally behind warlords and march off to their deaths?

I infer from the record two motivations. The first was a sort of frenzy driven, perhaps, by poverty and desperation and no doubt partly by deep-seated antagonisms. The "other fellow" could be presumed to be rich or at least richer than most, and he was also defined as a foreigner and therefore an enemy. The second was the propensity to follow a leader who embodied characteristics that compelled obedience. Whether driven by greed or fleeing from danger, one could not sit still.

Ibn Khaldun would not have been surprised that the Shahs of the seventeenth and eighteenth centuries made a virtual profession of dissipation. Nor would he have been surprised that long after the Shahs had ceased to be victorious generals, and the "worm of indulgence" had gnawed into the "apple of power," the dynasty still for a while enjoyed the fruits of its former power. Shah after shah lived in splendor, bedecked with jewels, eating the most delicious foods, fawned upon by his courtiers, and his every whim catered to by hundreds or even thousands the country's most beautiful women. All of this occurred while outside his palace was hunger, shabbiness, and envy. Inevitably, as Ibn Khaldun had predicted, the now effete rulers and their supporters, the privileged few, eventually became the target for others who were on the rise. Thus, he held, the history of societies is characterized by patterns that are neither linear nor cyclical (as many Western philosophers of history have asserted) but that oscillate in a wavelike pattern—rise, stabilize, decline, and fall. This pattern does not depend on chance events; over the long run, no society can avoid decline and fall.

Ibn Khaldun's theory was played out in eighteenth-century Iran. In the years after the death of Shah Abbas the Great, the Safavid dynasty weakened.

Within a generation after Abbas' death in 1629, his successors were disappearing into their harems in a haze of liquor and opium. It was better for their peoples when that was all they did; worse was exemplified by Shah Soleiman, who, when drunk, lashed out at everyone within range. In his few years in office, he conducted purges that were at least as damaging as those with which Stalin later plagued Russia. Army commanders, court officials, and even members of the royal family were cut down. Fortunately for Iran, Soleiman drank himself to death by the time he was 47 years old. But his successor was no better. Shah Sultan Hossein kept the old vices and added new ones. He sent agents around Iran to abduct attractive women for his huge (and very expensive) harem. His government did little besides cater to his lust. It could no longer defend itself or Iran. As it tottered toward collapse, new waves of poor, hungry, and wild Baluchi tribesmen rode in from the southeastern deserts.

*J*n fear of the wild tribesmen, as Ibn Khaldun would have predicted, the Shah fled, but his doing so merely opened the center of Iran more completely to invasion. It began in 1719, when the 19-year-old Ghalzai chieftain Mahmud of Qandahar led a force of ten or eleven thousand Afghanis across the formidable Dasht-i Lut desert to seize the city of Kerman. Two years later, after a number of smaller battles, he laid siege to the metropolis of Isfahan.

The capacities of the ruling establishment had fallen so far that the Shah was lulled into a sense of safety by being told that his troops would become invisible if they drank a magic soup.[2] Drink of another kind disabled the best of the city's defending units: The soldiers of the Georgian guard regiment, charged with guarding the most dangerous part of the walls, were slaughtered in their sleep. The regime's leadership was gone, but surprisingly its valor remained. In an attempt to avoid the slaughter of the whole population, Shah Sultan Hossein walked out of the main gate of Isfahan to meet his conqueror, Mahmud, just as the Abbasid Caliph Al-Mustasim had done four and a half centuries earlier in Baghdad to meet the great Mongol conqueror, Hulagu Khan. The gestures were supreme examples of courage, but they did not save the inhabitants: Like the Baghdadis, so the Isfahanis were slaughtered in the thousands.

However, Shah Sultan Hossein's bravery was not lost on the conqueror. As the fallen Shah removed the symbol of monarchy, the *jiqa,* from his turban and placed it on Mahmud's head, Mahmud tried to console him with words that Ibn Khaldun might have written: "Let not grief take up its abode in your heart," he was reported by the Armenian interpreter to have said. "Such is the mutability of human grandeur. Allah, who disposes of empires as he wishes, causes authority [over them] to pass from hand to hand and from one nation to another, as it pleases him."[3]

His sudden access to wealth and power seems to have "destabilized" Mahmud. His actions became erratic and dangerous even to his own followers. In fear of his rages, his own guards murdered him at the height of his wealth and power. At 26 years of age, he died seven years younger than Alexander the Great, who died a few miles away two thousand years before. The results of their ambitions were similar. The English novelist James Morrier, who gave us the delightful spoof on Iranian life, *Hajji Baba of Isfahan,* visited the ruins of the once flourishing Isfahan half a century later and found it, as he wrote, still desolate: "One might suppose that God's curse had extended over parts of this city, as it did over Babylon," he wrote. "Houses, bazars, mosques, palaces, whole streets, are to be seen in total abandonment; and I have rode [*sic*] for miles among its ruins, without meeting any living creature, except perhaps a jackal peeping over a wall, or a fox running to his hole."[4]

*E*ighteenth-century Iran also offers a test case for Ibn Khaldun's theory on how a new dynasty can be established.

In the chaos that followed the death of Mahmud, the one remaining son of the last Shah proclaimed himself Shah Tahmasp. He had one great asset: He still had the key ingredient in the cause of legitimacy, the dye of kingship, but he had almost no other resources. So he sought an ally—or as he would have thought, a servant—who had military power. Foremost among those he sought was a tribal leader from Khorasan by the name of Nadir Quli Beg. Nadir, like a man we will meet later, Reza Shah, began his rise to power by learning how to employ the latest military technology. For Nadir, this meant learning to use a matchlock musket; he became known as a musketeer, a *tufangch.* Rising through the ranks by skill and bravery—as well as an adroit marriage alliance—he finally became the strong right arm of the dissolute, weak, and cowardly Tahmasp.

Nadir apparently often considered how he could become Shah. But he appears to have realized that doing so without the coloration of the dye of kingship was too dangerous. So, for a decade, while he exercised effective rule, he prudently worked behind the façade provided by Shah Tahmasp as his principal minister and army chief. Finally, in 1736, Nadir decided that he was strong enough and accepted widely enough to dispense with this pitiful remnant of Safavid majesty and assert his claim to kingship. Apparently, he originally thought he would simply proclaim himself Shah and overwhelm any group or individual who stood in his way. But on the advice of one of his closest companions, he decided to sanctify his position by using an old and well-known Central Asian political rite: He summoned all the chief men of Iran to a meeting that resembled a Mongol *quriltai* or an Afghan *loya jirga*.

Quriltais and *loya jirgas* were often vast affairs with hundreds of participants and often lasted for weeks or even months. They were aimed, ostensibly, to ascertain the wishes of the whole people, but in practice they were the means by which uniformity could be imposed on the people. They were restricted in two ways: First, "the whole people" meant the clan and tribal chieftains, senior army officers, ranking government officials, and religious leaders. Second, although that select group was encouraged to participate and a restricted amount of posturing was allowed, real opposition was dangerous. After a decent period of time had passed, a binding consensus was demanded. Thereafter, any reconsideration was considered treason.

Nadir took no chances. He had informants circulating among the participants, and, on discovering that complete agreement was unlikely, he struck. One influential senior man, being overheard expressing opposition, was seized and, in front of the whole assembly and Nadir himself, was strangled. Opposition ceased, and Nadir took the crown.[5]

Nadir had the power, but the legitimacy of the inheritance of kingship eluded him. He vainly publicized his vague connections to the great Turkish and Mongol khans, and he even tried a peculiar ploy in the religious sphere: He urged Iranians to give up the central feature of Iranian Shiism, belief in the eschatological role of the Twelfth Imam, to focus instead on the Seventh Imam, Jafar as-Sadiq, whom he thought to be a less controversial figure. He proposed that Iranians would henceforth follow a sect he called "Jafariyah." But in Iranian terms, this was a far more radical move than Henry VIII's break with the papacy. What it would have entailed, by comparison, would have been for Henry VIII to force the English people to give up the notion of Christ returning to earth to raise the dead on the Final Day. Why Nadir Shah, as he had become, did this has never been satisfactorily explained. Indeed, he made sure that it was not explained. Whatever his motives, Nadir quickly backed away. He was wise to do so because "Twelver" Shiism had become deeply entrenched in Iran, as it remains today.

What Nadir Shah could do he did powerfully and with great effect. He was, above all, a military leader, and he threw his weight into building consensus by successful wars. Blocked by the Ottoman Empire to the west, he perceived an opportunity in the east. With his senses sharpened by having closely observed the fatal weakening of the Safavid Empire, he detected a similar decline in the Mughal dynasty that then ruled the Indian Empire. Having long observed the obsession of Iranian Shahs for wealth, he realized that the far vaster Indian Empire would have enabled its emperors to acquire wealth beyond the dreams of avarice. He loved jewels for his own adornment, and he needed money to pay his ever more demanding soldiers. So, six months after his coronation, he set out on a trail blazed by the great Mongol conquerors toward the great Mughal capital of Delhi. His attack aimed not to conquer India but to rob it. The prosperous city of Lahore bought him off with a ransom, but Delhi could not. He wanted it all, and he got it: He and his troops ransacked the whole city; he seized, packed up, and sent off to Iran the royal throne, the most expensive chair in the world, known as the "Peacock Throne"; and he even abducted a young Mughal princess for his son's enjoyment. Delhi gave him the title that his biographers have found fitting: "The Last Great Asiatic Conqueror."

After his death, Nadir was followed as Shah by his nephew, who, in the manner of his uncle, quickly put the last of Nadir Shah's sons to death and killed off all other claimants to the throne. But Adil Shah—the reign title he affected—could not inherit from his uncle the dye of kingship that his uncle did not have, so he was unable to establish a secure title to dynasty. His reign was short and vicious.

When Adil died, what was left of the family quickly faded, and Iran fell under the control of a man who, much like the shoguns of Japan, ruled under the nominal sway of the emperors. Karim Khan Zand did not take the title *Shah*, calling himself a *Vakil*,[6] but he took control of the army and the organs of the state. Having no claim that he had the dye of kingship or the sanction of religion, he took up a most uncharacteristic position for an Iranian ruler—his claim to power was public acceptance. Iranians were exhausted by the oppression of Nadir, and, at least relatively, they found Karim Khan to be a kind ruler. Riding the swell of public approbation, Karim Khan changed

his title to one without precedent and, sadly for Iran, without succession—
"*vakil* of the people"—which more or less meant that he pretended to be
their ombudsman. At least in part fitting his new title, Karim Khan actually
did rule Iran for years with one of the most enlightened regimes it was ever
to enjoy.

*T*hen after this relatively peaceful and even prosperous interval, another
strongman reached out for the monarchy. He was a Turkmen from a tribal
people known as the Qajars, who had come to Iran seven or eight centuries
previously and had become supporters of the Safavid Shahs. When the
Safavids declined and fell, the Qajars made a bid for supreme power. Many
of their chiefs failed, were driven into exile, or were killed. One young man
survived but while held captive was viciously castrated to make him unsuitable to contest power. He refused to let his incapacity stand in his way
but would always be known in Iranian history as Agha (the eunuch)
Muhammad.

In 1779, Agha Muhammad escaped the prison in which he had spent 20
years to seek refuge in the northern Iranian province of Mazandaran on the
Caspian Sea, where the Qajars were respected by the local tribal groups. While
there, the then 37-year-old Agha Muhammad began to build a modern military force of musketeers loyal only to him. Using this force as his strong arm
and profiting from the collapse of the Zand regime, he quickly took over
northern Iran and then moved south to seize the central province of Fars.

Agha Muhammad had no more satisfactory a claim to kingship than did
Nadir Shah and Karim Khan, and his position ever depended on his proof of
farr. The quest for this proof and the need to maintain it with military power
were often displayed in his willingness, one is tempted to say eagerness, to
use violence and engage in cruelty. In his campaign against Kerman, which
after all was an Iranian city, he "ordered that all the male prisoners be killed
or blinded and the women and children handed over to his troops as slaves.
Kerman, systematically plundered and devastated, did not recover before the
20th century." When the governor of Kerman, who had escaped before the
city fell, was captured, Agha Muhammad "ordered him to be raped by his
slaves, blinded and taken to Tehran, where he was tortured to death."[7] His
every campaign had its tale of horror. When he took Tiflis, then regarded as
a part of Iran, he devastated the city, massacred most of the men, and sent fif-

teen thousand women and children into slavery. An Armenian eye witness spoke of the city streets "paved, as it were, with carcasses . . . the bodies of women and children slaughtered by the sword of the enemy; to say nothing of the men, of whom I saw more than a thousand, as I should suppose, lying dead in one little tower!"[8]

After he had reconquered most of the territory of Iran ruled by the Safavids, Agha Muhammad Khan decided to take the title Shah in 1796, and he chose to do so by carrying out two ceremonies. He assembled what amounted to a second *quriltai* in the same place where 60 years earlier Nadir had held his *quriltai*. Then, after a suitable acclamation, he had the sword of Shah Ismail brought to the shrine of the founder of the Safavi religious order and girded to his waist. Five years later, at the height of his power, Agha Muhammad Shah, as he was then known, was murdered by two men whom he had intended to kill. The episode must be one of the most bizarre events in the history of royal tyranny. It seems that the Shah was annoyed, possibly awakened, by a dispute between two of his servants, and he ordered that their heads be lopped off. Because it was Friday, a holy day, he postponed their execution until the following day and, astonishingly, allowed them to remain loose in his sleeping quarters. Knowing that they were doomed, they waited until Agha Muhammad Shah fell asleep and then killed him, pocketed such valuables as they found in his quarters, and fled.

After his death, Agha Muhammad Shah's body was taken in great state to the city of Najaf (now in Iraq and then a part of the Ottoman province of Baghdad) to be buried in the holiest shrine of the Shia world, the sanctuary (*haram*) of the Imam Ali. There it was proclaimed that he, almost like Ali himself, had been a martyr (*shahid*) who had died in the struggle against the unbelievers. Building on this claim, Agha Muhammad's Qajar successors proclaimed their right to rule Iran as Shahs because they were empowered by the dye of religion. These moves were clever, but they failed to endow the dynasty with religious charisma.

Seeking religious charisma was to be a major quest of the Qajars, and preventing them from attaining it was to be a constant activity of the religious establishment throughout the next century. To illustrate this formative period of modern Iran, I now deal with the way Shia Islam organized itself and the way it related to the monarchy.

The Shiism practiced in Iran since the time of the first Safavid monarch, Shah Ismail, shares with all Muslims a belief in the mission of the Prophet Muhammad. In the Quran, Muhammad is described as the "messenger" (*rasul*) whom God appointed to deliver the true religion, which was said to be the same religion as Judaism and Christianity, to the Arabs in their language, Arabic. Sunni Muslims stop there. They believe that Muhammad was the "Seal of the Prophets" and that the Quran completes the message of God. However, all Muslims realized that the Quran emerged fitfully from the memories of men in the decades after the death of Muhammad and with occasional contradictions, omissions, and different interpretations. (This is, of course, also true of the Bible.) Even when written, different readings had to be dealt with. This was partly because, like other Semitic languages, Arabic is usually written without vowels (so that the phrase you just saw would read "lk thr Smtc lnggs rbc s slly wrttn wtht vwls.") Because of these problems, generations of scholarly commentators, many of whom were Iranian, subjected the Quran and Traditions (*Hadith*) of Muhammad's acts and sayings to intense scrutiny. Their scholasticism set the basis for moral and legal standards.

Where Shiism most fundamentally differs from Sunnism is in its assertion that God chose to continue the mission of Muhammad. Continuation of the task was necessary, Shiis believe, because, after Muhammad's death, some of his followers, particularly the first three caliphs, distorted his mission. Shiis believe that Muhammad's cousin and son-in-law, Ali, should have been his successor. When Ali, who finally became caliph (the fourth in the succession), tried to stop this process, the new Islamic community was plunged into a civil war. Ali tried to find a peaceful way to heal the schism, but he was caught between extremes and was killed. His enemies then established what is known as the Umayyad caliphate.

It was in reaction to the rule of the Umayyad caliphate that a sort of rebirth of what we can term Iranian cultural and religious nationalism began. It found its voice not in a return to the old regime or even to the old religion, but in the appropriation and conversion of Arab and Muslim events and causes.

What had happened was a remarkable cultural and religious transformation. As Iranians, for a variety of reasons, began to join the dominant community, that is, become Muslim, they necessarily immersed themselves in the vision, the symbolism, and the language of the Quran. However, while accepting much, Iranians were not prepared to give up being Iranian. So their language, modern Persian (like Ottoman Turkish, Urdu, Malay, and Swahili) is an amalgam of the native language and Arabic. As with language so with other aspects of their culture, and they retained in their evolving system of belief, ritual, law, and social organization a number of customs, rituals, and propensities of their traditional religion, Zoroastrianism. Unconsciously, no doubt, they were proclaiming, "We are Muslims just like the Arabs, but we are also Iranian, and therefore the way in which we act as Muslims springs from our own culture." Perhaps the most important of these traditions is their tapping into the wellspring of the ancient Iranian propensity to assume and attempt to atone for guilt: The Zoroastrian "weeping of the Magi" over ancient failures to act bravely and protect a cause or person is one of the most striking aspects of Zoroastriansim. In the events following the death of Ali, the Iranians found a familiar theme. Ali's sons, particularly Husain, tried to lead the Muslims back to what they regarded as the true path. In a battle between opposing Arab forces, Husain was killed and thus became a martyr for the true faith. His martyrdom forms the emotional core of the Shiism. Today, Iranian Shiis still take personal blame for "their" failure, which happened 14 centuries ago, to support and protect Husain, and seek to atone for their guilt with personal sacrifice.[9]

These intense emotions are generally not shared by Sunni Muslims. Yet the relative austerity of Sunni Islam provoked even among Sunnis a quest for a deeper emotional involvement. This quest, manifested in the brotherhoods of Sufis and in the cults of saints, spread across the whole Islamic world from Morocco to Indonesia among both Sunnis and Shiis and has been a persistent theme in Iranian history for a millennium. It remains so today.

Allied to their sense of personal guilt for the failure of early Muslims to protect Husain and their belief that the religious mission did not end with Muhammad, Iranians focus sharply on what may be regarded as the core belief of their brand of Shiism. That belief is that, in some mystical and understandable way, God ordained that the "spirit" (*ruh*) he had granted to Ali was passed down from generation to generation among designated members of his progeny. These men became known as *imams.* The original use of the word *imam* was to designate the person who stood in front of a group of men who were performing prayers to lead their actions. As employed by the Shiis, it was magnified to mean the figure who stood before the whole world to lead it in the divine path.

Iranian Shiis believe that a sequence of twelve imams followed the Prophet Muhammad until, in AD 874, 242 years after his death, the Twelfth, Muhammad al-Mahdi, "disappeared." The term used for his disappearance is *ghaybat*. To indicate that it is not a simple event, scholars translate it with a purposefully obscure word, *occultation*.[10] As used by Iranian Shiis, to whom it is the cardinal belief (the *vilayat*), *ghaybat* means that the Twelfth Imam is in a sort of abeyance, ready to return to earth on the Last Day. The similarity of this belief to the Christian interpretation of the disappearance of Jesus' body and his projected reappearance has impressed many commentators. Neither is believed to be "dead" in the sense that we know, but rather is in some mystical sense "removed." Because of their belief in the occultation and return of the Twelfth Imam, Iranian Shiis are called "Twelvers," just as those who believe in the divine role of Jesus are called "Christians."

Iranian Shiism treats the result of the withdrawal or disappearance of the Twelfth Imam in a special way that colors the history and politics of Iran: Between the occultation of the Imam nearly twelve hundred years ago and his reappearance on the Last Day, there can be no legitimate guide or ruler for humankind. Even the most holy and learned man of religion cannot speak infallibly on the most fundamental issues of life on earth. Final judgment must await the return of the Hidden Imam.

If this is their belief, what can be the makeup and role of the religious establishment?

The *ulama* or *olema* (men knowledgeable in religious matters) of Iranian Shia Islam were quite different from the Christian priesthood of western Europe. First of all, they were not members of a "church," so they were not appointed by a higher authority. They are perhaps best compared to the faculty of a university, a self-perpetuating and loosely connected collection whose members guard access by agreed criteria of knowledge, reputation, and acceptable mores. If members of this "faculty" are well chosen and perform well, they are esteemed by others, attract students, and exercise influence. How the process operates in practice is often difficult for even the members to comprehend. Consequently, outsiders, particularly European visitors to Iran, were often baffled in trying to understand who the *ulama* were, what they did, how they were chosen, and how they related to the rest of society and particularly to the monarchy.

One of the few contemporary foreigners who accurately described the elite of the *ulama*, the *mujtahids*, as they existed in early-nineteenth-century Iran was the English historian and visitor Major General Sir John Malcolm. As he wrote,

> They fill no office, receive no appointment, have no specific duties, but are called, from their superior learning, piety and virtue, by the silent but unanimous suffrage of their countrymen, to be their guides in religion, and their protectors against their rulers; and they receive a respect and duty which lead the proudest kings to join the popular voice, and to pretend, if they do not feel, a veneration for them.[11]

Mujtahids, wrote Malcolm, long existed, but their authority, he found, had risen in the years before his visit. There were seldom more than three or four men of this rank.

> Their conduct is expected to be exemplary, and to show no worldy bias; neither must they connect themselves with the king or the officers of government. . . . [They] exercise a great, though undefined, power over the courts of the Sherâh [the *Shariʿah*], or written [religious] law; the judges constantly submit cases to their superior knowledge; and their sentence is irrevocable, unless by a mooshtâhed [*mujtahid*] still more distinguished for learning and sanctity. But the benefits derived from the influence of these high priests are not limited to their occasional aid in the courts of justice; the law is respected from the character of its ministers; kings fear to attack the decrees of tribunals over which they may be said to preside, and frequently endeavour to obtain popularity by referring cases to their decision. The sovereign, when no others dare approach him, cannot refuse to listen to a revered mooshtâhed when he becomes an intercessor for the guilty. Their habitations are deemed sanctuaries for the oppressed; and the hand of despotic power is sometimes taken off from a city, because the monarch will not offend a mooshtâhed, who has chosen it for his residence, but who refused to dwell amid violence and injustice.

Beneath the *mujtahids,* the *ulama* were divided into several groups. The vast majority were what are called *mullas.* The word is said to be a corruption of the Arabic *maula*[12] but is similar to an old Persian word, *mobad,* which was the name for the Zoroastrian equivalent of the Shia *mulla. Mullas* can be compared to village priests in medieval Europe, and in Iranian villages they were hardly differentiated from other peasants except that they usually could read and write. With that ability, many served as teachers of the Quran. When disputes arose in the villages, they might also act as arbitrators. Those who lived in the cities and who had more education might serve as tutors in the house of a wealthy man or work as agents for the higher-ranking *ulama* in such tasks as notarizing papers. Overall, the *ulama* gave the settled Iranians—practically none lived with the nomadic tribes—such education as they could hope to have, ministered to their bodily needs in times of great stress, decided their legal disputes, and married and buried them.

Another large category in the religious establishment was composed of students. A student was known as a *talib,* a "seeker [of knowledge]." Today we are more familiar with the plural, *taliban.* Students often began their studies in religious schools, *madrasas,* when very young. As in Western schools, many dropped out along the course of their studies and so could function only as *mullas,* but if they continued toward higher education, they tended to cluster around a master to listen to his lectures on the religious literature. At this stage of their studies, they often gathered informally in mosques or even in the houses of a respected *mujtahid.* Thus, *mujtahids* could be thought of as "professors." A *mujtahid* was one who was recognized—indeed given a diploma—for having "studied deeply" (the basic meaning of the title) the corpus of the vast Shia literature on Islam. They were the professionals of the Shia intellectual world and were responsible for maintaining and increasing its academic lore.

A select few of the *mujtahids* were accorded the additional title *ayatollah.*[13] They were recognized, usually on the basis of their writings and their reputations, as the closest human approach to the wisdom of the Hidden Imam. What gave the *ayatollahs* their prestige, as Sir John Malcolm wrote, was the approval of their followers. What gave them their power was that they were recognized as an accepted source of legal opinions. They were called the *marja-e taghlid* (the "resource for emulation"), to whose definitive rulings the less educated were *moghallid* ("bound").

Separate from these formal religious "ranks," but often overlapping with them, were men who acquired a special status from their claim to have descended from the family of the Prophet Muhammad, *sayyids.* Although this claim did not automatically give them religious authority, they often combined it with membership in the *ulama.* They can be spotted because they usually wear a black turban, as Ayatollah Khamenei does today.

Like all practical people, Shiis realized that life must go on and that decisions, however imperfect they may be, will be made before the Last Day.

So, particularly under strong rulers and particularly in dealing with secular or military matters, religious leaders devised ways to cope with this "interval" before the return of the Hidden Imam. Thus, they generally acquiesced in the rule of the Shahs and their agents. But the theory, which the religious establishment increasingly tried to enforce, was that everyone, even the Shahs, were bound (*moghallid*) by rulings of the *ayatollahs.* The comparison is far from exact, but in some senses we may think of this relationship as being like the American president and the Supreme Court. The one asserts his power while the other attempts to impose the restraints of law. But in Iran, this sometimes resulted in a bitter and dangerous confrontation when strong Shahs tried to overcome restraint on their power while the religious establishment tried to enforce the religious law. Although the balance between the royal government and the religious establishment shifted frequently in Iranian history, a sort of "flywheel" helped to smooth the relationship: They needed one another.

Shahs found that approval of the *ulama* was often necessary to prevent civil war because military force alone could not legitimate their rule. To be secure, a ruler needed to be seen as a religiously acceptable administrator of worldly activities pending the return of the Hidden Imam. Thus, at the end of the eighteenth century, Shahs began to style themselves as the "shadow of God" on earth. They often bypassed the *ulama* to associate themselves directly with the symbols of religious leadership. But they also cultivated a relationship with the *ulama:* Some bribed pliable *mujtahids,* and nearly all Shahs flattered them in one way or another. Occasionally, a Shah would threaten a recalcitrant *mujtahid* or exile him. Toward the end of the eighteenth century, Qajar dynasty Shahs pushed forward the practice of appointing religious men to the partly official and partly religious position of leader of the congregational mosques, the *Imam-i juma,* who pronounced the politically important Friday sermon, the *khutba.*

On the side of the *ulama,* Shiism justified, within limits, acceptance of worldly power. To carry out the practical affairs of daily life, the *ulama* were prepared to acquiesce in the activities of the Shah and his officials provided they did not subvert the religious law in too blatant a fashion. They also, to a lesser degree, occasionally acted as a buffer between the population and the rulers. But their major functions were carried out in direct contact with the people for whom they provided guidance—in matters of faith as well as virtually every sphere of social life. Because Islam is, above all, a system of law, the reach of the authority of the *ulama* was wide and deep. Moreover, through the endowments they controlled, the *ulama* provided many of the services that Westerners associate with the role of government, including definition and administration of law, provision of education, some aspects of public health, and such social services as existed. It would not be much of an exaggeration to say that they were, at least in the eyes of most of the population, the real government, while the Shahs, officers, and officials were the froth on the top of the society.

The role of the royal establishment was essentially, indeed almost solely, to protect Iran and, therefore, the Shia Islamic faith. Orthodox Shia thought (*fiqh*) held that the *ulama* should restrict itself to the "social" sphere and not aspire to take over government. To go further, to create a theocracy, would expose the *ulama* to corruption. The only way to avoid this danger was to await the return of the Hidden Imam, who would turn over government to the *ulama*.

This was the traditional Shia view, but after the fall of the Safavid dynasty, rulers could no longer show a convincing religious justification for their authority, often failed to protect Iran, and were mired in ever more blatant corruption. By roughly 1800, the thought of leading Shia *mujtahids* was shifting toward assertion of the right to take a larger role in political affairs. In the nineteenth century, the Shia leaders moved progressively from restricting themselves to giving advice on matters of public policy to insisting on their rulings. Because the Shahs refused to acquiesce in this restriction of their role, and as they came to be perceived by the increasingly politically active population as the allies of non-Muslim foreigners who aimed to subvert the country and destroy the faith, they came to be viewed as mere tyrants. This gap between government and the people, led by the *ulama,* went through a series of stages[14] in which the reach of the religious establishment grew, while that of the Shahs declined. The cardinal issue between them came to be the role of non-Muslim foreigners in Iran, and to that I now turn.

*U*nder the Mongol rulers of what became Iran, a few Christian missionaries were allowed to establish themselves in Tabriz. Later, the Safavid ruler, Abbas I, permitted others to live in Isfahan, but none of these outsiders left much of an impact on Iranian society, nor did the fleeting diplomatic missions. It was commerce, not religion or strategy, that created the first of the long series of contacts that would ultimately bring about the first Iranian revolution.

The first sustained Western venture[15] into the Iranian sphere came a few years after Columbus sailed for America. In 1507, a Portuguese fleet arrived in the waters off the southern coast, and in 1515, the Portuguese seized the island of Hormuz at the eastern end of the Persian Gulf. Hormuz was Iran's window on Asia and Africa; it was the hub of a vast seaborne traffic by Chinese junks and Arab dhows that plied the Indian and African coasts and ventured to the Philippines, Indonesia, and China. Some of the Chinese and Arab ships were far larger and more sophisticated than the Portuguese galleons, but they were intended for commerce, not war. They lacked artillery and were not trained to engage in combat in formations. So the Portuguese quickly overwhelmed them. Shah Ismail of Iran, who claimed suzerainty over Hormuz, was infuriated by the Portuguese intrusion but, having no fleet to defend his coast, had to acquiesce in their conquest. Hormuz was the first part of Iran to be lost to a Christian power.

Half a century later, the English began to explore the possibilities of trade with Iran. Their first ventures were along a mostly land route through Russia, which had conquered the lower Volga and so opened access to the Caspian Sea. To sell English cloth and buy Iranian silk, the English founded the first of their great trading consortiums, the Muscovy Company. But the Russian hold on the route was weak: In 1569, the Central Asian Tatars sacked the entrepôt of Astrakan, 75 miles up the Volga, and the next year they burned Moscow. The English had to look elsewhere for a route into Iran. The Iranians helped them find it.

Shah Abbas, desperate for revenue, had monopolized the silk trade, but he was cut off from European markets by the Tatars to the north and by the Ottomans to the west, so he sent missions to Europe to encourage trade by way of the Cape of Good Hope. It was not until 1616, however, that the English began to take up the offer. Fearful of the Portuguese, a group of English merchants arrived at the little port of Jask in 1616 and landed their first cargo the next year. By that time, the English were ready to fight the Portuguese: In 1621, to the delight of Shah Abbas, an English fleet defeated a Portuguese flotilla. Focused as he was on the Portuguese danger, the Shah looked on the English as allies whose ships and cannon would enable him to retake Hormuz. This was the first of many times that an Iranian government would seek to use foreigners to accomplish its objectives, but, then as later, there was a price to be paid. Part of the deal was that the English were to be granted free access to mainland Iran with virtual extraterritorial status.

Seeing the English success, Dutch merchants quickly followed and soon nearly ruined the English trade in Iran. The Dutch Oostindische Compagnie could sell at great profit the spices they acquired at their newly acquired base in Indonesia while the English were often forced to pay for the silk they bought with silver. So Iran was a net drain on England's hard-earned specie, the very thing that its mercantilist economists most dreaded. The Dutch prospered, and when the English tried to stop them, the Dutch sank the English Indian Ocean fleet. The Dutch were nearly as heavy-handed and ruthless as the Portuguese had been. Over what was apparently a minor dispute a few years later, the Dutch navy bombarded the principal Iranian trading port on the Indian Ocean, a town later known as Bandar Abbas ("the Port of [Shah] Abbas"). This was the first case of what was later called "gunboat diplomacy." It would set a pattern that often would be followed in the years to come as the western European powers used their military power to create or maintain the "rights" they arrogated to themselves over Iran.

Meanwhile, Shah Abbas, learning from the foreigners, fostered an Iranian endeavor somewhat like the trading ventures of the English and Dutch. He moved a large colony of Armenians from the Iranian Empire's northern province to Isfahan. There, he created a sort of ghetto for the Armenians, enabling them to run their own affairs as virtually an autonomous "nation" within the Iranian state. Taking advantage of their opportunity, the Armenians established workshops, bought Iranian manufactured goods and processed Iranian raw materials, and began to sell them. Soon they branched out to seek markets abroad. Their first significant undertaking was to set up a trading station at the Mediterranean city of Aleppo, where they sold their goods to merchants from all over Europe. Venturing further, they reversed the English and Dutch companies' ventures into Iran by establishing their own outlets in Holland and England. They even sent trading missions across the Caspian Sea and up the Volga to Moscow.

This was not the way the English thought commerce with Asia should work. Feeling themselves bypassed, they tried to persuade the Armenians to deal only with them at their base in Isfahan. But the Armenians had learned how "unfree" trade was with the Europeans, and they replied that they would not fall into the monopoly trap; they would trade where they could among the potential purchasers. The English were not pleased. From that lesson, they would push toward the combination of military power and political control that would shape the growth of their Indian empire and their twentieth-century policy in Iran.

As I have pointed out, after the death of Shah Abbas, despite periods of relative stability (under Karim Khan Zand) and military power (under Nadir Shah), Iran fell behind Europe in technology and organization. The Iranian economy also suffered. The English soon found that they were able to buy silk, long Iran's most important export, more cheaply in India; so instead of taking in English silver in return for Iranian silk, Iran found itself having to pay with silver for English and Indian textiles. Even worse than this reversal of the balance of trade was the wild extravagance of the monarchy. It had begun before the time of Shah Abbas, but by the beginning of the eighteenth century, it had become, as a perceptive French observer wrote, a "bottomless pit."[16] The dimensions are astonishing: The royal establishment, including the women of the harem (which amounted to about five hundred wives, daughters, and concubines and perhaps four thousand slave girls), was thought to have soaked up about half the state revenues while the army, which had long since ceased to be an effective fighting force, soaked up the other half. Expenditures always outran revenue, so, to meet the shortfall, Shahs auctioned off the state offices, the customs, and the collection of taxation. Squeezed for more revenue than they could produce, the peasants lost their lands to urban merchants and in some areas even fled their villages. The currency became so debased that merchants refused to accept it as payment for goods. As the country weakened, it still attracted merchants but increasingly also caught the attention of foreign rulers. The eighteenth century was the beginning of the period of domination of Iran by non-Muslim powers. Early among them was the Russia of Peter the Great.

When Peter returned from his sojourn in western Europe, he was determined to build Russia into a great and modern power. Even during the 21 years of his war with Sweden (1700–1721), he kept an eye on his southern frontier. There, he saw, was what he needed to begin Russian industrialization, money to be made from the transit trade in silk and perhaps gold, it was rumored, in the Oxus River, as well as the raw material for manufacturing cotton. He was encouraged by a member of the Georgian royal family, which then owed allegiance to Iran, to believe that Iran was ripe for conquest. The way to reach it was down the Volga and into the Caspian Sea. So Peter constructed a small fleet. To land it, he demanded that the Iranians give him the port of Baku. Naturally, the Iranians refused. So, while beginning to set up advance bases for the invasion of Iran, Peter sent a diplomatic intelligence-gathering mission to probe the capacities and will of the Iranian government. This mission reached Isfahan in 1717 and was joyously received until the Iranians discovered that the Russians, far from coming as friends or merchants, were already on the move toward Iran. Even worse for the Russians, the Iranians also learned that the eastern pincer of Peter's move south, through Central Asia, had been virtually destroyed by the troops of the little principality of Khiva. Perhaps, the Iranians concluded, the Russians were vulnerable. Peter was undeterred. To him, the defeat at Khiva was a minor setback. The prize was still there: The prize he really had in mind was the vast empire of India.

Thus began what would become a duel between Russia and Britain, often played out in Iran, for India. Their conflict was sometimes just a figment of the heated imagination of military and intelligence establishments but sometimes involved real clashes in the remote mountains of Central Asia. It has become known as "the Great Game."

In what to Peter was probably a minor, if welcome, fringe benefit of his invasion of Iran came an event that played a major role in Iranian affairs down to our own times. In the course of his investigations, Peter learned that just outside of the port he chose as the springboard for his move through Iran to India was a vent where oil bubbled up from an underground field. Like the "fiery furnace" in Iraq, mentioned in the Bible, the Baku "furnace" had been known in antiquity: The Zoroastrians tapped it for one of their fire temples, and oil was gathered and sold all over Iran for heating and light. Peter issued containers of kerosene (the only part of petroleum then regarded as usable) to his troops for cooking and sold the rest of it to help pay for the expedition. He thus became the first foreigner to profit from Iranian oil, which at the end of the nineteenth century would become a major reason for foreign control of Iran.

For both England and Russia, Iran was a minor issue to which they gave sporadic but occasionally devastating attention. Toward the end of the eighteenth century, the intensity of contacts increased. For a while, Iran, under the determined Agha Muhammad Shah, held its own. In 1781, Agha Muhammad managed to dislodge the Russians from their foothold on the Iranian Caspian coast and two years later stormed back into the breakaway province of Georgia. Then, following the death of Catherine the Great, Russia lost interest in Iran. But the lapse was temporary. Alexander the Great picked up where Peter the Great had left off. During the time that Europe-oriented histories tell us that the Russians should have been completely focused on Napoleon's invasion, they were pressing into the Caucasus; in 1812, they won the battle of Aslanduz (on the modern Iranian frontier), and in the peace settlement, the 1813 Treaty of Gulistan, they forced the Iranians to cede much of what had for centuries been Iranian territory in the Caucasus and to give up all claims on the rest. This is known as the First Russo-Persian War, and in its wake came one of the most vicious occupations the Middle East ever experienced. The Russian viceroy, a general by the name of Alexei Yermelov, became famous for kidnapping and selling Chechen women and for destroying whole villages of Circassians.[17] As stories of what was happening in the Caucasus reached Tehran and the government failed to respond, the leaders of the *ulama* threatened to organize a *jihad* against the hated Russians. Forced to act, the then crown prince, Abbas Mirza, was defeated in what is known as the Second Russo-Persian War. Russian troops occupied Tabriz and in the Treaty of Turkmanchai in 1828 imposed huge indemnities on Iran and turned the Caspian into a Russian lake.

Having demonstrated that Iran was virtually defenseless, the Russians converted their triumph into humiliation. One clause of the 1828 Treaty of Turkmanchai called for the repatriation of Caucasians, now theoretically Russian citizens, so the head of the Russian treaty supervision mission in Tehran determined to flush them out of Iranian households. This violation of the sanctity of each household's private area (*birun*) or harem by foreign agents was, of course, bitterly resented. As word spread, a crowd, spurred on by members of the *ulama,* assembled to march on the Russian enclave, the equivalent of the modern Baghdad "Green Zone." When they reached its outside wall, Russian troops fired on them. The firing did not stop the crowd, but it did infuriate them. Enraged, they killed as many of the Russians as they could find. For the first time, "the people" had taken upon themselves the defense of the Iranian cause. From this time onward, we may say, a sort of nationalism became a popular driving force.[18] Soon this new form of nationalism was suffused with a religious cause.

*J*n part, presumably, to try to recapture prestige and being unable to do anything in the north (against Russia) or in the west (against the Ottoman Turks), the Iranians attacked and recaptured (from the Afghans) the former Iranian city of Herat in 1856.

At this time, Britain and Russia were again hostile to one another. Having just emerged from the Crimean War, the British government and its prodigious offspring, the East India Company, were alarmed by what they thought might give the Russians, who had encouraged the attack on the Afghans, a useful base to threaten India. As they reviewed their confrontation with Russia in Central Asia, the British saw that both they and the Russians had fared badly. The Russian expedition against Khiva in 1839 and the British occupation of Afghanistan in 1842 were disasters, so they were in a mood for compromise. The key element was a Russian promise not to advance farther into Central Asia but to leave the principalities there as a buffer zone. It was a promise the Russians did not keep. The British made no promises but pushed ahead again to dominate Afghanistan. This time they appeared to have "won," at least temporarily, but the "hawks" within the British establishment, particularly those in British India, viewed Afghanistan as the gate to India. They regarded Iran as Afghanistan's gatekeeper and feared that it was willing to open the gate to the Russians.

As strategists so often do, the British misread their opponents: As we now know, what the Russians actually wanted was to distract the Iranians from the Caspian, which was their real objective. But the British were obsessed with the danger of a Russian move south toward India from the late eighteenth century right down to the twentieth century Cold War. India was the jewel of their empire; indeed, without India, they had no empire.

So when they received news of the Iranian capture of Herat, the British panicked and declared war on Iran. They then sent an expeditionary force from India up the Persian Gulf, where it fought a short battle with the Iranian army. (Ninety years later, they would do almost the same again, stopping just short of a full-scale attack on Iran.) The war was deeply unpopular in England, and the government speedily settled the conflict in the 1857 Treaty of Paris, which forced the Iranians to recognize Afghan sovereignty and specified that in any future dispute between Iran and Afghanistan, Great Britain would arbitrate. The settlement came none too soon because a far more serious threat to Britain's position in India was posed by the 1857 Sepoy Rebellion in India.

Still smarting from the Crimean War and sensing opportunity in Britain's distraction in the Sepoy Rebellion and its aftermath, the Russians again pushed south. Piece by piece, they took over the Central Asian steppe and oases. In 1866, they seized Tashkent and Samarqand, and two years later they forced the ancient Iranian city of Bukhara to become a satellite. Khiva followed in 1873, and Marv, which Shah Ismail had conquered in 1510, appeared to be next on their agenda. Marv sounded warning bells for the British. They acted as if by being there the Russians were practically in India.[19] Indeed, the British were to spend much of the nineteenth century listening for the thundering hooves of Cossack horses.

To a small group of senior Iranian officials, the Anglo-Russian rivalry sounded quite a different note. To them, pounding hooves announced a threat that might enable them to overcome their disunity and opportunism and to bring about desperately needed reform. The leader of the group, Mirza Hossein Khan, had served for 12 years as Iranian ambassador to the Ottoman Empire.

But what Mirza Hossein thought of as modernization the *ulama* saw as Westernization, and they were horrified. In the eyes of the senior religious leader, the *Rais-al-Mojtahedin* (chief of the *mujtahids*), Hajji Molla Ali Kani, the most dangerous change was the one that Mirza Hossein proposed in the central preserve of the religious establishment, law. Not only was law the philosophical and social core of Islam, but administering it was also the principal way the *ulama* earned their living. So when Mirza Hossein moved cases dealing with foreigners from religious courts and put them under the Foreign Ministry, he struck at the *ulama*'s livelihood as well as their beliefs. Even worse was another move: He intervened in the selection of judges. His aim was to make the legal system more just and efficient by weeding out the men who were incompetent, but control of the judiciary had always been the preserve of the *ulama*. Thus, he called into question their claim to competence. I have compared the *ulama* to university faculty, and it will be clear to those who have been teachers how jealously they protected their "turf" from outside interference. But Mirza Hossein was to do even worse, and it was his next move that destroyed his reform program and ended his career.

To get the funds needed for any serious attack on Iranian backwardness, Mirza Hossein in 1872 pushed through a concession to Baron Julius Reuter. Formerly known as Israel Beer Josaphat, Reuter was a naturalized English subject who had made a fortune by establishing the Reuters news agency. His company was to be required to build a railway—then thought of as the essence of modernization—in return for a concession to exploit minerals (including oil) and forests. It was also to be allowed to open a bank, which would, so critics observed, reach into the pockets of Iranians in every town and city. So vast was the grant that it amounted to turning over virtually the entire Iranian potential for economic growth and allowing this foreign company to design Iran's future. (Using foreigners to design the country's future is a theme that would recur in Iran after the First World War and would come to fruition after the Second World War as I describe later, but in the nineteenth century, it was literally a revolutionary idea.) To solidify the Shah's support for his program, Mirza Hossein suggested a move that was, in its own way, almost as radical as the granting of the concession: The Shah should tour Europe to see for himself what the modern world was like. The Shah was thrilled by the prospect.

So, accompanied by various officials, guards, aides, and Mirza Hossein, the Shah set out in 1873. Accustomed as he was to his own household with its harem, the Shah insisted on taking along his wives and other female attendants. Embarrassment lurked and disaster followed. The women were in purdah. Their segregation would have been easily accommodated in medieval Europe, but there were no longer facilities or customs to deal with them in the nineteenth century: Europe had changed, but Iran had not. Finally, after several embarrassing incidents, the Shah decided to send his women home while he continued onward. His move solved the protocol predicament, but it infuriated the women. Feeling humiliated, the Shah's favorite wife, a power behind the curtain, blamed Mirza Hossein because she could not blame her husband. So, on her return, she set out to destroy him. In her vendetta, she found eager allies. The *ulama* were delighted to have a friend in the Shah's bedroom. Their leader, Hajji Molla Ali, denounced Mirza Hossein for "being an infidel" (in the Farsi expression, he *taghfir*ed or *kaffar*ed him) who wanted to sell Iran to the foreigners and Christianize it. Other senior officials and members of the royal family who aspired to influence rushed to join the lynch mob. They feared Hossein's reforms and probably were angry at not being included in the trip. So, by the time the royal party reached Iranian territory, a near revolt forced the Shah to dismiss Mirza Hossein.

With Mirza Hossein out of the way and at the strong urging of the Russian government, which did not want an invigorated Iran and certainly not one under the control of the English, the Reuter Concession was eventually canceled. So Mirza Hossein's program followed him into limbo. But the forces that had fueled the original grant—above all, the prospect of the graft that was involved—survived. So a more limited but similar concession was given to a Russian subject, Baron von Falkenhagen, while Reuter was given a new concession to search for oil and to found the Imperial Bank.[20]

Modernization was also a contentious issue for the Iranian army. There also, it was difficult, if not impossible, to differentiate modernization from Westernization. Since the time of Napoleon, Europeans assumed that the Iranians would welcome any offer to increase their military effectiveness and would therefore ally themselves with those who helped them. Anxious to prepare a base for operations against British India and to distract the English from Europe, Napoleon sent a small military mission to Iran in 1807. The mission soon lapsed and was briefly replaced by a British military mission. Neither made much of an impact, but the Iranians began to make feeble efforts to copy what their neighbor, the Ottoman Empire, was then doing by forming a Western-style "new" army, the *Nizam-e Jadid*. It did not prosper. The Iranian army had so declined from the time of Agha Muhammad Shah in the previous century that it could hardly mount a parade.

But military training missions and arms supply had won a place in diplomacy that they would hold to the present day. Each foreign power worked on the belief that establishing a cadre of men trained in the doctrine of its own army would give it "friends in court" and potentially the court itself. So in 1833, the British undertook to develop and fund what was called a "rifle corps" with suitable small arms and ammunition. It also withered and died. A long period of inactivity followed. Then in 1878, the Russians tried their hand. They established an Iranian brigade under Russian officers. Their venture got off to a bad start for reasons that seemed to the Russians obtuse but to the Iranians crucial: The recruits objected to being dressed in Western-style uniforms. From their already considerable experience with Central Asian and Caucasian Muslims, the Russians hit on a solution: They dressed the soldiers of the new brigade in Cossack uniforms. The Iranians found the uniform acceptable, and, as it became better trained and equipped, the Iranian Cossack Brigade became the most—virtually the only—effective military force in Iran. It would eventually enable one of its Iranian officers, Reza Khan, to seize the monarchy and found a dynasty.

Meanwhile, another development, also of ultimate great significance in Iran, began. In the second decade of the nineteenth century, the first group of young Iranians was sent to study in England. As with missions from other Middle Eastern countries, the Iranian program's aim was to create technicians in fairly rudimentary fields of endeavor. The program was not popular.

At midcentury, there were fewer than 50 Iranians studying abroad. It was not until shortly before World War I that significant numbers went abroad to study.[21]

Meanwhile, education on Western models was being offered in Iran by French, American, and English missionaries. The American Board of Commissioners for Foreign Missions was setting up schools, hospitals, and printing presses all over the Middle East and among the American Indian tribes. In Tehran, the first modern, or at least secular, school was founded in 1851 and began to spread rudimentary education among the children of wealthy urban families. As the years passed, a surprisingly large number of Iranians found their way abroad to places where their command of Persian and Turkish offered relatively easy access to a different educational environment, mainly the Ottoman Empire and India, but some also went to what had become Russian-dominated Georgia. Particularly in these places, the Iranians came into contact with more open educational systems and (to them) novel ideas. Because much of what passed through their hands—particularly newspapers but occasionally also translated books—was smuggled into Iran, an increasing number of younger Iranians at least vicariously experienced life abroad.

Even without the support of Mirza Hossein (who was exiled to a provincial governorship in Khurasan, where he died in mysterious circumstances in 1881), Nasir ad-Din Shah continued to flirt with schemes to modernize Iran. Everything, he realized, depended on the money that he did not have. So on yet another tour of Europe, his third, in 1890, he finalized a deal to give an English company the monopoly on the Iranian tobacco trade. In return for the concession, the Imperial Tobacco Corporation agreed to pay the government £15 million (which was approximately the equivalent of $700 million in today's money). It was not a vast sum, but Iran had few other options and many urgent needs. The Shah apparently thought it an excellent deal. But opposition sprang up almost immediately, as it had to the Reuter Concession and a proposed gambling concession. All over Iran, merchants (who saw a loss in revenue) and *ulama* (who saw the insidious hand of the Christian West) joined in protests. The government cracked down. When the religious leader of Shiraz threatened to kill any foreign tobacco agents, he was kidnapped and hustled off into exile. Troops fired on demonstrators. But the religious establishment then "fired" its major weapon: A religious order, a *fatva*, was issued by the supreme authority, the *Marja-e Taghlid*, making the use of tobacco a mortal sin while the concession was in force and the foreign salesmen were active. All over Iran, the match went out; with one accord, the entire nation gave up its addiction to tobacco. Defeated, the Shah bowed to the *ulama* and canceled the concession. Doing so did not enhance his popularity, and for Iran it was a costly move: Britain forced Iran to pay an indemnity equivalent to 33 years of what the concession would have earned. Since Iran did not have the money, it had to borrow it, at considerable additional expense, from the British Imperial Bank. The indemnity was Iran's first foreign debt.

Less spectacular than the monetary blow to the country was a political blow to the monarchy. Since the early years of the century, the religious leadership had asserted that the Shah, like all Muslims, was *moghaled*. That is, he was legally (according to Islamic law, the *Sharia*) bound by the rulings of the religious authority, the *Marja-e Taghlid*. The Shah's acquiescence in the ruling on the Tobacco Concession was the first time that a monarch had accepted this principle.

During these years, there came into prominence one of the most remarkable Iranians of the century. Jamal ad-Din was born in the town of al-Asadabadi in western Iran but took the *nom de la politique* "al-Afghani" so that he would not be identified as a Shii when he moved in Sunni countries. Learned in Muslim law and culture, he was a passionate advocate of the protection of the Islamic world from European imperialism. Protection or preservation, he realized, required "reform," but for him, reform did not mean modernization in the sense Mirza Hossein Khan understood. Rather, for Jamal ad-Din, it meant something comparable to Protestant Christian Puritanism: a return to First Principles.[22]

Extraordinarily vigorous and persuasive, Jamal ad-Din worked with Shahs and sultans, government officials, the *ulama*, merchants, and indeed anyone who would listen or read the articles he wrote and published in Egypt, the Ottoman Empire, India, and even Russia, as well as in Iran. After years spent as the quintessential gadfly of the Islamic world, he finally despaired of winning over Nasir ad-Din Shah, who had brusquely thrown him out of Iran. Thus, when a young disciple of his proposed assassinating the Shah, Jamal ad-Din probably condoned and certainly did not oppose the deed. Mirza Reza Khan shot the Shah in May 1896.

Living in exile and protected by the sultan, Jamal ad-Din died of cancer the following year. He had carried on through example and teaching the most remarkable *jihad* of the century.

Money was still in such short supply in Iran that Nasir ad-Din's successor had to borrow from the British Imperial Bank the money to pay for his coronation. He then borrowed more from Russia to pay for his excursions to Europe. So resented were these moves that the *ulama* accused him of selling Iran.

Mozaffar-ed-Din Shah, proved a weak and incompetent ruler, and his ten-year reign brought to a climax the confrontations over foreign intrusion that had marked the long reign of Nasir ad-Din—the shift toward the influence of the *ulama*, the growing hatred of the monarchy, the decline of the country's ability to protect itself, and the growth of a new class of men not associated with government. These trends would lead to the first Iranian revolution, to which I now turn.

Four

FROM POLITICAL REVOLUTION THROUGH SOCIAL REVOLUTION TO VIOLENT REVOLUTION

*I*f Jamal ad-Din "al-Afghani" had hoped that the assassination of Nasir ad-Din Shah would help to restore Iranian independence, he must have been shocked by the first steps of the new Shah. When he came to the throne, the already aging Mozaffar-ad-Din Shah was in ill health and needed a level of medical care that Iran could not then provide. To go to Europe to get it, he needed money. So he engaged a Belgian team of financial experts. Led by a man the British and Iranians regarded as an agent of the Russians, Joseph Naus, the financial team took charge of the government's major source of revenue, customs. With that as a base, they quickly moved into other areas so that, by 1903, Naus functioned as Director-General of Customs, Minister of Posts and Telegraphs, High Treasurer, Head of the Passport Department, and Minister of the Supreme Council of State. That a foreigner would occupy any one of these positions was unprecedented; together they amounted to Naus running the Iranian government. Wielding such power, Naus secured a Russian loan for the Shah on the stipulation that Iran would bank only with Russia. Iranians began to feel that their worst fears were reality: Iran was being sold to foreigners. Already regarded by the Iranians as arbitrary and oppressive, Naus, with almost unbelievable insensitivity, allowed himself to be photographed at a costume party dressed as a *molla*. The photograph became a sort of symbol of government subversion. This impression seemed to be substantiated by acts of Iranian officials throughout the country: Troops fired on demonstrators even in the shrine of Imam Reza, Iran's most sacred location, and in other cities, *mujtahids* were publicly bastinadoed when they opposed royal governors.[1] Riots erupted all over the country, and even the Shah began to receive veiled threats. Despite or because of these breakdowns of public order, the Shah, always desperate for money, asked for a second Russian loan. Watching the course of events, the always suspicious *ulama* found a new purpose for their traditional alliance with the bazaar merchants. The only question was how to manifest their opposition.

The coalition of *ulama* and merchant was joined by men who were the modern version of traditional class known as "notables" (*ayan*) and also by the still-small group that was forming an intelligentsia. Grasping for words to put these secular intellectuals in an Iranian context and to differentiate them from religious intellectuals, the *ulama*, the contemporary Iranian cleric Nazem-ol-Islam called them "men of intellect" (*uqqal*) from the Arabic word for "reason" or "knowledge." Together, these four quite different groups— *ulama*, merchants, *ayan*, and *uqqal*—united in a move that was at once both traditional and revolutionary: Some two thousand men abandoned their houses and work places to take *bast* in a shrine where the government dared not attack them. From that act in December 1904 may be dated the first Iranian revolution.

Bast was the traditional Iranian means of taking asylum. A political opponent of the Shah or an official who had fallen from favor—or even an outlaw—could enter a sanctuary where he became immune to arrest. By the end of the nineteenth century, the *bast* wasn't just limited to traditional sanctuaries—mosques, shrines, and the houses of religious leaders—even telegraph offices and foreign embassies had achieved this status.[2] *Bast* was so common in the nineteenth century that sheltering outlaws became virtually the main occupation of the Shia holy city of Karbala. That was traditional, but what was revolutionary about what happened in the December 1904 *bast* was that it was used as a protest. In this guise, we can compare it with the tactic used by Mohandas Gandhi, *Satyagraha* (organization of nonviolent resistance), when he began his campaign for the liberation of India. Like Gandhi's *ahimsa* (nonviolence), *bast* was peaceful and so was difficult for a government to attack without appearing tyrannical.

*A*s in the contemporary Russian revolution, Iranian protesters in the 1904 *bast* were vague about their demands. They even lacked a vocabulary to express their objective. But the word that they used encapsulated the old while grasping for the new: They demanded an *edalatkhaneh* (literally a "house of balances").[3] Exactly what this was to be did not become clear until later.

Deeply embarrassed by the size of the demonstration, the fact that it was carried out not by a mob but by leading citizens, and by the attention it got abroad, the chastened Shah issued a decree in his own handwriting promising the protesters what he understood of their demands. Elated by their unaccustomed bravery and feeling that they had won a victory of some sort, the protesters peacefully returned to their homes.

That, they quickly learned, was a mistake: The Shah did not keep his promise. At first, the leaders of the *ulama* believed that the Shah was personally well intentioned but misled by the corrupt officials who surrounded him. "Good ruler, bad advisers" is a recurring theme in the history of revolutions and was the initial position of the Russians in their 1905 clash with the tsar. The ruler, both the Russians and the Iranians thought, was the father of his people and, if he was properly informed, would act with justice and kindness. So, the senior Iranian *mujtahids,* like the famous Russian priest George Gapon, carried their demands respectfully to the monarch. From their audience with the Shah, they came away believing that he was in sympathy with their aims. To give him the benefit of the doubt, it is possible that the Shah did not understand exactly what the protesters wanted because it was without precedent in Iranian history and because the clerical leaders of the protesters kept assuring the Shah that they loved him, prayed for him, and depended on him.[4] What was without precedent was that they were requesting, not demanding, an *institutional* means to deal with a traditional problem—the deplorable conditions of the people caused by corrupt officials. What they told the Shah of the conditions of his people made a shocking story: Thousands of villagers had been forced to flee even into the Russian-dominated Caucasus while peasants on the verge of starvation were reportedly being forced to give their daughters to tax collectors when they could not pay. Somewhat vaguely, to be sure, the *mujtahids* assured the Shah that such abuses and the steady encroachment of the hated British and Russians would be ended if the Shah allowed the formation of an *edalatkhaneh,* a place where balances could be struck.

While the senior members of the *ulama* were covertly negotiating with the Shah, their secular allies were carrying on activities that were even more of an innovation: They were engaged in a propaganda campaign. It was a sign of the spread of education in Iranian society that the radicals assumed they could build support by laying out their grievances and demands on posters to be *read*—rather than just listened to—by people in the streets. How much was understood by those who read the *shabnamehs* that flooded the streets and were pasted on every wall is not known, but they certainly understood the essential message that the government had become a corrupt tyranny that was subverting the essential balances that regulated Iranian life.

To the senior *ulama,* the reply of the Shah was evasive: They should silence those subversives who spread evil talk and just pray for the sovereign's good health; to the secular protesters, the Shah replied in quite a different medium—whips, sabers, and bullets were delivered by the Russian-officered Cossacks. The protesters felt they had been cheated. That motivated them to speak more forcefully and to sharpen their demands. Arrest of protesters added fuel to the fiery rhetoric. The secular protesters as well as the senior *mujtahids,* led by two outstanding clerics, Muhammad Tabatabai and Abdullah Behbahani, grew increasingly radical and strident. They told the Shah point-blank that his role was limited but unambiguous and that when he failed to fulfill his duties or exceeded his authority, the nation had the right to choose another Shah because "A king is an individual like any one of us." Nothing like this had ever been heard in Iran before.

Stirring rhetoric is important, but revolutions always seem to need the emotional "trigger" provided by a martyr. Americans will remember that it was the 1770 "Boston Massacre," in which British troops killed a small boy, that triggered the final moves toward the American Revolution.[5] A similar act occurred in Iran when a group of religious students attempted to rescue a popular cleric who had been arrested by the Cossacks. In the scuffle, one of the students, who happened also to be a descendant of the Prophet, a *sayyid* (Farsi: *seyyed*),was shot and killed. A crowd quickly assembled, picked up his body, and headed for the great congregational mosque, where they joined in enacting Shia public mourning rituals: self-flagellating, shrieking and moaning, hoisting the dead man's bloodied shirt as their banner. The mourning procession turned rapidly into a mass demonstration. The bazaar and all shops closed. . . . [T]he popular protest acquired sacred form, for the killing of a *seyyed* was a sin as well as a crime—this time carried out by soldiers under government instruction. . . . [The religious students, the *taliban*,] roamed in the streets and the closed bazaar carrying the bloodied garb of the dead, hailing the Imam of the Age [that is, the Hidden Imam]. They were followed by women and children wailing and lamenting: "O Muhammad, your community is destroyed."

Whatever confusion they may have initially felt about their aims, the members of the loose coalition of protesters had certainly learned a new means of political action—the mass demonstration. So in July 1906, a far larger demonstration was staged. This time more than twelve thousand men took *bast*. The lesson would not be forgotten: Mass demonstrations overturned the last Shah in 1978 and 1979 and protested the outcome of the presidential election in June 2009. Like the 2009 demostrators, the 2006 protesters took to their rooftops, shouting "*Ya Allah*" and "*Allahu Akbar*."

From the way they moved, we can infer that the *ulama* saw their aim in somewhat different terms than the others did. They went *en masse* to Qom, the intellectual center of Iranian Shiism. At the same time, thousands of merchants, notables, and "men of intellect" took *bast* in what was, in view of their fear of foreign subversion of the nation, the most unlikely place, the British Legation in Tehran. As we now know, the choice was even more surprising because the British were giving money to the Shah to enable him to pay the troops who were firing on them. But, oblivious to these things, they poured into the Legation grounds, where they constructed a tent city. Each tent was supervised by a *molla*, so there was an evident patina of religion, but among the tents the vast assembly quickly formed what amounted to an open-air university with lectures, study groups, and steering committees. In the process, the separate groups began to formulate a coherent set of demands that focused on and attempted to anchor in Islam the revolutionary notion of constitutional government. So novel was this concept that it also required the coining of a new word, *mashrutiyyat*, from the Arabic word meaning "to set conditions." A constitution was a means to end arbitrary rule by setting the conditions in which government could operate.

Faced with this demand, Mozaffar-ed-Din Shah and his chief minister temporized, attempted to divide the *ulama* from the others, offered bribes to selected leaders, and threatened dire punishment to others. But to no avail. Although they did not directly participate in the *bast* at Tehran or Qom, similar coalitions were formed in other cities. In his attempt to protect himself by blaming others, the Shah dismissed his hated prime minister. But he acted too late. Led by the *ulama*, the protesters held to their demand. Finally, on August 5, the Shah issued a handwritten order authorizing a *Majles-e Shoray-e Melli* (a national consultative assembly) to be open to men of the several religions and of all classes. Learning of this assemblage, the *ulama* returned in triumph from their monthlong *bast* at Qom, the bazaar reopened, and the tent city within the British Legation was dismantled. At that moment, the fundamental question of the revolution was posed by an official of the British Legation: "Are we witnessing the Dawn of Liberty in Persia, or the beginning of a sorry farce?"[6] The answer soon became clear.

The Shah was fundamentally opposed to the demand of the new movement and, indeed, to the very existence of such a movement, whereas the key figures in the movement were united only in opposition to him. Among themselves, the religious leaders (avidly courted and even lavishly bribed by the Shah) had doubts about the merchants, and the merchants had even stronger doubts about the newly emerging "men of intellect." Among themselves, they had trouble even naming their objectives so that, although terms from European languages were freely adopted, the ways in which these foreign words were understood varied from group to group. These differences focused on politics, but they arose from ways of life, traditions, and even mode of dress that made the proposed institutional assemblies uncomfortable and the political alliances fragile. Inevitably, these problems offered the by-then frightened members of the reactionary opposition opportunities to recoup their leadership. Religion was a major weapon in their hands.

Religion immediately became an issue because, almost at the last minute, the protesters had substituted the word *melli* ("nation") for *Islam;* the new body, *Majles-e Shoray-e Melli*, was to be a *national* consultative assembly rather than an Islamic consultative assembly, a *Majles-e Shoray-e Islami*. That change was important, the framers of the new institution felt, to prevent the reactionaries from accusing its members of *infidelism* (the term for accusing them of being *kafirs*, unbelievers, is *takfir*), a very dangerous charge in Iranian society then and today. The emphasis on "nation" also appealed to the secular "men of intellect," in that it opened the assembly to Christians, Jews, and Zoroastrians. But in Persian (as in Turkish and Arabic), the word *melli* did not then mean "nation" in the sense they intended: Each community—the Muslims, the Christians, the Jews, and the Zoroastrians—was a separate *melli* divided from the others by custom, religion, dress, diet, and sometimes language. So the other members of the coalition, who were Shia Muslims, were not accustomed to consorting with, and certainly not sharing their decision making with, members of the minorities and were easily stirred against them. Thus, the *Majles* began with a built-in weakness that its enemies found easy to exploit.

When the leading members of the coalition met to design an electoral law, they ran head-on into the opposition of the Shah. With the active intervention of the British Legation, the initial obstacle seemed to have been overcome, and elections, the first ever in Iran, were held in October 1906. Naturally, they were deeply flawed: Old social forces, landlords, members of the royal family, and the very rich prevailed locally even if they were weakened nationally. Where existing social credentials might not have carried the day, bribery, vote rigging, and intimidation ensured that the candidates were mainly those approved by the powerful. But that did not make the new *Majles* acceptable to the Shah. With his almost constant need for new money, the Shah was particularly disturbed when, in one of its first moves, the *Majles* voted to deny the government the right to contract foreign loans.

In response, the Shah took a sort of *bast*. He retreated from Tehran. Outside of the turbulent capital but within striking range of it, he set up his command post. There he assembled those troops of his army in whom he had confidence as well as a jail, where he confined, tortured, or executed those members of the opposition who fell into his hands. Like a spider in a web, he sat and waited for his enemies to attack one another; he wasn't just passive, however, but sent emissaries in the time-honored way to bribe and importune the deputies. Many of those who resisted also feared for their lives, particularly among the "men of intellect" who were already members of various secret societies, and went underground. In the midst of this turmoil, just a week after signing a decree granting a constitution on January 7, 1907, Mozaffar-ed-Din Shah died and was replaced by his even more violent son.

Muhammad Ali Shah did not feel bound by the compromises his father had, half-heartedly, offered, nor did he try to win over the deputies. Rather, he chose to use the weapon the Russians had given him—the Cossack Brigade. The Russian commander of that brigade, with the Shah's approval, bombarded the *Majles*. Moving in, his troops arrested and took away in chains the man the *Majles* had elected to be prime minister; even more shocking to the Iranians, they arrested the two leading *mujtahids*. Then his troops looted and burned what had become the symbol of the new order, the building in which the Assembly was held.

Worse was to come from a different direction when a delicate balance between the Russians and the British was solidified in 1907. Then, as a British ambassador said of one of the ongoing Iranian crises, "the two Governments acted throughout with complete accord."[7] Having struggled against one another for decades in the "Great Game," with their secret agents trading blows and tracking one another in the high mountain passes while their ambassadors cajoled, bribed, importuned, and threatened officials in the palace, the two powers suddenly agreed amicably to divide Iran. This *volte-face* came about partly because Imperial Germany had set out to build a huge navy to match the Royal Navy, and Britain thought it needed Russia as an ally. Russia was ready to cooperate. Both powers had recently been chastened in their lust for empire: The Japanese administered a sharp defeat to the Russians in the Far East, while the Boer Afrikaans gave Britain a painful lesson in guerrilla warfare in South Africa. The public in both countries was tired and favored a more modest approach to empire. In Iran, modesty equated to an amicable slicing of the map. The Iranians who sat on the map were not consulted or even informed of the Anglo-Russian entente; the British and the Russians drew the lines on the map. In their deal, the Russians got the lion's share—the entire north, which was agriculturally the richest part. In that area, the Russians enforced "security," collected taxes, and essentially created a new colony like those it had conquered in the Caucasus and Central Asia. The middle of Iran became a sort of no-man's land—or, more accurately, "both-men's land"—in which companies and individuals of both powers could compete for concessions. The British got the south, which appeared to be the poorest part of Iran but satisfied the primary British aim of blocking the road to India.

Not then in the British zone, into which it would be incorporated eight years later, was the Bakhtiari tribal area along the Iraqi frontier, which turned out to have the only major resource of the country, oil. The existence of oil in that area, in at least small quantities, was already known. It had been used locally for centuries to waterproof buildings and bind bricks. More recently, several geologists had published the results of their explorations. One of the geologists, a Frenchman by the name of Jacques de Morgan, decided to capitalize on his findings. Because he did not have sufficient money to pursue his aim, he made contact with an English entrepreneur, William K. d'Arcy, who had made a fortune prospecting for gold in Australia. D'Arcy was sufficiently intrigued to send a team to Iran in 1901 to negotiate a concession. The team received strong British support but met with even stronger Russian opposition. The Iranian grand vizier, who wanted the concession to be granted, allegedly tricked the Russians out of their opposition by giving them a Persian-language text of the grant, which they did not manage to translate before the Shah had publicly affirmed it.

The original area of the concession was vast—nearly two-thirds of Iran—and was to run for 60 years. D'Arcy's group, which grew into the Anglo-Iranian Oil Company (AIOC), was to pay Iran 16 percent of its net profits. The company drilled its first test well in 1902 and, after a number of financial and technical mishaps, struck oil in commercial quantities inland from the Persian Gulf in 1908. The first shipment was not made until 1912, just before the First World War. Thereafter, oil would become the mainstay of the Iranian economy and would float Britain to victory in the war, but it also would become the major issue of contention between Iran and Britain.[8]

Other than oil, the Iranian economy was a mess. Taxes were collected in a haphazard fashion—with the rich paying too little and the poor too much—and in such a harsh and exploitative fashion as to diminish productivity, often driving the nearly starving peasantry to rebellion or flight. Much of what was squeezed out of them disappeared in the pockets of the rapacious collectors, and even the money that actually reached the government coffers often simply disappeared. Iran had no budget. Not only was there no system to check on what came in and allocate what went out, but there also was no competent personnel. In what passed as a finance ministry, the only officials were men known as *mostowfis* (collectors, literally "those who seek to get what is due"), who were not subject to oversight. Because their positions were often hereditary, some were not even adults. Handling state revenues could be a lucrative sinecure, but it was often a dangerous undertaking because the Shah, members of the royal family (a vast number because many Shahs had scores of children), their hangers-on, and powerful officials all had their hands in the purse. Attempting to draw the purse strings was sure to get a zealous official dismissed, imprisoned, tortured, and sometimes even murdered, so none, as far as is known, tried to work out plans for expenditure or investment.

Recognizing that money was the key to reform but that attempting to control it was extremely dangerous, the first *Majles,* in one of its last brave acts, decided to seek outside help. It recognized that turning to either the British or the Russians was to use the fox to guard the henhouse; so in 1907, it turned to the distant and virtually unknown—to the Persians—American government. In turn, the American government recommended a lawyer, publisher, and banker with experience in managing customs in the then American-controlled Cuba and the Philippines. William Morgan Shuster was commissioned as Iranian Treasurer-General and Adviser to the *Majles* with the task of bringing order into the nation's finances. He met with fierce opposition in every step he took from those who had profited from the previous financial chaos and from the Russians, who saw him as an obstacle to their dominion over Iran. Sizing up the obstacles he faced and determined to prevail, Shuster formed what amounted to a small private army, the Treasury Gendarmerie, to collect taxes from those who had avoided paying them. Initially, particularly among the less powerful delinquents, he moved with impunity, but offenders turned out to include Russian subjects, so when he tried to effect the law, he infuriated the Russian government. Some wealthy Iranians, members of the royal family, and their hangers-on also came to hate him, accusing him of "lack of tact," which presumably was a polite way of saying that he did not accept bribes.

At first, Shuster was not aware of the growing anger. As the British minister reported, "probably through ignorance [he] was showing an utter disregard of the privileged position of Russia and England in Persia."[9] Elated by his success in gathering in the revenues and bringing some order in the way they were disbursed, he took pride in his work. More important to a professional, which he undoubtedly was, he thought he was on the way to success. He reached the conclusion that Iran *could* become self-sufficient if it acted, as he proposed, intelligently. But he made a fatal move when he ordered the confiscation of the property of the Shah's uncle, who had been exiled to Russia.

For the Russians, that was the last straw. They were not interested in protecting the prince but wanted to seize his property and sent their Cossacks to do it. The Cossacks clashed with Shuster's gendarmes and lost. That was humiliating to the Russians. Worse was to follow. In part buoyed by Shuster's example, groups of Iranian nationalists in the Russian zone began boycotting Russian goods—even their favorite and virtually indispensable drink, tea. Some even waylaid Russian troops. Now really alarmed, the Russians sent twelve thousand troops marching toward Tehran to quell the resistance. The reopened *Majles* was closed, and the deputies were warned that if they attempted to reconvene, they would be put to death. The Russians also demanded that Shuster be fired.[10] He was in December 1911. From his experience, Shuster wrote a book whose title tells it all: *The Strangling of Persia: A Story of the European Diplomacy and Oriental Intrigue That Resulted in the Denationalization of Twelve Million Mohammedans, A Personal Narrative.*[11]

The First World War brought Anglo-Russian relations to a head: Russia had long sought to control the "plug" in the passage that joined the Black Sea to the Mediterranean, the great city of Constantinople (now known as Istanbul). The narrow channel up the Dardanelles and through the Bosporus was the only route along which enemy fleets could attack the southern Russian coast, as the Russians had learned during the Crimean War, and they were determined to control it. Britain had long resisted the Russians because, from their point of view, the passage had exactly the opposite meaning: Only if Russia could be threatened by the Royal Navy would Russia be deterred from using its huge army overland against British interests. So the British were determined to keep the Russians out. Those considerations form the essential background to Anglo-Russian relations throughout the nineteenth century. So Britain should have demanded a high price for agreeing that, after the Germans were defeated, the Russian spoils of the First World War would include Istanbul and the Straits. The price it got was control over the rest of southern Iran, including the area where the oil fields were located. As it turned out, Britain got what it wanted, but Russia did not: The tsarist regime was destroyed in the 1917 revolution, and the ensuing Bolshevik regime was hemmed in by the Western powers.

Meanwhile, during the wartime Russian onslaught against Iran, most of the men who had helped to form the *Majles* either went into hiding or fled the country. A number found their way to Germany, where some of them had studied. Since the Germans had never attempted to conquer or control Iran, the Iranians regarded the Germans as less dangerous than the British or Russians. So, when the war broke out, the Iranians declared neutrality, saying that the conflict among the Europeans was not their affair. The Germans saw this Iranian attitude as an opportunity to cause their opponents trouble, so they jumped into Iranian affairs in a series of small-scale, bold, but not well-organized moves. The first was an attempt by their version of Lawrence of Arabia, the diplomat-turned-guerrilla-leader Wilhelm Wassmus, to raise a revolt by the tribes of southern Iran. His campaign was valiant, but it didn't work.[12]

Less romantic but more practical was the campaign of the German ambassador to the Iranian government, Prince Heinrich Reuss. As the Russians marched down toward Tehran, Reuss urged the Iranian government to quit the capital before they arrived. If the Iranians would take the gamble to support the Central Powers, Reuss promised, Germany would guarantee an end to the Anglo-Russian domination. To Iranian nationalists, Reuss' offer seemed plausible since at first nearly everyone thought that the Germans were winning the war: The German army had virtually annihilated the Russian army in August and September 1914, capturing or killing hundreds of thousands of Russian soldiers, while the British were proving unable to break past Gallipoli through the Straits to the Black Sea and were bleeding to death in the trenches of France. More locally, Germany's allies, the Turks, proclaimed a *jihad* against Britain and Russia, seized Tabriz in the north of Iran, and attacked the Suez Canal in Egypt. India seemed on the point of another "mutiny" against the British, much like the 1857 Sepoy Rebellion. Thus, betting on the Central Powers seemed to many Iranians a good gamble. Furthermore, the Iranians were terrified of a repeat of the brutal Russian suppression of Tabriz in 1911. At the urging of the then prime minister, virtually all the members of the *Majles*, along with influential *ulama* and merchants, decamped first for the religious haven of Qom and then went on to form a government in exile in Kermanshah. Even the Shah was on the point of fleeing to set up a new government in Isfahan when he was stopped—almost literally as he was stepping into his carriage—by the British and Russian ambassadors.

What the Germans had unsuccessfully encouraged in 1915 received a renewed impetus when the tsarist regime was overthrown in 1917. As the Germans forced the communist government to withdraw from the war in the 1918 Treaty of Brest-Litovsk, they got the Russians to agree to the creation (under German "influence") of a separate state from the former Iranian province of Georgia. Strategically, this was of little significance to the Germans, but in one of those curious accidents of history, it happened that the chief German negotiator at Brest-Litovsk had been born in Constantinople (Istanbul) and was personally deeply interested in Middle Eastern affairs. He also had in his entourage several Iranian émigrés who prevailed on him to demand that the new Russian government renounce all the concessions the tsars had won during the previous two centuries and evacuate Iran. In no position to resist and perhaps agreeing in principle, the Russians accepted.[13] Even more dramatically, Lenin dispatched an emissary to Tehran to apologize for past Russian misdeeds and to offer compensation if the Iranians would defend themselves against Britain.

The Iranians were unable to fight the British, but the Russian communists were. The revolution had left the Caucasus and Central Asia in chaos: There, Trotsky's new Red Army faced a "White" army under tsarist officers. Fearing that the Whites would lose and that the Reds would pour into Iran, the British sent a small army toward the Caucasus. "Dunsterforce" marched right across Iran from the British base in Iraq, but it was unable to turn the tide, and the British government decided to give up the campaign. So, after defeating the Whites, the Red Army set up "soviet" republics in Georgia and Armenia but did not then attempt to invade Iran proper, leaving Britain to exercise what little control there was.

Iran was virtually in chaos. In the eyes of the Iranians, Iran had virtually ceased to exist as a separate state. That indeed was the attitude of the British. When Iran attempted to be represented at the 1919 Paris Peace Conference, the British prevented the delegation from admission.[14] President Wilson was deeply disturbed by the British action, as he was on Britain's (and France's) position on the rest of the Middle Eastern issues, but his voice sounded in the wilderness of imperialism.[15] Meanwhile, in Tehran, the British set out to realize the dream of the senior British statesman, Lord Curzon, that Iran would be one of the "vassal states" Britain planned for the wide swath of territory stretching from Egypt through Iraq to Iran and from Iran across Afghanistan, India, and Burma to its bastion in Singapore. For Iran, the British wrote a treaty that would clamp on Iran's government British "advisers" (whose advice must be taken) and a British-officered army and police force; it also deprived Iran of any voice in foreign affairs. Britain was beginning to impose (with a combination of bribes, offers of aid, and threats) this new treaty when it ran into a wave of anti-British nationalism. Humiliated by what the British demanded, the Iranian member of the "joint" military commission took the only course he felt that a Persian nationalist could then take: When ordered to agree to the British demand, he shot himself and left a suicide note, saying that he was a patriot and could not yield to British imperialism. His attitude, if not his deed, was echoed throughout the thin layer of "men of intellect," who, realizing their own weakness, regarded the monarch and those who acquiesced in the subjugation of the nation as traitors. The British paid no attention to the nationalists and had the Shah appoint pliant ministers of their choice. As the British ambassador to Washington admitted, Britain "in effect advocates a virtual British protectorate of Persia [putting the country] exclusively in our hands. . . ." However, the British minister in Tehran realized that the Iranian prime minister was in danger if he supported the Anglo-Iranian agreement and officially extended "to [his] Highness their good offices and support in case of need, and further to afford [his] Highness asylum in the British Empire should necessity arise."[16]

With much of the country in revolt and people starving in the hundreds of thousands—about one in four Iranians died[17]—and fearing that the British had subverted their country, the Iranians were ready for another of those "men on horseback"—men like Ismail Shah, Nader Shah, and Agha Muhammad Shah, who always appeared in the midst of chaos and despair.

*R*eza Khan, as he was known before becoming Reza Shah, was born in 1878 in a village with a population of less than a thousand people, situated high in the mountains in the northern Iranian province of Mazandaran. His father died shortly after his birth, and his mother took him to Tehran to live with her relatives. Reza later took pains to obscure this part of his life,[18] but when he was about 16 years old, in 1893 or 1894, he enlisted in the Cossack Brigade. He seems to have served additionally as a guard in the German Legation. In 1911, while serving under the Qajar prince and then governor, Abdol-Hossein Mirza Farmanfarma, he learned how to use the Maxim machine gun, then the technological marvel of battle, and was known, for a while, as Reza al-Maxim. His skill, determination, and bravery got him promoted to captain, and although he had no formal education even in military matters, he rose rapidly through the ranks of the Cossack Brigade. To have done so, he must have enjoyed close relations with the Russian officers, who then commanded the brigade, but it seems that he resented them and their presence in Iran. So, when the Russian Revolution occurred, Reza took part in a conspiracy to get rid of the Cossacks' commanding officer, who was accused, probably falsely, of being procommunist. Then, when the Shah, under British direction, decided to remove all the Russian officers in October 1920, Reza, already a senior officer, quickly caught the eye of the British commander of what was called the Northern Persian Force ("Noperforce"). He was at the right place, Qazvin, where the Iranian Cossacks were tightly disciplined, rather than in Tehran, where the British thought they were out of control. The British decided to build the Qazvin contingent into the nucleus of an Iranian security force and began to provide it with arms and training and paid its salaries and expenses. To command it, they picked Reza. With British encouragement, Reza marched on Tehran. There, the British assisted him by preventing the newly formed Swedish-officered gendarmerie (which outnumbered his force about four to one) from opposing him and by "advising" the Shah to accept his advent as a successful coup d'état.

Reza needed skills and contacts that he did not then have, so he joined forces with one of the new "men of intellect" to help reorganize the government. Seyyed Zia ad-Din Tabatabai, a former journalist who was known as pro-British, was imposed on the Shah as prime minister, and Reza became commander of the military forces. With what must be read as a gesture of protest, even this British-appointed prime minister signed a new draft treaty, negotiated by his predecessors before the coup, with the Russians. The treaty was apparently popular with the Iranians, but its Article 6 contained a "sting" that would later prove painful: It gave the new Soviet Union "the right to introduce its troops on to the territory of Persia in order to take the necessary measures in the interest of self defence." It was, of course, the Russians who would decide whether Iran was being used against Russia or its allies. Iranians were not bothered by this clause because the treaty seemed to provide a balance against the imperialist demands of the British. In any event, the Iranians must have realized, Russia would have intervened regardless of what any treaty said if it felt endangered; so the treaty was more psychological than strategic.

At that time also, Seyyed Zia pleased the men of his class, the "men of intellect," when he convened the *Majles*, which had been closed throughout the war. Even more popular was his rejection of the British-drafted treaty that would have made Iran a virtual colony, dismissal of the various "advisers" the British had sought to install to run the government, and disbanding of the South Persia Rifles. He became the Iranian hero of the moment. Almost universally, the elated Iranians foresaw an end to the symbols of British rule: the oil company, the bank, and the telegraph company.[19] But in his lunge to create a new Iran, Seyyed Zia stepped on too many feet. The privileged class, the notables, turned against him, and his erstwhile ally Reza came to distrust his ambition. So just three months into his tenure as prime minister, Reza exiled this remarkable man who might have changed Iranian history. He was not to return until the middle of the Second World War.

Effectively on his own, but in command of the only significant military force in the country, Reza struck out at the centers of revolt. In the north, he led his Cossacks against Tabriz, which had long sheltered the radical wing of the Constitutionalists and was then trying to achieve autonomy or perhaps independence as *Azadistan* ("the free land"). When they took Tabriz, the Cossacks killed the leader of the *Azad* movement; next, Reza overwhelmed the short-lived quasi-Soviet government in the Gilan provincial city of Rasht; turning, he led his troops south to overwhelm the Arab and Qashghai tribesmen in the British-protected area along the Persian Gulf. In these ventures, also, Reza followed the path staked out by Ismail Shah, Nader Shah, and Agha Muhammad Shah. Unification was always the top priority of vigorous Iranian rulers.

Unification was only the first step for Reza. Despite, or perhaps because of, his complex dealings with the Russians and the British, he was determined that Iran again become strong and independent. In this effort, he profited from the dealings of his second prime minister. Ahmad Ghavam al-Sultaneh wanted to find a source of finance and advice not under British or Russian control. With Germany no longer available, the obvious answer was America. So Ghavam instructed his minister to go to the United States to seek American investment and advice. The investment didn't come to much, but the quest for advice got Iran another American financial expert like William Morgan Shuster. The new man was Arthur C. Millspaugh.

Millspaugh had roughly the same mandate as Shuster and served remarkably well despite powerful, mainly Iranian, opposition from the same forces of privilege that had ruined Seyyed Zia's efforts. He reformed the tax system so as to avoid the evil of auctioning tax collection to city merchants—

a practice that had virtually destroyed peasant agriculture—and stopped dependence on foreign borrowing, which had kept recent governments in thrall to foreign powers. But eventually, his emphasis on a strict budget, something Iran had never had, infuriated Reza, who thought of the state treasury as his personal "wallet" and who wanted to devote at least 50 percent of all revenues to his new 40,000-man army; so in 1927, he dismissed his "Treasurer General."[20]

Meanwhile, Reza plunged ahead with ruthlessness, energy, and a range unprecedented even among such powerful rulers as Ismail, Abbas, and Agha Muhammad. Perhaps, up to that time, the only leader comparable to him was Kemal Atatürk, who was remaking the Turkish government, army, and society from the wreck of the Ottoman Empire. It is usually assumed that Atatürk became a model for Reza, and in some activities, this is true. Reza tried to copy Atatürk but failed in some of his efforts. For example, Atatürk purged *Osmanlu* Turkish of its huge Arabic vocabulary to create modern Turkish, but when Reza tried to do the same with Farsi, it proved too complex. Atatürk dropped use of the Arabic script, which was cumbersome when applied to Turkish. Reza did not even try to do that; Persian is still written in a modified Arabic script. More important, Reza rejected the path that Atatürk had taken when he founded a republic. Why he did is debatable. Perhaps it was due to the opposition of the Iranian *ulama*. They were disturbed to discover that Atatürk had abolished the caliphate. Even though the caliphate was a Sunni institution, it was Muslim. So the *ulama* identified republicanism with secularism and strongly opposed it. (Ironically, as we see, republicanism became an aim of the *ulama* nearly half a century later.) Reacting to their opposition, or perhaps taking advantage of it for his own purposes, Reza met with the leaders of the *ulama* and told them that he had given up the idea of forming a republic.

If not a republic, what was Iran to be? Reza's answer was the monarchy. But in the traditional sense, he had no satisfactory claim to it. Of humble birth, he could hardly assert a royal heritage. So he made a clever tactical move: On October 31, 1925, he ordered the *Majles* to depose the last Qajar Shah and to "elect" him. To be *elected* was quite a revolutionary concept, useful in the short run but dangerous in the long run. So having accomplished his purpose through election, he sought to obscure this route to the monarchy. The best means to obscure it was cosmetic: He adopted the reign name "Pahlavi," by which he identified himself with the ancient Persian tradition.

He and his son Muhammad Reza built the image of the regime on Iranian monarchial glories from the time of Cyrus the Great.

What about the other traditional claim to kingship? The Safavis had grounded their claim to the monarchy, as I have shown, on the "dye of religion." Although the Qajar Shahs could not so identify themselves, they made continuous and, for a century, generally successful efforts to win the approval of the *ulama*. It was not, as we have seen, until nearly the end of the nineteenth century that a gulf widened between the monarchy and the religious establishment. That separation had been a major cause of the 1905 revolution and, although Reza could not have have imagined it, would be the cause of the 1979 revolution.

After using the *ulama* to avoid pressure to establish a republic, Reza not only dropped them from his entourage but embarked on a program to halt all their traditional activities—administration of the law, granting of public charity, and provision of education—from which they received the bulk of their income. When Reza introduced Western-style, secular courts to administer criminal and commercial law codes in 1925 and a general civil code, based on European models, in 1926, he accomplished two objectives: On the one hand, he weakened, fatally he mistakenly thought, the *ulama,* and he justified abolishing the "capitulation" system under which foreigners lived in a sort of extraterritorial legal limbo. On the other hand, he began to undermine the educational monopoly of the *ulama.* Eventually, lay teachers were allowed to teach even courses on Islam, which had theretofore been the monopoly of *mujtahid*-licensed *ulama.* In 1935, Reza founded the University of Tehran as the capstone of the new and greatly enlarged secular school and technical training system. Finally, he confiscated much of the *evghaf* (pious foundation) property. His essential aim, I believe, was political, but contemporary observers thought he was also motivated by the desire to show Europe that Iran could be "modern." It was certainly in this spirit that he decreed the wearing of Western-style dress and in 1936 outlawed the veil for women.

In addition to undermining the religious establishment, Reza decided to destroy the tribes, who then comprised about one Iranian in each six or seven. In his view, the tribes were the domestic enemy: They disrupted Iranian society, made and broke dynasties, allowed themselves to be used or provoked by foreign invaders, and, above all, were independent. So he devised two ways to destroy their autonomy and power. The first was military. He divided them to pick them off one at a time: Some he flattered, and some he attacked; he brought their leaders to the capital, some to be fêted, others to be murdered; more generally, he decreed that tribesmen could no longer migrate with the seasons as their herds required, but he forced them to settle in areas to which they were unaccustomed; many contracted malaria and other diseases. Finally, he imposed on them a heavy new burden of taxes. These measures gravely weakened the tribes, but, most important of all, he imposed on them a military conscription program that carried away their young men. In the opinion of one of the most knowledgeable historians, "there is hardly a blacker page in the history of Pahlavi Iran than the persecution to which the tribal population was subjected. . . . For some tribes, only the abdication of Reza Shah in 1941 saved them from extinction."[21]

Reza certainly did not understand the economic contribution of the nomads. Iran, as I have pointed out, is mainly desert and steppe; only small areas have sufficient water to sustain settled agriculture. Pastoralism is the only possible use of the drier areas. Ranging over large areas enables nomads to harvest the scant grasses that each area provides, and it enables animals to be moved, seasonally, from dry lowlands that cannot sustain them in the heat of summer to relatively lush and cool uplands and to return when snow and ice make the uplands unlivable. Viewed in overall economic terms, by using what could not otherwise be used and by providing the produce of their animals, the tribes played a significant part in the Iranian economy. Reza appears neither to have understood this nor to have cared. This was evident to all observers, but his policy had another dimension that has not been appreciated.

Reza's brutal program to weaken the tribes and augment his army merged with his more benign policies to create an urban labor force to man the new state-financed and state-run industries with which he hoped to make Iran self-sufficient. Those objectives he accomplished, but the side effects, planned or accidental, created a social revolution that he certainly did not anticipate. Although not well understood, what happened in Iran—and happened in Egypt at a later period and is happening in India today—is a transformation that cuts to the sensitive nerve of politics through powerful economic and subtle social processes.

In embarking on his programs, Reza realized that if his country was to become strong, it must convert the traditional part, the overwhelming bulk, of the society into what I have called "the New Men." Viewed from this perspective, the national economy may be compared to a boat with men at the oars. Of Iran's population of eight or so million in the 1930s, less than one in a hundred was "rowing." The others could not reach "the oars" of a modern economy. That is, they did not use mechanized equipment or power tools: They plowed, planted, and threshed with hand or animal labor; they transported goods by camel or mule back rather than by train or truck; and such little manufacturing as they did was in cottage industry. They could not produce steel or even turn their abundant raw materials into products suitable for the world market. The only significant exception was the oil industry, and that was effectively denationalized under British control and run in part by foreign labor.[22]

Reza wanted the Iranians to "row." To this end, he tolerated modern education, fostered technical training, and brought women out of purdah. But he realized that the whole of traditional society had to be transformed to effect his program of making Iran strong. His policy certainly did not aim to be "democratic" nor did it necessarily raise the social status of those who profited from his ventures to join the modern economy—the vast majority of lower-class men and women remained lower class—but it aimed to give them new skills and to change their outlook, dress, and habits so that they could participate more effectively in the modern economy.

All developing societies seek to do essentially what Reza did. Like many other leaders of what today we call the Third World, Reza used the army as the incubator to hatch these new figures. He jerked men out of villages and cities by imposing conscription and, during their two years of service, dressed them in "modern" clothes, disciplined them, and trained them in new skills. Even driving a truck for a person who had never known any means of transport other than a donkey brought about a significant change of perspective. Casting off tribal or village clothing, as Reza decreed, and putting on a uniform, adopting a family name, leaving his peasant relatives behind, visiting or moving to the cities, seeing unveiled women in daily life, and perhaps learning to read were all, in the terms of the traditional society, revolutionary.[23]

Whatever his motivation and whatever his realization of what he was doing, Reza set this social revolution in motion. Unknowingly, he also prepared the way for the violent revolution to follow in the time of his son, when the growing capacity of the people was not matched by a widening of political empowerment. That lay far off in the future and the possibility probably never crossed his mind, but while Reza fostered modernization, he became particularly sensitive to and angry about the one element in Iran that was already "modern," the oil industry. The Anglo Persian Oil Company, as it was then known, occupied a whole province in the southwest of Iran, which its owners and managers treated as a virtually independent state. In its dealings with the Bakhtiari and other tribes, the company carried on what were effectively its own foreign relations. Internally in its zone, it treated the Iranians as a virtual serf population, keeping them low-paid, unskilled, and segregated. More galling yet, it gave Iran what the Iranians regarded as an unfair return on its exploitation of their oil. The payment was said to be 16 percent of the net profit, but the Iranians, who had no access to the company accounts, had no way to tell what the net profit was. Worse yet, governed by world markets, the company produced Iranian oil on a scale over which the Iranian government, which was dependent on its royalties, had no influence. Even in "normal" times, the company would produce oil in amounts it chose from its various sources on the basis of criteria over which Iran had no control or even knowledge.

Eventually, as he grew stronger, Reza would no doubt have moved against the company, but the sudden fall in revenue caused by the Depression following the 1929 "Crash" triggered a reaction. In 1932, he announced that he was canceling the Anglo Persian Oil Company concession. This was a typical first step in an Iranian bargaining process, the daily practice of commerce in the bazaar, but the British took Reza's move as a final decision and reacted furiously. The company, which was controlled by the British government, refused to negotiate, and the government sent a Royal Navy flotilla to the Gulf in a show of force designed to intimidate the Iranians. ("Gunboat diplomacy" was already anachronistic, but, as we shall see, it would be tried again on a much larger scale 55 years later in the so-called Abadan crisis.) When intimidation didn't work, the British finally agreed to negotiate. In the following year, they and the Iranian government worked out a deal in which royalties and supplementary benefits were marginally increased in return for the extension of the concession for an additional 60 years. The new deal included the significant additional proviso that the concession could not be unilaterally canceled. That proviso was to become the major issue in Iranian politics and in Anglo-Iranian relations at the end of the Second World War.

Foreign visitors and observers usually regarded Reza as a great reformer and generally approved his regime. He had twisted the "lion's tail" and survived. He had "liberated" women and reunified the country. If his regime was brutal and oppressive, that was not then unusual. The Contemporary fascist regimes in Greece, Italy, and Spain; the Nazi regime in Germany; and the communist regime in Russia were at least as brutal to their own people, and Britain and France tyrannized peoples in their colonies. Thus, outsiders were not shocked by the coercive police state that Reza created. But those foreigners who were closest to him had doubts at least about his personality and some even about his sanity. The English diplomat and essayist Harold Nicolson wrote in 1926 that Reza was "secretive, suspicious and ignorant," and a few years later, the head of the British Foreign Office, Sir Robert Vansittart, described him as a "bloodthirsty lunatic."[24] Their comments may perhaps be somewhat discounted because the British were the objects of Reza's (and Iranians') anger, but the Germans, who were Iran's major trading partners and "best foreign friends," held not dissimilar views of Reza. German Ambassador W. von Blücher described his first meeting with this creator of modern Iran in these memorable terms:

> Heavily-built and with broad shoulders, he stood erect, both hands in his broad leather belt. He wore a plain uniform, consisting of a yellowish-brown blouse which almost reached his knees and blue riding britches. Heavy high boots, a curved sword and a kepi, which he kept on, completed his outfit. Across his chest the ribbon of an order and aside from that there were two or three simple decorations. I could discover no insignia of rank. . . . On the herculean body was a head which . . . bore a certain resemblance to that of a bird of prey. . . . The powerful, broad eagle's beak sprang boldly forth and achieved something singularly irregular from the scar between the eyes. The eyes were dark and unfathomable. . . . No expression moved the face. A strong current of strength, energy, and brutality flowed from the whole personality. . . .

It was this man whom the British and Russians were to overthrow in September 1941 when he tried to enforce Iranian neutrality to the detriment of those two traditional enemies of Iran.

When Reza was bundled off to exile in the Transvaal in South Africa, the main beneficiary was his son, Muhammad Reza Pahlavi. Having been designated crown prince by his father, he took the office of Shah immediately but did not actually crown himself Shah until 26 years later in a grandiose ceremony. For the first few years of his reign, during the Second World War, he had little to do. Russia and Britain regarded Iran not so much as a state than as a "pipeline" through which supplies were sent from America to the beleaguered Russians. With neither the Russians nor the British interested in Iranian internal affairs, provided they did not jeopardize the route to Russia, the young Shah spent much of his time in games, sports, and love affairs. In this relatively permissive atmosphere, the "men of intellect," the *uqqal,* who were growing in number, began to experiment with politics in ways that Reza had not tolerated. When in November 1943, at the Tehran Conference, President Roosevelt insisted that Churchill and Stalin affirm Iranian sovereignty—the first significant action by an American government in Iranian affairs—the scope of their political life seemed to Iranians to have been opened as never before: Articles and books proliferated, and discussion "circles" (*dowrehs*) sprang up in the cities as they had not since the 1905 revolution. Iranians, for the first time in nearly 20 years, were able to take the *Majles* seriously as the focus of national affairs.

As the war ended, the justification for foreign occupation simultaneously ended. The pipeline from the Gulf to Russia fell empty. Impoverished and exhausted by the war, British voters threw Churchill and the Conservatives out of office and voted in Attlee and Labour. Under pressure from the voters to cut all expenditures, the new British government withdrew from the south, except, of course, from the oil-producing area. Facing no comparable public opinion demands, the Russians remained in control of the north, where, under their protective wings, two "Soviet" republics had come into existence: the Republic of Gilan in Azerbaijan and the Mahabad Republic in the Kurdish area. The Soviet government, naturally, wanted to protect these extensions of communist rule, but, at the same time, reviving old imperial aims, it wanted an oil concession in Iran. Using the conflict of these ambitions to get rid of both of them was one of shrewdest statesmen that Iran ever produced, Ahmad Ghavam.

Ghavam was a member of the former ruling family, the Qajars, as was the younger man who helped him achieve his aims, Dr. Muhammad Mossadegh. Together they would shape Iranian affairs in the postwar years. As a brilliant speaker in the *Majles,* Mossadegh laid a trap for the Russians, and, as prime minister, Ghavam sprang it: Mossadegh had persuaded the *Majles* in the midst of the war, in 1944, to pass a law stating that no concessions could be given to foreigners without its approval. As the war ended, Ghavam warned the Russians that the continued presence of Russian troops on Iranian soil would probably cause the upcoming elections to result in a majority in the *Majles* that would make the concession impossible.[25] Caught in the dilemma, the Russians opted for the concession and dropped their support for their friends in Gilan and Mahabad. No sooner had they done so than Ghavam sent the Iranian army to depose the dissident leaders and reclaim the provinces for Iran.

At that point, Ghavam's master stroke of diplomacy produced an unintended and tragic result, one that would have long-term effects. The young Shah, looking for a national role and finding a suitable model in what the more violent Shahs of the previous dynasties, Ismail, Nader, and Agha Muhammad, had done, went with the troops as their commander in chief and ordered them to commit a bloodbath.[26] The wounds of that assault were to infect Iranian politics for the next half century and shape the political persona of Muhammad Reza Shah. This was a tragic immediate result, but Ghavam's strategic purpose was achieved by Mossadegh: At his urging, in October 1947, the *Majles,* with near unanimity, voided the results of the oil concession negotiations with the Russians. The Russians were furious. With what turned out to be a supreme irony, they attacked Mossadegh as a British lackey. Undeterred, in the coming years, he would navigate the dangerous, difficult, and twisting course that he believed was required in the Iranian national interest. Unfortunately for Iran, Ghavam's reward was to be dropped as prime minister just a month later.

With the Russians having raised the issue of oil concessions in a dramatic form but having been pushed out of the way, all Iranian eyes focused on the British oil company, by then known as the AIOC. The *Majles* bill rejecting the Russian concession contained a provision requiring the *Majles* to review the AIOC concession to see if it fully protected the rights of Iran. Both the British and Iranian governments realized that at least cosmetic changes had to be made in the concession. The figures suggest why: From the beginning of production in 1911 to 1950, Iran received 9 percent of the total value of oil exported while the British government received approximately 36 percent and other (foreign) shareholders about 4 percent. In any given year, Iran never received more than 17 percent of the value of the oil produced from its fields. These figures do not tell the whole story because large amounts of the company revenues went into investments in subsidiaries abroad and into the acquisition of a fleet of tankers.[27] Under Ghavam's successor as prime minister, an army general, a compromise was reached to increase Iran's share, but the *Majles* rejected it. Compared, as of course all Iranians did, to the "fifty-fifty" split in revenue made on January 2, 1951, in Saudi Arabia by the American consortium ARAMCO, the AIOC offer was unsuitable, unfair, and "un-Iranian." Perhaps even more galling to the Iranians was AIOC's policy of employing Iranians only as unskilled laborers, whereas ARAMCO was already working to create a new middle class of entrepreneurs and builders.

Meanwhile, Mossadegh had chaired a *Majles* committee to work out what the *Majles* would find suitable, fair, and in the national interest. The committee reported in February 1951 that AIOC would not accept being "reformed,"[28] and therefore recommended that it be nationalized. The then prime minister stood against that recommendation and, for his implicit support of AIOC, was assassinated. An indication of the mood of the country was given by the next action of the *Majles:* It gave a pardon to the assassin. It was clear that no Iranian could have supported a continuation of the concession on the existing terms and remained in office so long as the *Majles* retained popular support and the Shah lacked the power to overturn it. Mossadegh had found his cause and had his finger on the national pulse. It was the fate of the AIOC concession that made Mossadegh Iran's first democratically elected prime minister.

At that time, Iranian politics were still played more as a tournament of heroes than a clash of party programs. Practically, the only organized party, the Tudeh, was communist and suffered from its connection with the Soviet Union; it was small but disciplined, determined, and active. Because Mossadegh had no party of his own, he would need the Tudeh's help in the months ahead because the program he was evolving, which focused on oil but included elements of social reform, was strongly opposed by the Shah and the conservatives. True, his long opposition to Reza Shah and his espousal of nationalism made him the idol of "the street" and the bazaar, but it did not give him a solid base of support. For consistent support, all he had was a loose coalition of members of the *Majles,* most of whom were "men of intellect," known as the National Front (*Jabha-yi Milli*). Each of these men regarded himself as a "hero." Like Don Quixote, each tilted at his own "windmill."

Mossadegh had no way to control them. Such power as he had grew from his skill as an orator and depended on the always fickle mood of the Iranian public. Thus, it was the focus on his personality and his political style that would set the scene for his downfall. He was, in the sense that I have laid out in this book, a quintessential Iranian, impassioned, mystical, mercurial, much given to display, rhetorically violent but also shrewd, occasionally ruthless, and a true nationalist. The Iranians idolized him and related even to his weaknesses, but he was not the kind of man with whom Western officials felt comfortable. The record shows that they were baffled by him. Worse, they were frightened by him.

His policy on oil was, of course, at the center of the Western hostility toward him. For decades, Britain had profited from the oil it extracted from Iran on the cheap. When Britain was rich and powerful, this was attractive; but when Britain emerged from the Second World War having sold off most of its foreign assets and was essentially bankrupt, getting oil from Iran cheaply appeared even to the new Labour government as nearly vital.

Oil had also become a major national concern for Iran because the country had embarked on a development program. In 1947, the American company Morrison-Knudson International was commissioned by the *Majles* to make an initial survey and lay out a preliminary plan for development; its plan was then elaborated by another American consulting firm, Overseas Consultants Inc., and these laid the basis for the Iranian development authority that the *Majles* created in 1949. This organization, known as the *Sazeman-e Barnameh* (the "Plan Organization"), began the first seven-year development program. The idea behind these efforts was that oil would fuel development.

Even more important than the financial importance of oil was its national symbolism. The vast alien city that was the production center of AIOC embodied the memory of generations of humiliation by the great powers. In Abadan, under the British flag, Iranians were not even treated as citizens, nor were they allowed access to information or training sufficient to know what was happening to "their" oil. Iranian employees were relegated to mostly low-level positions, whereas educated government officials were prevented from access to company books. Thus, although Russia was regarded as more brutal, Britain was thought to be more sinister. In the Iranian estimation, the British had defrauded, subverted, tricked, and cajoled Iranians ever since their merchants and traders arrived at the court of the first of the Safavid Shahs. The Iranians uniformly thought that the British were the evil force behind every failure they experienced; they were sure that Britain intended to keep Iran weak and backward; and the more informed and culturally adept the British were, the more Iranians feared them.

Iranians had long believed that the deal they had with AIOC was unfair. Hence, figuring out what to do about it was regarded as the most important task for the *Majles* in 1950. This task was turned over to a committee of members chaired by Mossadegh. Mossadegh decided there was no hope of getting the British to agree to an arrangement that the Iranians would regard as suitable; so, as I have said, he proposed to nationalize AIOC. That set off a complex process that was more international than national, and so I have dealt with it in the final section of the book. Here, to anticipate, I simply relate that Britain threatened to invade Iran, sanctioned it, boycotted its oil on the world market, and froze its financial assets. When none of these ventures caused Mossadegh to change his policy, Britain's secret intelligence service, MI6, proposed to the Central Intelligence Agency (CIA) an overthrow of the Mossadegh government.

Ironically, on October 29, 1954, three months after the CIA and MI6 engineered a coup, the new government, although created to shore up the British position on oil, settled the dispute with AIOC. AIOC agreed that nationalization was legal in return for $1 billion from the foreign companies that became its successors and an additional smaller payment from the Iranian government. The fields and facilities were placed under the jurisdiction of the National Iranian Oil Company. In turn, NIOC turned over operations to a consortium of foreign oil companies (in which AIOC, renamed British Petroleum, retained a 40 percent ownership and in which, for the first time, American companies were allowed to participate). The post-Mossadegh government granted them a 25-year renewable concession. These arrangements, ironically roughly what Mossadegh had offered before he was overthrown, quadrupled Iran's income from oil.[29]

Oil was not the only source of funds. To enable the Shah and his new prime minister to push through a purge of the National Front, build up security forces, and get the economy moving through a redesigned seven-year economic plan, the United States came forward with what was then a large-scale aid program—nearly $1 billion in the decade after the 1953 coup. The United States had replaced Britain and Russia as the major foreign actor in Iranian affairs. As one of the most able American officials specializing in Iran, Gary Sick, later wrote, the coup "abruptly and permanently ended America's political innocence with respect to Iran. . . . [T]he belief that the United States had single-handedly imposed a harsh tyrant on a reluctant populace became one of the central myths of the [Iranian-American] relationship. . . ."[30] The coup also positioned the Shah as a puppet of America in the eyes of most Iranians. He struggled for years against that image. However, while projecting an image of imperial majesty, he had put his hand into America's pocket.

*H*aving put the Shah back in power, America was committed to him. As a later American ambassador, William Sullivan, wrote, "Our destiny is to work with the shah." For America during the next 26 years, Iran became the Shah, and the Shah became Iran.

Consequently, to understand the events leading to the revolution of 1979, assessing the Shah's character is as important as analyzing American interests and detailing the programs he undertook. From my many meetings with him and from the observations of others, I came to see the Shah's personality outlined by three experiences. Growing up under the shadow of his violent father, of whom he was terrified, he became indecisive and furtive. Installed on the throne by the British and the Russians the day after they overthrew Reza Shah, he was forced to participate in, and benefit from, what was essentially the political "murder" of his father in order to possess what had been his father's "bride," Iran. Thus, without pressing the point too far, I believe that he suffered from what could be described as a sort of Oedipus complex. Finally, having panicked and fled the country when confronted by the Mossadegh crisis, he struggled to overcome his sense of personal cowardice. Even those officers of the CIA mission that put him back in power "had almost complete contempt for the man . . . whom it derided as a vacillating coward."[31]

The effects of these experiences were visible throughout his reign: He would alternate weakness with cruelty, secretiveness with grandiose display, and contempt with fear. In one of my meetings with him, in which we were discussing the American government's hope that he would widen the political process to allow more popular participation, he chose to show me how he despised even his closest associates. He called in a cabinet minister, gratuitously humiliated him, and turned toward me, saying, "Do you expect me to share power with *that*?"

With such an attitude, he could not have expected loyalty, and he didn't. Rather, he put his trust in fear. To effect it, in 1957, he created a security service known as *Sazman-e Ettilaat va Amniyat-e Keshvar* (SAVAK), similar to the *Staatssicherheit,* the *STASI,* of communist East Germany. SAVAK grew to vast size. The publicly known figure was approximately six thousand officers, but this was multiplied, as *STASI* was then doing also, by an unknown but apparently huge number or covert or part-time officers and informers. These agents penetrated virtually every organization of civilian life—not only *monitoring* the activities of students, professors, journalists, and other categories of the proliferating class of "men of intellect," industrial workers, and the *ulama* but also *creating* puppet organizations, such as labor unions, to co-opt their activities and expressions. SAVAK became one of the most important organs of the Shah's state and demonstrated that his conception of rule was not fundamentally different from that of his father, Reza Shah.

Like Reza, Muhammad tried to destroy all opposition. The communist Tudeh Party was, of course, a prime target, but it was only one of several. Perhaps the most important was what remained of Mossadegh's National Front. That movement had given Iran its most important move toward democracy. Had it survived, it might have prevented the 1979 revolution.

The people whom SAVAK rounded up as suspected dissidents—a wide definition—were often tortured. Indeed, as Amnesty International reported in May 1976, "torture of political prisoners during interrogation appears to be routine practice, but persons may be subjected to torture again at any time during their imprisonment." This charge was backed up by other investigations, including the International Commission of Jurists.[32] If such prisoners were to be tried, they were usually brought before military courts. In all, perhaps twenty thousand Iranians were hustled into prisons in which many simply disappeared. This aspect of the Shah's regime was, to say the least, unfortunate for him personally because it made his people hate him.[33]

During the Eisenhower administration, America turned a blind eye toward the Shah's violations of human rights. Having helped to overthrow his opposition, it could hardly have done otherwise. But when John F. Kennedy became president, he sought to put Iranian-American relations on a more democratic and sustainable basis. As a member of the Policy Planning Council, I played a role in that effort. My colleagues and I mildly encouraged the Shah to spread the benefits of Iran's growing revenues more equitably among the people, to curtail the rush toward militarization, and to open the government to political processes. The Shah was furious. In one of our meetings, he told me that he had identified me as the principal enemy of his regime. He set out to do precisely the opposite of what my colleagues and I had recommended.

The truth is that we had not recommended much. Americans did little to help the Shah and did quite a lot to endanger his regime. Perhaps the most important act detrimental to his regime happened in 1964, when the U.S. Department of Defense insisted that the Iranian government issue a "status of forces" law that essentially extraterritorialized the personnel of the military assistance program. From the American point of view, this was simply standard procedure among countries receiving American military assistance. Moreover, it had been practiced in Iran during the Second World War for the thirty thousand American troops who were engaged in shipping supplies to the Soviet Union. Years later, in 2008, it would also be demanded of the newly installed government in neighboring Iraq. But from the Iranian point of view, it brought back still fresh and painful memories of imperialism when the Great Powers imposed on Iran and other African and Asian countries a comparable system of extraterritorialization that was known as "capitulations." Capitulations were regarded by the Iranians as the hallmark of imperialism. Indeed, one of the most popular moves made by Reza Shah, the father of Muhammad Shah, was to abolish them and make foreigners subject to Iranian courts and law in 1935. So the status-of-forces agreement evoked memories that provoked a political storm in Iran and tended to unite the secular nationalists with the religious establishment in opposition to the Shah's regime. Reinstating "capitulations" under a new title was what Muhammad Reza was charged with doing. Worse, right after the new law became known, the U.S. government granted Iran a $200 million loan. So the critics of the regime also saw a repeat of the early years of the century, when the government seemed to be "selling" Iranian sovereignty.

Although the Shah made little effort to be beloved by his people, he deserves praise for some aspects of his policies.[34] Like his father, he was intent on making Iran independent and strong. To this end, also like his father, he fostered the spread of education and training. During the last 15 years of his reign, as oil income rose, the number of schools, colleges, universities, and training schools multiplied. Outreach programs, particularly the "Literacy

Corps," became active even in remote towns and villages. Enrollment in secondary schools tripled to about three-quarters of a million while enrollment in various kinds of technical training schools went from about fifteen thousand to a quarter of a million. On the eve of the revolution, higher education enrollment also reached a quarter of a million. The government added new faculties as well as new campuses to the University of Tehran, which the Shah's father had founded, and duplicated it in a dozen cities throughout Iran. Those figures should be measured both against the size of the population, which was then about thirty-four million, and against what had happened before the Shah's reign. One of the most important categories of students was those who went abroad to study. At the end of the First World War, about five hundred Iranian students were studying abroad, whereas by the 1960s and 1970s, at least sixty thousand, many with government financial support and all with at least government tolerance, were studying just in America at any given time. Those who went back to Iran constituted a virtual social class, whereas the original group of *uqqal*—the secular intelligentsia—half a century earlier at the time of the first revolution had numbered less than a hundred or so.

The "motor" bringing about these and other changes was the *Sazeman-e Barnameh* ("The Plan Organization"), which had been established by the *Majles* in 1949 and began the first seven-year development plan with a budget, largely drawn from the World Bank and the U.S. government, of $350 million. In the early 1950s, it was derailed by the boycott on oil exports—and consequently the fall of oil revenue, sanctions, refusal of the U.S. government to assist Iran under Mossadegh, and the coup against his government—but it was reconstituted after the return of Muhammad Reza Shah. The second Plan, due to be completed in 1962, envisaged expenditures, increasingly drawn from oil revenues, of more than $1 billion. More ambitious planning was under way. With the help of the Ford Foundation, economic and planning specialists were drawn from Harvard University under Kenneth Hansen to advise Dr. Khodadad Farmanfarmaian, who as head of the economic bureau of the Plan, was its chief architect. The ambitious Third Plan was budgeted at $2.5 billion. But the Third Plan was partially sidetracked when the Shah decided on a more direct program to deal with Iranian poverty and backwardness in what he termed his *Enghelab-e Safid* ("White Revolution"). Although often derided as a public relations stunt to build support for the regime, the White Revolution was seriously undertaken, and particularly its core, land reform, begun in 1962, was significant. Under it and the

Literacy Corps, the peasant society of rural Iran began to be transformed: The number of agriculturalists who owned their own land rose from about 1 in 20 to 15 in 20.

Although the intent was laudatory, planning on such a vast scale was inevitably defective, and the execution often fell short. The fundamental problem with land reform was that most holdings were too small to sustain what had come to be regarded as a decent standard of living. Not enough was done to provide credit, seed, and instruction. So, although about two million peasant families were encouraged to believe that they were entering into a new age of prosperity and independence, they soon saw that they did not have the means to do so. Consequently, most peasant farmers came to see land reform, like many of the new reforms, as façades behind which the old systems of landlord control, moneylender usury, and poverty continued. Disappointed in their villages, many migrated to the cities, where opportunities seemed greater. The result was a massive shift in the population and the growth of a new urban proletariat.

With insufficient attention being paid to what actually happened "in the field," the government focused on the planning process. Development plans grew, one after another, to enormous proportions as oil revenue rose steeply. Particularly after the 1973 Arab-Israel war, Iran's yearly income from oil more than tripled to $18.6 billion. As the plans took hold, Iran achieved astonishing rates of growth; indeed, for years, they were the highest in the world. By the time of the Fifth Plan, the aim was for a 15.4 percent rise in Gross Domestic Product, or about five times what was considered a reasonable target for a developing economy.

Judged in financial terms, what Iran was doing under Muhammad Reza Shah was a spectacular success, but the impact was uneven. As I have explained, developing societies naturally favor those of their citizens who are most capable of adding to national wealth, the modern rather than the traditional sectors of society: that is, those who can "row the boat." Thus, the Plans aimed to empower these people and tended to leave behind groups such as the urban poor and the rural peasantry. Those left behind were particularly bitter, but they were soon joined by others. Seeing this discontent but feeling that he was doing what Iran needed, the Shah determined to smash all opposition.

What particularly infuriated him was that demonstrations against his policies and his regime were led by the *ulama*. So important were the *ulama* to become, as I shortly describe, that Muhammad Reza Shah's attitude toward them must be emphasized.

As we have seen, his father, Reza Shah, began the process of impoverishing the *ulama* and removing from them their traditional activities (and sources of income) as judges, teachers, and administrators of pious foundations. Muhammad Reza Shah regarded them with a mixture of contempt and fear. He once described to me their leaders, the *mujtahids,* as "lice-ridden, dirty old men." But he recognized that the Iranian people revered them as the anchors of their lives—in the accepted phrase, the *marja-e taghlid* ("resource of emulation") in a sea of tempestuous change.

These feelings were manifested when, in 1962, the government sought to impose a new law regulating the election of local councils. On the face, the measure was a step toward democracy and emancipation of minorities, but the *ulama* saw it as an attack on religion and began to agitate against it. Particularly for the younger *ulama* and the seminary students, this agitation was the first introduction to politics. They rose to the occasion. Even more important, they "won." The government gave in to their protests and canceled the law.

They had tasted blood, but their leaders were still cautious. As in the early phases of the 1905 revolution, so in 1962, they avoided criticizing the Shah directly but blamed the government action on his prime minister. As I have pointed out, this is a common first step on the road leading to revolution. Muhammad Reza Shah misread their hesitation as weakness. That too is common in the early phases of revolution. So an almost mechanical process began that would lead, seemingly inexorably, toward the final phase in 1979.

During those years, like his father, Muhammad Reza Shah made little attempt to deal with the *ulama.* Indeed, like earlier Shahs, he sought to preempt their sanctity by making highly publicized pilgrimages to holy places, but his main effort was to suppress or get rid of them. As seen by many Iranians, Muhammad Reza Shah was echoing the activities of his brutal, anti-Muslim father. Reza Shah, as I have mentioned, had sent his troops into the holy sanctuary in Mashad in 1935, where they fired into a prayer meeting; in the same month, almost 30 years later, in March 1963, Muhammad Reza Shah sent his paratroopers into a religious school in the holy city of Qom, where they severely beat a number of students and killed two. What was different was that Iran had changed in the intervening 30 years. A new figure had arisen among the *ulama.*

Ayatollah Ruhollah Khomeini had become the most popular teacher in
Qom. He was already well known for the criticism he made of the monarchy
in a book he had written 20 years before, *Revealing Its Secrets.*[35] Following
the attack on the seminary, he delivered the first of his stinging attacks on
Muhammad Reza Shah, comparing his action that day to Reza Shah's 1935 attack and accusing the regime of being fundamentally opposed to Islam itself.[36] Two weeks later, Khomeini was arrested and taken to Tehran. But the
government did not know what to do with him. It released him, rearrested
him, and finally exiled him. This indecision would be echoed in the events
leading up to the revolution, when the Shah could not make up his mind
what to do. The Shah's despotic and even brutal actions, but also his indecision, created the opportunity that Khomeini seized.

From his exile in the Iraqi holy city of Najaf, Khomeini mounted a powerful propaganda campaign against the Shah's government. As he poured
forth a torrent of letters, pamphlets, tracts, and audiocassettes, his campaign
enrolled not only thousands of *mollas*, teachers, and students but also the by
then disaffected urban poor and rural farmers. His most important work
was an assemblage of his lectures known as *The Rule of the Islamic Jurist* (*Vi-
layat-e Faghih* in the popular Farsi version), which he published in 1969. In
it, he asserted that the men of religion, the *ulama*, constituted Iran's only legitimate political authority; that the recognized leaders of the *ulama*, the
most senior jurists, the upper ranks of the *mujtahids*, known as the grand
Ayatollahs, constituted the ultimate authority, the *marja-e taghlid* (the "resource for emulation"), to which those less trained in theology were bound
(*moghaled*) and must submit; and that the country as a whole must be reformed on Shia Islamic principles. In short, he proclaimed that Iran must
become a theocracy under the rule of the senior clerics, who alone had the
knowledge required to make fundamental decisions, and that even the Shah
must obey them.

*M*eanwhile, thinking that he had overcome opposition, the Shah pushed
ahead at full speed with the development program. But the ability of Iran to
absorb the enormous infusion of money and to manage the proliferating
projects was limited. Too fast a pace began to "overheat" the economy and society. Bottlenecks developed as transport, for example, could not keep pace
with program requirements and electrical generation fell short of demand.

The economic crisis came in 1975–1976, when at least some in the government, led by the then prime minister, the American-trained economist Dr. Jamshid Amuzegar, cautioned that Iran needed a period of retrenchment. The Shah would have none of that advice. Many of his courtiers and some foreign "experts" encouraged him to continue full speed. He did agree to several measures that he thought would ease the strain, but they were either ineffective or self-defeating—indeed, some were even trivial or infuriating.[37] So, in the ensuing rather mild recession, while Iran remained essentially prosperous, the dream of wealth that the Shah had proclaimed collapsed. To the people, this dream was spelled out in better houses, new cars, and all the accoutrements of European or American society; to the Shah, it meant power and dignity.

As K. S. MacLachalan has written, the Shah

> apparently came to believe that he could transform Iran into a state economically the equal of countries of Western Europe, and could encourage a "resurgence" (*Rastakhiz*)—the name he picked for [the] political party, the only legal party, he created in 1975—of Iranian civilization. Political hegemony in the Persian Gulf [where he offered to take over from the British in attacking rebellious tribes] and an important rôle in the international arena were to be parallel aspirations in this grand plan.[38]

These aspirations became particularly evident in the military sphere.

Even more than economic development, the Shah aimed at military power, which he thought was quite distinct from the economic, social, and intellectual capacity of Iran. In 1963, I convinced at least some of my colleagues in the U.S. government that it would be to the interest of Iran, and even to the interest of the Shah, if he would at least slow down or better stop his already large military buildup. There were many reasons. First, at that time, Iran's resources were much smaller than they later became, and such funds as he commanded were needed for civil programs. Second, Iran could not hope to offset the power of its northern neighbor, the Soviet Union, as it appeared to think possible, but a significant buildup would seem provocative to the Russians and so would potentially destabilize their relations. Finally, in the Iranian military, although it was the recipient of lavish favors, rumors of coup planning abounded. I feared that if the military continued to grow but was not balanced by less glamorous and less favored countervailing institutions, such as a vigorous *Majles*, an independent judiciary, and a reasonably free press, Iran would simply become another military dictatorship.

Mine was a lonely voice—and Muhammad Reza Shah knew it because he received a constant stream of congressmen, U.S. Department of Defense officials, journalists, and industrialists who assured him that what he was doing had America's firm approval. In fact, although it was detrimental to Iran and undercut our own policies, that was correct: Americans in and out of government encouraged his purchase of equipment because it helped pay for the oil we bought and increased the profits of what President Dwight Eisenhower called our "military-industrial complex." The most the U.S. government would do was to urge the Shah essentially to follow the advice William Morgan Shuster and Arthur C. Millspaugh had given—to get his finances in better order. The advice was not taken. The Shah embarked on a 20-year shopping binge.

Expenditure was already large in the Kennedy administration, but particularly after President Richard Nixon and Henry Kissinger visited Tehran in 1972, the Shah's passion for armaments became a frenzy. Within less than five years, he had placed orders for about $10 billion worth of the most sophisticated equipment America was then producing. Ironically, it was due to Mossadegh's nationalization of oil that the Shah had the means to engage in this massive military program. Instead of urging him to spend less on guns and more on the real needs of his people, as I had done in the Kennedy administration, Secretary of State Kissinger issued instructions that the Shah was to be given anything he wanted. Ultimately, this would also include nuclear weapons technology and equipment, thus setting the stage for the American-Iranian confrontation 30 years later.

Once undertaken, this military buildup was almost impossible to control, as Jimmy Carter was to find when he became president in 1977. Carter had campaigned for a reduction of American arms sales abroad but was almost immediately hit with demands by the Shah for a whole fleet, some three hundred of the latest American jet fighters together with supporting aerial and ground control systems and sophisticated ships, radar, and other forms of weapons. Reluctantly, Carter agreed to most of what the Shah demanded. When the 1979 revolution occurred, he had placed orders for an additional $12 billion worth of military hardware. All that equipment, as Ayatollah Khomeini bluntly put it, was no more useful than "scrap metal." When push came to shove in the events leading up to the revolution, his vaunted and much-privileged army and police either laid down their weapons and went home or joined the protesters.

Meanwhile, most Iranians remained poor, frustrated, and illiterate. In the economic turndown two years before the revolution, many were unemployed and some even hungry. For them, neither armaments nor grandiose projects mattered. They followed the one major national institution the Shah had not coopted—the religious establishment.

The religious establishment was, for Americans, the least understood part of Iran. In the huge volume of reporting from the American embassy on events in Iran, it was hardly mentioned. Indeed, in 1964, when a young diplomat wrote an analysis of it, he was reprimanded by the ambassador for wasting his time. In the dozens of books then being published on Iran (as well as those published after the revolution), less than half a dozen made serious attempts to understand the culture of the religious community, the *ulama,* from which Khomeini came,[39] and probably less than a dozen Americans had read Khomeini's plan for the government he wanted to install—and did install—in Iran.[40]

"Americans approached Iran from a position of almost unrelieved ignorance," commented the Iran specialist on the U.S. National Security Council, Gary Sick. If the public was ignorant, the government was little better. It was almost totally lacking in understanding of what was happening in Iran. As Mr. Sick continued,

> The quality of information available to U.S. policy makers on Iran was indeed dreadful. . . . There was a general tendency in the embassy's reporting to explain away the "exaggerations" and "distortions" in non-official news reports and local rumors, although many of these reports and rumors later proved to be more accurate than the government's official line. . . . The CIA [as the House of Representatives Select Committee on Intelligence reported in January 1979] . . . had produced two separate analytical pieces about Iran over the previous year that entirely failed to prepare Washington decision makers for the problems they encountered in late 1978. In August 1977 a 60-page study entitled "Iran in the 1980s" was based on the assumption that "the shah will be an active participant in Iranian life well into the 1980s," and that "there will be no radical change in Iranian political behavior in the near future."[41]

The second analytical study by the CIA, produced in August 1978, held that "Iran is not in a revolutionary or even a 'prerevolutionary' situation."

The fact was simply that American diplomats, intelligence analysts, and journalists missed the meaning of the significant events that created the "pre-revolutionary situation." These events were anchored in Iranian history, religion, and culture and required knowledge of that background to be understood. I have laid the background out in earlier parts of this book; here, I show how one particular custom embedded in that tradition created a crescendo of events that first led first to a "prerevolutionary situation" and then to a revolution.

The first event came in January 1978, when the Shah instigated a newspaper attack on the exiled but still very-much-in-touch and deeply venerated *ayatollah,* Ruhollah Khomeini. Given what is known of his life, the article was not only scurrilous; it was ridiculous. It accused him of leading "a licentious life in his youth, indulging in wine and mystical poetry, and [saying] that he was not really an Iranian [because] his grandfather had lived in Kashmir and his relatives used the surname Hendi (Indian)."[42] Outraged by this attack on their teacher and guide, whom many regarded as a saint, religious students in the city of Qom went on a rampage. They made common cause with the shopkeepers in the bazaar and marched on the local police station to present a large agenda of demands. Feeling under attack, the police fired into the crowd and killed a number of people—the estimates vary from two (by the government) to 70 (by the students).

At the request of the students and in the absence of Ayatollah Khomeini, one of Iran's other senior religious leaders, Ayatollah Kazem Shariatmadari of Tabriz, declared a mourning ceremony for the dead. In Islamic custom, such a ceremony is held 40 days after the death of the person, and in Shia Iranian custom it is highly charged emotionally. So, 40 days after the clash in Qom, crowds gathered and marched singing slogans in a number of cities, particularly in the traditionally highly politicized city of Tabriz. Then, either feeling frightened by the outpouring of antigovernment feeling or, alternatively, as he so often did, feeling both justified and powerful, the Shah decided to meet the protests with overwhelming force. As he had done 33 years previously against the breakaway "Soviet" republics of Gilan and Mahabad, the Shah mounted a large-scale military action against the dissidents. This time he had better equipment—tanks and helicopters—and he used them ruthlessly. So a new group of "martyrs" was created to be commemorated 40 days later. That event would produce another round of marches, prayer meetings, and riots, but this time they engulfed practically all the major towns and cities of Iran. What had begun in a relatively minor way in the seminary city of Qom had become a national movement. The organizers had learned how to mobilize crowds, and large and increasing numbers of people had become accustomed to demonstrating.

But the Shah still wavered between repression and apology. Repression came first. In the first week of September, the Shah declared martial law, banning all demonstrations and arresting known or suspected organizers. Crowds assembled anyway. On Friday, September 8, special army units fired into a large demonstration in Tehran, wounding or killing a number of people and giving rise to rumors of a virtual slaughter. Strikes then spread all over the country, and more commemorations were held as casualties increased. The Shah realized he could no longer hope to control them by repression. So he turned to apology. He went on national television on November 6 and, in what to him was a generous but humiliating address, admitted his "past mistakes, unlawful acts, oppression and corruption,"[43] described the "waves of strikes, [as mostly] quite justified," and acknowledged that the Iranian people "arose against oppression and corruption."[44] He promised to abide by the constitution he had repeatedly violated and to allow free elections for the virtually moribund *Majles*. He was too late.

*A*merican officials had not understood the sequence of popular protest, army massacre, and religious denunciation that had turned opposition into revolution. The sequence was unlike other revolutions and was distinctively Iranian. Forty-day mournings had become a nationwide cascade of growing sadness and anger. Soldiers began to refuse to fire on demonstrators, who were their neighbors, friends, and relatives. Some joined the demonstrators. With remarkable rapidity, the institutions of the state began to collapse. The huge army, nearly half a million men, simply disintegrated, and the police vacated their posts. Soon, at the urging of Ayatollah Ruhollah Khomeini, ministries closed their doors even to their ministers.

Under pressure, the Shah's latent indecisiveness paralyzed him. One day he proclaimed his determination to suppress the rebellion, and the next day he would say that he would never use his army against his people; one day he appointed a new and presumably resolute army commander as prime minister, and the next day he deprived him of authority; one day he talked of creating a new government, and the next day he spoke of leaving the country;

one day he even talked of inviting Khomeini into the government, and the next day he discussed having him assassinated. Repeatedly, he turned to the Americans not so much for advice as for the decision he could not make. What he really wanted was for the United States to tell him how to save his crown and, more important, to help him do it. The American ambassador told him, "You are the shah and you must take the decision as well as the responsibility."[45] The Shah did not want to do this. The words were never used, but from my knowledge of him, I believe he quietly wished that Kermit Roosevelt, who masterminded the CIA coup in 1952, could come back to Tehran.

That was not the game of President Jimmy Carter. His position, as he summed it up in a small press conference on December 7, 1978, was quite simple: He hoped that the Shah could survive in some fashion, but whether or how was up to the Iranian people: "We have never had any intention and don't have any intention of trying to intercede in the internal political affairs of Iran. We primarily want an absence of violence and bloodshed, and stability. We personally prefer that the shah maintain a major role in the government, but that is a decision for the Iranian people to make."[46]

This was not good news for the Shah. It was particularly disturbing that, just after he and everyone in Tehran had read the president's remarks, large numbers of Americans—there were then perhaps twenty-four thousand living there[47]—began to leave Iran on what were called extended vacations, designed to prevent any ugly incidents if public order deteriorated. There was a major reason to fear incidents because the commemoration of *Ashura*, the tenth day of the Islamic month *Moharram*, when it was believed the Imam Husain was killed, always was the occasion for a great outpouring of religious emotions. It is always a day of tense excitement, but in 1978, *Ashura* belonged to the Shah's great critics, the *ulama*, whose leader, Ayatollah Ruhollah Khomeini, had already linked America and the Shah as the enemies of Islam and Iran. Not only the *ulama* but many others—certainly including the Shah himself as he later often said—believed that President Carter's remarks were intended to show that the Shah did not have unqualified American support and so could be overthrown. In the event, on December 11, the streets of Tehran were said to have been flooded by an estimated four million marchers shouting "The Shah must go."

So, as the Shah told the American ambassador, he had no good options: He could try to crack down on the militants, but it was already clear that even if the soldiers would obey orders, they probably could not control the huge crowds that had demonstrated on *Ashura,* who probably could be called out again and again by the *ulama.* Events then followed in such quick succession that no one—not the Shah, the army, SAVAK, the secular government, or even the *ulama*—could control them. In a last-ditch effort to avoid what was predicted to be a bloodbath, the Shah considered turning to what remained of Muhammad Mossadegh's National Front, most of whose leaders had spent years in his prisons. Or he could leave Iran. He wavered between these options and finally tried a combination of them. He tried first to suppress the revolution; when he failed, he tried various moves to blame others, even turning against some of his most loyal supporters, imprisoning and throwing to his enemies as a sop the man who had been for 13 years his prime minister and his security police chief. Finally, the Shah managed to convince one of the National Front leaders to form a government, but on the condition that the Shah leave the country, which he did on January 16, 1979.

Three days later, the streets of Tehran were thronged with a million people who celebrated the end of the monarchy. Then, on February 1, the Grand Ayatollah Ruhollah Khomeini returned to Iran.

Five

THE REVOLUTIONARY REGIME

hen the Shah fled on January 16, 1979, he left behind as his last appointment a moderate as prime minister. Shapour Bakhtiar balanced two Iranian traditions: He was the son of a tribal chieftain, and he was a modern version of the "men of intellect," the *uqqal*, who had been inspired by the 1905 revolution and who later formed the "National Front." He was close associate of the American-overthrown Prime Minister Muhammad Mossadegh. His father had been murdered by Reza Shah and, he had been imprisoned various times for a total of six years for criticizing Muhammad Reza Shah's despotism. So his credentials seemed impeccable—but only in the abstract. His ideas were grounded in the liberal democracy that the CIA-MI6 1953 coup and Muhammad Reza Shah's dictatorship had crippled. To the younger generation of Iranians, they were a distant memory rather than a current license. Moreover, Bakhtiar, a cautious and orderly man, was out of his element in the chaos of revolution. He seems not to have understood, much less approved of, the fierce passions let loose by the collapse of the old order. Disregarding his lifetime of dedication to Iranian freedom, a million people took to the streets of Tehran to demand that he resign.

Two weeks into the Bakhtiar government on February 1, after an absence of 13 years, the 76-year-old Ayatollah Ruhollah Khomeini returned to Iran. On his arrival, he was greeted by delirious crowds that were estimated at between three and six million people—an astonishing one in ten or perhaps even one in five Iranians. The country literally threw itself at his feet. Bakhtiar tried to follow their lead, but Khomeini would have nothing to do with him or his government.

Khomeini had long since asserted his right to rule and had no hesitation in doing so. On the day of his arrival, he was quoted as saying, "I appoint the government," and proclaiming that the government he appointed "was God's government," so failure to obey it amounted to disobedience of God. Khomeini's prime minister–designate was the 72-year-old French-trained engineer Mehdi Bazargan.[1] But the Shah's appointee, Bakhtiar, remained in the prime minister's chair. So, for ten days, Iran had two mutually incompatible governments headed by men who were surprisingly like-minded. Then on February 11, Bakhtiar resigned and went into exile in Paris, where, 11 years later, he was tracked down and murdered.

Like the 65-year-old Bakhtiar, Bazargan was dedicated to the rule of law and believed in gradualism. Long in opposition to the Shah, he also had spent time in prison and surrounded himself with men who had shared his experiences. His colleagues were mainly middle-class professionals who had been active in the push for democracy. Bazargan thought that, because the Shah had left and a new government (his) was in office, the long-sought aims of his generation had been accomplished. It was time to get on with reconstruction. It would not be far-fetched to think of him as the Aleksandr Kerensky of the Iranian Revolution: the man who thought the revolution had happened—it was over. He was wrong. The revolution had just begun.

As one of the foremost students of revolution, Crane Brinton remarked on the nature and course of the French and Russian revolutions, "In such a chaotic condition, indeed, it would seem that the action of the moderates is a uniformity of revolutions. Their sentiments and training impel them to try and put a stop to disorder, to salvage what they can of established routines."[2] That generally is an almost impossible task. Bakhtiar and Bazargan were no more successful at it in Iran than early leaders of revolutions in Russia or France.

The first event that the Bazargan government had to deal with was an attack on the American embassy by a large group of young people. The embassy was in no condition to protect itself and offered no resistance. So the young "students," as they said they were, took the ambassador and his staff prisoner. When word reached Bazargan, he turned to his associate, Dr. Ebrahim Yazdi, an American-trained doctor, who had long been active in the Iranian student protest movements in America and had become closely associated with Ayatollah Ruhollah Khomeini during his exile in Paris. He asked Yazdi to move quickly to free the Americans. Yazdi ordered them out, and the students meekly complied. Then Bazargan had the embassy surrounded for its protection. In the chaotic conditions of those days, the only group of would-be guards he could muster was decidedly informal. Some of the American officials described it as "ragtag." That was the best he could do because neither Bazargan nor anyone else really controlled any formal security force. But, at least for a while, the "ragtag" peacekeepers accomplished their mission. The first Iranian-American crisis ended more or less painlessly in just a day. Worse was to come nine months later.

Observing how weak Bazargan was, Khomeini cut to the heart of the revolutionary violence. Immediately realizing that the new regime would need its own security force, he resurrected but also adapted a tradition long practiced in Iran and Iraq: Senior clerics customarily had mustered their students and the street gangs (*lutis*) to protect them and enforce their edicts. So, in May 1979, Khomeini created his own security force, which came to be called the Revolutionary Guard (*Pasdaran-e Enghelab*). Its role was the traditional one—to protect the *ulama* and enforce their rulings. In addition, it was to act as a counterweight to the American-trained regular army and the remaining secular political parties, each of which had its own armed guard. So the Revolutionary Guard had to be cast on a far larger scale and to be better organized than the traditional militias. It would ultimately grow almost as large as the regular army and be better equipped.

Small and informal though it was, the Revolutionary Guard gave Khomeini striking power, which he used initially to decapitate the old regime and would later turn against his contemporary rivals. But even Khomeini could not completely control the pent-up angers, desires for vengeance, jealousies, and social hostilities that permeated Iranian society and drove demonstrators into the streets and gangs into each other's houses and work places. Not just the army and police, but virtually all forms of governmental, industrial, and even informal organizations quickly collapsed in the face of popular fury or were incapacitated by mutual suspicion.

What had happened was precisely what neither Bakhtiar nor Bazargan had understood: The fall of the Shah had voided Iran's "social contract." That is, it shattered the intricate web of customary, legal, and organizational relationships that actually governed daily life. Consequently every action occurred within a formless or fluid situation. Nothing was stable or even predictable: Shared custom was deprecated as probably immoral, civil statutory law was considered void, and nonreligious organizations had simply melted away. Respect was replaced by fear, tolerance by distrust, and mutual protection by avariciousness. So, as the great English philosopher Thomas Hobbes warned his contemporaries in a comparable period of anarchy in late-sixteenth- and seventeenth-century England, when government falls apart and people lapse into the "state of nature," the hand of every man reaches out against his fellow. Thus it happened in Iran. When civic order failed, individuals needed protection from one another and some means to secure the necessities of life; consequently, they gathered into small groups, and the country fell under what can only be termed mob rule.

Foremost among the mobs were informal organizations known as *komitehs* ("committees") that were roughly comparable in function but more scattered than the *Comité de salut public* that formed in "The Great Terror" during the French Revolution and the *soviets* that sprang up in the early days of the Russian Revolution. In Iran, their original purpose was at least partly benign, distributing scarce necessities. But they soon seized the military forces' arsenals and armed themselves with half a million guns so that almost everywhere they were the most powerful and determined organizations in the country. As they grew in number—Tehran was said to have had about fifteen hundred *komitehs*—and their members increased to well over a hundred thousand, they became the lynch mobs of the revolution. They took upon themselves the task of ferreting out opponents to the regime, rather like the way the French Revolutionary *comités de surveillance* did. They robbed the houses of the members of the former regime and carried out both political and personal retribution; they abducted people, some of whom they imprisoned and others whom they executed. Not even Ayatollah Ruhollah Khomeini could control them. Rather than try, he encouraged them to hunt down and destroy opposition to him and his program.

The *komitehs* often functioned on their own but sometimes worked in league with "Revolutionary Tribunals" (*Dadgah-ha-e Enghelab*) that were set up by members of the *ulama,* who acted as prosecutors and judges. They also call to mind historical parallels: They carried out the functions of the *tribunals révolutionnaires* of The Great Terror during the French Revolution.

The first one was established less than a week after Khomeini returned to Iran and immediately executed the first group of "defendants," all senior army commanders. In the following months, at least another one thousand would be executed, often on vague charges, with little or no evidence and without a chance to speak in their own defense. Included among them were former Prime Minister Amir Abbas Hoveyda, his cabinet, and other senior civil and military officers. The "hanging judge" of the Revolution, Ayatollah Sadeq Khalkhali, ruled that having belonged to the previous government in almost any capacity was sufficient proof of guilt. But, many of the victims were private citizens who had fallen afoul of neighbors, rivals, or enemies. Again, the parallel to the French Revolution is both suggestive and sobering: In The Great Terror, between twenty thousand and forty thousand were executed in similar processes and for a variety of similar reasons. In Iran, judges, although drawn from the *ulama,* acted with little attention to the well-defined codes and procedures of Islamic law. They moved fast and to enforce their jurisdiction, they employed their own gangs of armed toughs.

Although he occasionally tried to bring the tribunals and the *komitehs* under at least his own control, Khomeini acted like Mao Zedong had acted in 1966 during the Chinese Cultural Revolution. As Khomeini said: Civil rights and legal procedures are nothing more than "a reflection of the Western sickness among us. . . . [T]he people on trial are criminals and should be killed." Like Mao, Khomeini wanted the regular institutions of government, which he saw as hindrances to the revolution, to be destroyed in the process.

Because this was Khomeini's objective and because he had the power to achieve it, Prime Minister Bazargan, appointed by but often undercut by Khomeini, lost authority over government agencies piece by piece. He was unable to bring the revolutionary tribunals, which he regarded as "shameful," under the Ministry of Justice or to affect their actions. Nor could he control "the street." Every attempt he made to achieve stability was regarded as an act of disloyalty. Worst of all was his attempt to find a new basis for relations with America.

Bazargan had met with the American ambassador before the revolution. As head of government after the revolution, he met with President Jimmy Carter's National Security Council (NSC) director, Zbigniew Brzezinski, more or less by chance at a ceremony in Algeria. These meetings opened him up to accusations of counterrevolutionary subversion. America was the enemy, the "Great Satan." That was not just Khomeini's designation of

America; rather, it was shared by "moderates" and professional men such as Bazargan and Bakhtiar. Because of the memory of the CIA-MI6 coup against Prime Minister Mossadegh, many, indeed probably most, Iranians believed that the United States was again preparing to put the Shah back on the throne with stealth, money, and violence. They were not completely wrong: That possibility had been discussed in the NSC and was advocated by its director, but President Carter rejected it. Behind what most foreigners regarded as Iranian paranoia, it must be admitted, was both recent history and current possibility.

As we now know, but as no one in either the Iranian or American government then knew, the Shah was in no position to be put back on the throne. He had long been afflicted with cancer, and it was getting worse. Previous treatments had not halted it, and he was undergoing strenuous medical treatment. Nor was the probably still proroyalist Iranian general staff in a position to effect a coup or work with a group like the one Kermit Roosevelt had put together 25 years earlier. They were already being thinned out by purges, and, in any event, it was highly unlikely that they would be obeyed by their scattered and disheartened troops. But plotting coups was the memory, and the memory set the context in which American actions were judged. The issue that focused all minds was whether the Shah would be allowed to enter the United States.

Through his friends Henry Kissinger, David Rockefeller, and John Mc-Cloy, the Shah had been trying to gain admission to the United States. The senior American official still in Iran, the chargé at the embassy, L. Bruce Laingen, advised against allowing his entry because he feared that doing so would damage American interests and further empower the Iranian radicals. President Carter took Laingen's advice. He urged the Shah's advocates to guide him toward a neutral country. They refused to do so. Carter thought that the Shah simply wanted a safe haven where he could settle down to enjoy life, but soon Carter was told of the Shah's illness. He was told further that the Shah's cancer—which had been complicated by jaundice—required a sophisticated medical treatment unavailable in his then place of exile, Mexico. As it turned out, this was not true, but Carter accepted this judgment as a fact. So, on moral grounds, despite the grave dangers he knew to be involved, he authorized the Shah's entry. Obviously very worried about his decision, he faced his advisers on October 19 and, with uncanny prescience, "wondered aloud what advice they would give him when the Iranians took the embassy in Tehran and held the Americans hostage."[3] He would soon find out.

Of course, at the time of President Carter's decision, the Iranians were not informed of the deliberations in the White House, nor did they know of the Shah's illness. For years, he had carefully disguised the fact that he had cancer, fearing the effect that knowledge of his condition would have on his regime. Consequently, when it became public knowledge, few believed the widely publicized diagnosis of his illness to be more than a cover for a plot to get him into position for a return to power on the turret of an American tank. His entry into America seemed to confirm Iranians' suspicions: "America was at it again." In the mistrust and fear that were integral parts of revolutionary ferment but also, as I have said, based on both history and current possibilities, those Iranians who decided events were sure that America was preparing another coup like the one the CIA had pulled off 25 years before. Worse, they were prepared to believe that a sinister group of anti-regime Iranians, like those who worked with the CIA, were involved. It seemed to many that probably Prime Minister Bazargan, who had shown some hesitation and lack of warm support for the revolution, was involved.

During the time that the American government was wrestling with the problem of the Shah's desire to enter America, the Iranians were working on the text of a new constitution. The task of preparing the draft was turned over to the "Assembly of Experts" (*Majles-e Khobregan*), but the guiding principles were set out by Ayatollah Ruhollah Khomeini. His instructions were simple: It must be "one hundred percent Islamic."[4] From this, he assumed that the members of the Assembly understood that the draft was not open for criticism by those who had not achieved mastery of Islamic learning. Only the senior members of the *ulama,* the jurist-consults (recognized *mujtahids*), were competent to judge what was Islamic. Thus, the "ignorant" among the Assembly members were to have no effective role in preparing it. But in a rare assertion of independence, the Assembly decided that all its members were competent.

Discussion, at least in the beginning, seems to have been vigorous, but the central issue soon came down to the role of Khomeini. He had set out in the lectures that subsequently became the book *Velayat-e Faghih* (*The Rule of the Learned Jurist*) what was required: a theocracy whose legitimacy derived from God and in which the supreme religious jurist, the *faghih,* would rule. That narrowed the field of possible rulers to two or three "grand" *ayatollahs* who were recognized as being the *marja-e taghlid*—that is, the religious leaders whose opinions were binding on true believers. (Khomeini himself had been granted that status by Ayatollah Kazem Shariatmadari in 1962.[5]) When relatively moderate members, who were in a minority, tried to restrict the role, Khomeini warned against "deviationists" and thundered that "The *Velayat-e Faghih* is not something created by the Assembly of Experts. It is something that God has ordained."

Khomeini, of course, prevailed. Then the delegates acted as if to expiate their lapse in questioning Khomeini by awarding him the post of "vice-regency" for life and setting out the role of the *faghih.* The *faghih* was to be superior to the president: He could appoint subordinate officials in the Council of Guardians, which would function like a combination of an upper house and a supreme court. He would also appoint all senior officials and commanders of the various armed forces.[6]

All discussions of the dangers of these decisions, carefully made so as not to appear to be critical of Khomeini but aimed only to clarify the procedure after his death, were brushed aside. Bazargan, who was technically the head of government as prime minister and was, after all, Khomeini's appointee, tried to persuade the Ayatollah that the Assembly had produced a document that endangered Iran's future and turned the *ulama* into a ruling class. (I later show how this in fact happened.)

Bazargan and perhaps others pointed to the fact that Shiism had traditionally held that religion would almost certainly be corrupted if the *ulama* took on the task of government in the sinful times before the Day of Judgment when the Hidden Imam would return to remove human corruption. Thus, he argued, future generations would blame his generation and even call the *ulama* into question for descent into the mire of politics. This was an argument that had been made before to Khomeini—during the time of the Shah—when his reply had been simply that "Islam *is* politics." He had not changed his view and was determined to push ahead.

Pushing ahead meant referring the draft constitution to referendum. That was done on December 2, 1979. The timing was doubly significant: The Iranians had just learned that President Carter had decided on October 21 to allow the Shah to enter the United States, and December 2 was the day after the emotional Shia Muslim celebration of *Ashura*, the tenth day of the Islamic month *Moharram*.

Khomeini had set both the emotional and electoral terms with great skill. On the emotional side, he proclaimed that those who voted "no" or abstained in the referendum would dishonor the martyrs who had died to chase away the Shah and bring the Islamic republic into being. That was the religious issue; the national issue was also disturbing. A show of indecision, voters were warned, might encourage American intervention. The Americans had intervened to overthrow an elected Iranian government and impose upon Iran the hated Shah. To put him back into power again and so get their hands on Iran's oil must be their aim. To encourage such events was thus not only sinful but treasonable.

On the electoral side, Khomeini posed the issue as one between a choice for anarchy, which probably everyone read as meaning a return of the monarchy, and the constitution. He set up the ballot so that there was no other option. It was the constitution as written, yes or no. Faced with the alternative of restoration of the hated monarchy, even Khomeini's strongest critics had to vote yes. They were followed by what was proclaimed to be 99 percent of all Iranian voters. By the time of the plebiscite, Mehdi Bazargan, who had manfully tried to restrain the plunge into theocracy, was gone. He had resigned two days after one of the most dramatic events of the revolutionary turmoil—the seizure of the American embassy by a large group of young Iranians on November 4, 1979.

Why the American embassy? If one seeks to understand the Iranians at that time and to evaluate the hostility and propensity to think the worst of the United States ever since, the question deserves a careful answer.

Throughout modern (that is to say nineteenth- and twentieth-century) Iranian history, foreign embassies, particularly the Russian and British embassies, as I have written, have been the command posts for foreign intervention. To Iranians, they also were the symbols of imperialism—foreign flags planted right in the midst of Tehran. In recent years, attention had shifted somewhat, but not entirely, from Russia[7] and Britain to America. Right on one of Tehran's main streets, the huge American embassy was particularly obvious. In less hostile times, it was once almost a place of pilgrimage for Iranians. I happened to be there a week after President John F. Kennedy was murdered and saw that thousands of ordinary citizens had come to sign their names on books of condolence. It was an unsolicited act of great sympathy. But whether through sympathy or hatred, everyone in Tehran knew the embassy.

The embassy, of course, housed the representatives of a host of American governmental agencies, including the CIA, that had worked closely with the Shah's regime. Even in previous years, long before the revolution, many believed, as sober and intelligent Iranians remarked to me, that inside the buildings were both the people who were pulling the strings on Iranian puppets but also the documents that listed all the Iranians who worked against Iranian interests. So, in the atmosphere of revolution, the embassy was an obvious target. Some Iranians called it a "den of spies." Students had already attacked it once in February. As I have mentioned, all over Iran, groups of people were taking the "law" into their hands; so it was not a complete surprise that on November 4 a group of several hundred young people calling themselves "Students Following the Imam's Line" rushed the embassy and took some 70 members of the staff hostage.

Hostage taking (*gerogan-giri*) is an ugly act; when used against the officials of a foreign government who are under the protection of a native government, it violates centuries of diplomatic practice. The sanctity of diplomats has been recognized for the practical purpose it achieves but has also been enveloped in religious sanctions even in primitive societies and ancient times.[8] As Herodotus wrote, hostage-taking was one of the ugly acts of the first Greek-Iranian wars. The students were not interested in diplomatic practice and seeing their action as a new tool in his revolutionary kit, Khomeini upheld their action. As he said, "It is . . . up to the dear pupils, students and theological students to expand their attacks against the United States and Israel so that they may force the U.S. to return the deposed and criminal Shah." It is perhaps significant that Khomeini's son Ahmad also jumped over the wall to congratulate the students. So, the students thought they had a clear mandate. They were right.

Apparently, the students were inspired by actions taken on a number of American university campuses by the Students for a Democratic Society (SDS) in 1968 and the "May 1968" strikes that were begun by students in universities in Paris and spread to the streets, involving millions of workers throughout France. In France and America, the militants did not take hostages, but they sometimes moved from threats into violence.

All three of these outbursts—American, French, and Iranian—were impelled by anger and fear but had no clear, long-term objective, although the French "May 1968" riots did nearly destroy the government of Charles de Gaulle, who, like the Shah had done in 1953, briefly fled the country. In Iran, although the student attack was aimed at the American embassy, its real target was domestic: It sought to demonstrate the weakness of the government of Mehdi Bazargan and to humiliate him. It did. Having seized the embassy, the Iranian students soon realized that they had taken the revolution to a new stage; indeed, as some of them put it, they had made a "second revolution." So, in a triumphant mood, they faced the issue of what to do with the hostages. They apparently had originally intended to release them in a few days, but, heady with their daring act, they decided not to do so[9]: They did not trust the government to use them to enhance the objectives of the revolution or even to keep them prisoner. So they locked some in storerooms and tied others to chairs. Housekeeping was a more difficult problem for the unemployed young people, but they managed to arrange a life-sustaining diet for their prisoners.

They immediately found that they had hit a gold mine. Although the American staff had tried to destroy the documents in the embassy, they had done an ineffective job. Many were still in file cabinets or boxes, while others were shredded but not burned.[10] So the students soon began to piece together the shredded documents, presuming, I imagine, that they were the most revealing and damaging. Ultimately, they translated and published nearly 50 volumes of these reconstructed papers in bilingual editions with lurid yellow covers emblazoned with the code words (e.g., *secret, noforn, do not disseminate,* etc.) and seals—particularly that of the CIA—that would lend authenticity and suggest sinister activity. With good reason, the prime minister and his colleagues were frightened of the wild young men and women.[11]

Demonstrating the confusion of the revolutionary chaos were contrary actions by some of Khomeini's closest associates: Bazargan was, after all, an appointee of the Ayatollah; and his foreign minister, Ibrahim Yazdi, as I have mentioned, had himself been a student activist and was Khomeini's aide during his exile in Paris. They both tried to get the students to release the hostages. Meanwhile, another close associate of Khomeini, a young *mulla* by the name of Hojjat-ol-Eslam Moussavi-Khoeini, was advising the students not to compromise and certainly not to release their prisoners to Bazargan or Yazdi. Khomeini wavered, but the Shah's arrival in America settled the issue.

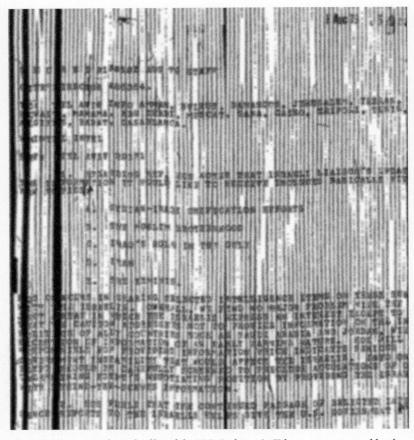

Shredded document from the files of the U.S. Embassy in Tehran, reconstructed by the "Students Following the Imam's Line" in November 1979

Khomeini flew into a rage, characterizing the Iranian moderates as "American-loving rotten brains [who] must be purged from the nation." Bazargan must have winced. He knew his time was up, and he quit. Ultimately, he would flee the country.

Meanwhile, at the White House, Carter's advisers tried to think of a means to rescue the embassy staff. As the "point man" on Iran at the NSC, Gary Sick relates their deliberations.[12] As he wrote, they considered three possible courses of action: mounting a rescue mission, warning the Iranians of a punitive strike if the hostages were harmed, and attempting to negotiate. Obviously, some form of negotiation was the least likely to endanger the hostages and that was tried first—and repeatedly.

The questions Carter and his advisers had to answer were: How to negotiate? And with whom to negotiate? As a result of a contact with one of the *ayatollahs* who was thought to have some influence over Khomeini, President Carter decided to send a mission to Tehran. He chose former Attorney General Ramsey Clark and former Ambassador William Green Miller. Both men were thought to be acceptable to the Iranians, and Miller, who had served in the consulate in Isfahan and the embassy in Tehran, was a Farsi speaker. They flew off to Turkey to await permission to enter Iran. It never came. Khomeini ordered the Revolutionary Council members not to receive them. Step one had failed.

In the meantime, just two days after their seizure, help arrived for the hostages from an unexpected quarter. Although the U.S. government regarded it as a pariah and had done much to weaken it, the Palestine Liberation Organization (PLO) offered to use its good offices to try to get the hostages released. Iran had espoused the Palestinian cause, and PLO chairman Yasser Arafat had been warmly received in Tehran. Possibly, the Americans thought, he had some influence with the Iranian religious leadership. Probably somewhat embarrassed by this generous and unsolicited offer, President Carter urged that the Palestinians try. So, on their own, three of the organization's senior officials flew to Iran and met with Khomeini at his headquarters in the seminary city of Qom. What then happened has never been revealed, but, apparently, they had a cold or even an acrimonious discussion. However, as a result of their plea, Khomeini decided to allow 13 relatively low-ranking or nonpolitical men and women to be released. They were out of Iran by November 19. The rest remained in captivity and, as the released men and women reported, were being treated severely, with at least some being bound hand and foot.

One group of American officials was not surprised by the failure to get the other hostages released. From the State Department's Bureau of Intelligence and Research, which over the years has proved to be the most competent of American intelligence analytical organizations, came the "finding" that

> there was by that time sufficient evidence to warrant the judgment that diplomatic action had almost no prospect of being successful in liberating the hostages and that no economic or other U.S. pressure on the Iranian regime, including military action, was likely to be any more successful in securing their safe release. Consequently, they [the analysts] concluded, the detention of the hostages could continue for some months.[13]

They were right. The detention would last almost 15 months.

With Bazargan out of the government, Khomeini had to find a replacement for him as president. He chose Abol-Hasan Bani-Sadr. Bakhtiar had been 65 years old and Bazargan had been 72, whereas Bani-Sadr at 47 years was a man of a younger generation with different memories. But like Bakhtiar and Bazargan, he had been devoted to Muhammad Mossadegh and, when very young, had been briefly a member of the National Front. Despite these apparent contradictions, he was known to be especially close, indeed almost a "devoted son," to Khomeini.[14]

Under other circumstances, Bani-Sadr might have become a liberal democrat, but he was caught up in the excitement of revolution. He too had been inspired by the 1968 Paris student revolt and saw in Khomeini's resistance to the Shah the best chance of creating Iranian freedom. He had accompanied Khomeini during the last part of his exile and served as his press officer in Paris, putting a "liberal" face on the Ayatollah. However, when he returned to Iran, he began to have doubts about the direction the revolution was taking. Indiscreetly, he even spoke of needing to rescue Iran from "a fistful of fascist *ulama*," and, dangerously, he opposed the growth of the cult of personality that was turning Khomeini into a demigod.[15]

Appointed as foreign minister, he was, officially at least, the man responsible for the hostages. In this capacity, he began to work on an Iranian offer that would give Iran both a moral victory—the United States would admit the guilt of the Shah—and a practical victory—the United States would return all the assets the Shah had lodged in America.

To work out the deal, Bani-Sadr sent representatives to the United Nations, where, through intermediaries, they reached a compromise agreement on steps to end the crisis peacefully. Under the proposed arrangement, the hostages were to be released and allowed to depart immediately, and Bani-Sadr was to address the Security Council, where he would call for an international commission to investigate human rights violations under the Shah. Iran could sue in American courts for the return to Iran of the Shah's assets, and both states would guarantee not to intervene in one another's affairs. Then the UN Secretary General would fly to Tehran to escort the hostages to safety. It seemed a "done deal." However, just as Bani-Sadr was getting ready to fly to New York and the Secretary General to fly to Tehran to conduct the hostages to safety, on November 28, Khomeini dismissed Bani-Sadr as foreign minister, replacing him with another member of his inner group, Sadegh Ghotbzadeh, who announced that negotiations were ended "at present."

While these various steps were being taken—or, more accurately, these various stumbles occurred—President Jimmy Carter had moved to create a bargaining counter and to put pressure on the Iranians to come to negotiations. He froze all Iranian assets, more than $11 billion, and banned imports of Iranian oil into America. These moves, although damaging to the Iranian economy, had not the slightest effect on the students or, apparently, on the religious leaders. The issue of the hostages would poison Iranian-American relations throughout the Carter administration.

Despite Bani-Sadr's dissident views on the revolution and his misstep on the hostages, Khomeini made him a member of the Revolutionary Council and cleared the way for him to become president after Bazargan's resignation. In the elections in January 1980, Bani-Sadr got more than 75 percent of the vote. Lest there be any doubt of his importance or his ability to speak for the supreme leader, Khomeini ruled that support for him was obligatory; Khomeini vested in Bani-Sadr further, at least nominal, authority, making him chairman of the Revolutionary Council, commander in chief of the armed forces, and ruling authority over the Revolutionary Guard.

With all these cards in his hand, Bani-Sadr felt secure enough to try to wrest the government from the *komitehs* and the Revolutionary Tribunals and to bring the Revolutionary Guard under government control. Although these undercut Khomeini's announced program, the Ayatollah approved Bani-Sadr's actions. On the Iranian New Year, No Ruz (March 21, 1980), he proclaimed "the year for restoration of order and security." In his text, Khomeini denounced the lack of discipline in the revolutionary movement and stressed the need to get the economy going again. Iran, he implied, needed to defend itself against all foreign powers. "We are as much at war with international communism as with the world-devourers of the West."[16] Khomeini's message was comforting to the battered population, until he reached the point in his address (read to the media by his son) where he attacked secular political groups, journalists, and the existing educational system and described the "men of intellect," the *uqqal*, which of course meant the heirs to Mossadegh and the National Front, as "the source of all our misfortunes."

Either undeterred or heedless of these dark hints, Bani-Sadr seemed to be making progress in the spring of 1980; he thought there was an opening for change toward moderation. Even the most conservative and senior of the *ulama* recognized that glaring abuses, abuses even of Islamic law, had occurred. The Ayatollah of the Shia shrine city, Mashad, Hasan Qomi-Tabatabai, took the lead in denouncing the revolutionary courts for "unwarranted expropriations, unwarranted jailings, unwarranted judicial decisions, unwarranted killings, unwarranted whippings. . . . [T]rials, tortures, judgments and confiscations of property perpetrated by the present leaders are all contrary to Islamic principles and rules." He went even further in what could only be a reference to Khomeini. Harking back to the traditional definition of the role of the *ulama* in general and the *mujtahids* in particular, he said, "Real clerics do not seek power. . . . Real clerics do not support those among the religious leaders who govern over us. The real task of the clerics is to enjoin the good and to enlighten the people."[17] His was a brave voice but a voice that was soon drowned in the revolutionary tempest.

Bani-Sadr, as a secular leader, wisely left such issues to the *ulama*, but on what seemed to him the major issue, that the United States was Iran's most dangerous enemy, he agreed with virtually all Iranians. He could not take a firm position on the hostages unless he could be sure both that the United States was not planning action against the revolution and that the United States would not rebuff his overtures. He also had to be sure, which he clearly could not be, that Khomeini would come out with a firm and unequivocal position in his support. Neither of these preconditions was likely enough for him to chance his career and perhaps his life.[18] Probably sensing this, opposition to him soon arose throughout the revolutionary movement, and Khomeini either failed to support him or actively undercut his authority. His period of order and security began to fade almost before it had begun.

Among the most important contributing factors to further radicalization was that the students who had seized the American embassy were piecing together and publishing its secret files. As they assembled this "evidence" of subversion, they found that they had a powerful weapon. In the prevailing atmosphere, they could implicate anyone they chose if his name appeared in a document. He need not have even met the American official who wrote his name; the official might be just drawing up a list of people working in various departments of the government. Suspicion was enough. The mention of one's name was occasionally a ticket to prison or the firing squad. Alert to the power in their hands, the students soon were using the reconstructed documents against Iranian government officials and even senior members of the *ulama*.

Bani-Sadr, while showing some support for the students' exposure of American diplomatic and covert activities, soon realized their action was detrimental both to him and to his programs. He needed to resolve the issue for, among other purposes, getting America to release blocked Iranian funds. As commander of the Iranian armed forces, he was also aware of how desperate their need was for spare parts. As he later remembered, "We had only 5 to 10 days' supplies."[19] In Iran's national interest, he had to negotiate with America. But he realized that almost any move he made, even any statement he made, could be used against him. The best move he could devise was to involve the United Nations. He worked out an arrangement with Secretary General Kurt Waldheim to get the process under way: Waldheim sent a commission headed by Swedish Prime Minister Olaf Palme to Iran to begin an investigation of Iran's charges against the United States while the Iranians were to transfer the hostages from their student jailors to the Revolutionary Council. It wasn't much of a move, but Khomeini refused to allow the Revolutionary Council to receive the hostages. Palme left Iran having accomplished nothing.[20]

Blocked from what had seemed a feasible, even an attractive, solution to the problem, Bani-Sadr decided to reverse course. He would drop the issue of the hostages and concentrate on the exiled Shah. If he could get the Shah back to Iran to be tried, he would meet the demands of those who had thwarted him and would become, in their eyes, a hero of the revolution. It was not a difficult move to make either emotionally or conceptually: He had no love for the Shah, whom he and everyone around him regarded as a criminal and a stooge of America, and there was ample precedent for extradition. The Shah was then in Panama, and so Bani-Sadr set out to get the Panamanian government to send him back. It might have worked; if it had, Bani-Sadr's career would have turned out quite differently. But when the Shah learned of the move, he hurriedly left Panama for Egypt, where he was reasonably sure he would be safe.

Thwarted by each attempt he made, Bani-Sadr decided to wash his hands of the crisis. But, of course, that was equally impossible for him. As his prestige weakened, he was forced to accept as prime minister Muhammad-Ali Rajai, a man he detested and whose aims were the opposite of his. When they clashed, Khomeini equivocated, and Rajai packed the cabinet with candidates of the more radical of the *ulama*. Increasingly, Bani-Sadr felt frustrated and was becoming more of a nuisance than a supporter of Khomeini; he was under attack by the religious establishment and by the carefully packed *Majles;* and he was the object of large demonstrations organized by the Islamic Republic Party. As a result, he was forced to resign in June 1981, just over a year after he had proclaimed his new policy.

Like Bazargan, Bani-Sadr also would flee Iran. After hiding for a month, he left Iran on July 29 in a hijacked Iranian air force plane flown by Iran's most famous pilot. Just a year later, his former foreign minister, Sadegh Ghotbzadeh, who had also been a close associate of Khomeini, was arrested and charged with an abortive attempt to bomb the house of the Ayatollah. Under interrogation and allegedly tortured, he implicated in the plot the Grand Ayatollah Kazem Shariatmadari, who held the highest title in Shia Islam's religious establishment and had once saved Khomeini's life. That a *Marja-e Taghlid* could be attacked showed that no one was safe. In an unprecedented move, he was "demoted" from grand *ayatollah* and was put under house arrest in Qom, where he remained until his death in 1986. His fall set a precedent. He was soon followed by Grand Ayatollah Hossein-Ali Montazeri who languished under house arrest in Qom until he was allowed to reappear in 2003.[21]

In summary, what these events showed was that the only safe place in Iran was the extreme wing of the ruling clerical establishment. They also showed that one must be there constantly since no previous service, relationship, or even clerical standing offered protection. Watching the fate of men such as Bakhtiar and even Bazargan and Bani-Sadr, those who hated what was happening to Iran and/or feared for their own lives decided to take action.

From Paris, Bani-Sadr announced a campaign to overthrow his erstwhile patron, Ayatollah Khomeini, while working together with the leader of the secular revolutionary Mojahedin-e Khalq, Masud Rajavi. Like most of the anti-Shah political groupings, the Mojahedin had grown out of Muhammad Mossadegh's National Front and split from it over the issue of how to fight the regime: To overthrow the Shah, the Mojahedin it was prepared to use violence, which the National Front was not. The Mojahedin carried through this tactic during the revolution but then turned its guns on the new organs of repression. Mojahedin-e Khalq provides the Iranian example of what happens when the means of political discussion and activity are blocked: It turned to the only means left—violence. This has been a response to tyranny since the American Revolution.[22]

Not having the means to match the repressive forces of the state in open combat—as it learned painfully in the last days of Bani-Sadr's government, when its marchers were set on by agents of the police—the Mojahedin-e Khalq organized its own version of The Great Terror. And spectacular it was. Even before Bani-Sadr had left the country, the first bomb was planted. It exploded during a meeting of the leaders of the Islamic Republic Party (IRP), killing virtually the whole leadership of the regime. Then, two months later, another bomb was set off in the office of the prime minister, killing the president (Bani-Sadr's replacement), the prime minister, and the chief of police.

In an event remarkably like the attempted assassination of Adolf Hitler by Count Claus von Stauffenberg on July 20, 1944, an aide to the commanding "Special Security Committee" placed a briefcase full of explosives beside the prime minister. Like Stauffenberg, Masud Kashmiri had the highest level of security clearance in his government; unlike Stauffenberg, he succeeded: Hitler escaped with minor wounds, but the Iranian prime minister was immediately killed. Other attacks followed. All over Iran, senior—and often hated—officials were struck down. By the time the Mojahedin moved from terror to propaganda, hundreds of men at the center of the regime had been killed.[23]

The regime must have been temporarily unbalanced, but by this time its supporters were so widely spread throughout the country and so deeply entrenched that it was able to strike back immediately. It did so with ferocity. The police, presumably with the help of the wide intelligence network of *mollas* who reached into every house in the country, were on the trail of the Mojahedin activists. Almost immediately, they ran to ground and killed the first group of them in a Tehran suburb. As a Reuters reporter found, within a week, the Revolutionary Courts had condemned and executed another 15 people. Within a year, Amnesty International documented another 2,946, but that was probably only a part of the real total. The Mojahedin believed that the true count of those "who lost their lives through execution, in street battles, or under torture in the short period from June 1981 to September 1983" was 7,746, of whom 9 in 10 were its members. At least half were high school or college students. Probably some of the others were innocent bystanders or even people trying to help the wounded. The Revolutionary Prosecutor-General announced that demonstrators were to be "tried in the streets," that is, lynched, and the chief of the Tehran Revolutionary Court proclaimed that "Islam does not allow wounded rebels to be hospitalized. They should be finished off." Most were.[24]

The killings did not stop in 1983, nor were they restricted to the Mojahedin. In *A History of Modern Iran*, Ervand Abrahamian gives a succinct account of the "Terror," in which he revised the figures he gave in an earlier work upward toward the claim of the Mojahedin: He believes that between June 1981 and June 1985,

> revolutionary courts executed more than 8,000 opponents. Although they targeted mainly the Mojahedin, they also went after others—even some who opposed the Mojahedin. The victims included [another underground group known as] Fedayins and Kurds as well as [the Communist Party, the] Tudeh, the National Front and [Ayatollah Kazem] Shariatmadari supporters. Many—including Shariatmadari, [former President Mehdi] Bazargan supporters and Tudeh leaders—were forced to appear on television and recant their previous views. Thus the toll taken among those who had participated in the revolution was far greater than that among the royalists.[25]

The executions did not stop there. As soon as the war with Iraq ended in 1988 and the government could afford to do so, in just one month of savagery, it hanged some 2,800 prisoners then lodged in its prisons.

Truly as Pierre Vergniaud wrote of the French Revolution, *Il a été permis de craindre que la Révolution, comme Saturne, dévorât successivement tous ses enfants.* (It is to be feared that the Revolution, like Saturn, devours one after another all of its children.)

In addition to the proportionately huge casualties they suffered, what really defeated the Mojahedin was that they had failed to create for themselves what that great guerrilla leader and theorist Mao Zedong had pointed out to be essential: a social environment. He called this environment the "sea" in which the guerrillas, like fish, could live. Perhaps creating such a condition was impossible in the Iran of that time. The general public was infiltrated, demoralized, and beaten down, and it lacked any organizational structure other than the religious establishment, which was, of course, the determined foe of the Mojahedin. As the casualty figures show, the Mojahedin could hardly find places to hide, much less people to lead. So what was left of the movement fled into exile. By the end of 1983, it was no longer a threat to the regime.

*I*n the meantime, another enemy had become a serious threat to the regime. On September 22, 1980, the Iraqi army launched an attack on Iran. The next eight years of fighting along the 2,000-kilometer (1,200-mile) front, the Iraq-Iran war, would become Iran's "quagmire," bankrupting its economy and killing tens of thousands of its people, but it was devastating for Iraq as well. The odds were always against Iraq: Its population was only a third of Iran's—fifteen million to forty-five million—which meant that its army was proportionally smaller. Although there was a long history of hostilities along the frontier and Iraq's then leader Saddam Hussein was clearly worried by the attempts of the Iranians to stir Shia and Kurdish Iraqis to revolution, what apparently convinced him to attack at that time was the chaos he perceived in Iran.

The 1979 revolution had virtually destroyed the army the Shah had so expensively and massively created. Ayatollah Khomeini rightly believed its officer corps to be opposed to the revolution and wrongly believed it was capable of restoring the monarchy. So, the revolutionary government's first act, as I have mentioned, just a few days after Khomeini returned to Iran, was to execute the senior commanders. Beginning with that act, it decimated the officer corps. As David Segal has written, the purge was "perhaps the most devastating destruction of a military force by its own government since Stalin's Red Army purges of 1936–1938. . . . [I]t would appear that more than 5,000 Iranian officers have been executed by their own government, while additional thousands have been imprisoned or forced into exile."[26]

The analogy to the Red Army—and also to the French army during France's revolution—carries forward to the next act. Out of the chaos, a new Iranian military force began to be created, and slowly, painfully, and at great cost it once again became powerful. Its first taste of combat was relatively minor: suppression of Kurdish separatists. Beating down Kurds was a traditional outing. It allowed the regime to detract attention from the divisive issues raised by the revolution. And it was "popular" because the Iranians knew that both the United States and Israel were helping the Kurds. Finally, it was militarily controlled and easy because the Kurds were scattered and only lightly armed. It was in the Kurdish campaign that the Revolutionary Guard, the *Pasdaran-e Enghelab,* began to learn its trade. But fighting Iraq would prove to be a very different challenge.

Fighting the large, well-equipped, and organized Iraqi army, which incidentally contained a high proportion of Shia Muslims, required the Iranian regime to "rehabilitate" the Shah's army. In the desperate challenge of combat, even the old officer corps was temporarily "forgiven." To get the air force into action, hundreds of pilots were taken direct from prison, many of them awaiting execution, back to their aircraft. But also the new organizations, the *Pasdaran-e Enghelab* and the *Sazeman-e Basij* (the militia), became fighting forces during combat with the Iraqis. Unable to match the Iraqis in equipment or organizational skills, their leaders learned their new trade literally under the gun and relied on tactics taken from the Chinese in the Korean War, "human waves." The costs were enormous: Before the fighting ended on August 20, 1988, perhaps as many as a million people died or were killed. Iran alone lost about 250,000 casualties, plus nearly that many more were disabled.

Less immediately evident than the tally of death was the reassertion of one of the characteristics of Iranian culture we have observed since the Zoroastrian "weeping of the Magi," through early Shiism, and that was constantly emphasized in passion plays and processions—the celebration of martyrdom. In the war against Iraq, hundreds of thousands of young men were marched through mine fields against prepositioned artillery and machine-gun emplacements. Tens of thousands were slaughtered. They became the heroes, indeed, the very symbols of the revolution and of its messianic culture.

During an extensive trip along the war's central front in 1986, I had occasion to see the effect of Iranian religious ecstasy on the Iraqi soldiers: It appalled them and eventually broke their morale. The effect on the Iranian "home front" is more difficult to judge. What appears is that the martyrdom of the youth, rather than horrifying and revolting the society, the way wars often do, gave the society an emotional stake in the revolutionary regime that went quite beyond mere nationalism. To criticize or oppose the regime became not only unpatriotic but also a sacrilege against the dead. Thus, it tended to halt the earlier attempts to ameliorate the most extreme elements of the doctrine that Ayatollah Khomeini had imposed on Iran. It certainly was a factor in the destruction of the Mojahedin opposition.

In a communication to undisclosed recipients, apparently written in 1988, Ayatollah Khomeini set forth his decision to accept a ceasefire. After outlining the terrible costs of the war, he wrote that the Iranian commander had informed him that "we can have no victory for another five years, and even by then we need to have 350 infantry bridges [brigades?], 2,500 tanks, 300 fighter planes" and that the commander had said that Iran would need "laser and nuclear weapons to confront the attacks." These measures, he said, were equivalent to drinking a cup of poison, so he decided to stop the war.[27]

When Ayatollah Khomeini died on June 3, 1989, at age 86, he appeared to have solved what he regarded as the most crucial problems faced by his regime: He had virtually destroyed the secular opposition, beaten down the breakaway challenge of the Kurds, and he had seen Iran through the terrible Iraq-Iran war. What he could not do was pass to anyone the essence of his role, being the supreme authority on literally everything pending the return of the Hidden Imam. A *faghih,* as I have explained, had to be anointed by the general consensus of the *mujtahids.* Only two of the *ayatollahs* could have met their standards—Muhammad Kazem Shariatmadari and Hossein-Ali Montazeri, and he had disqualified them.[28]

Lacking a senior *ayatollah,* the Constitutional Reform Council named to the post of *Rahbar* ("Supreme Guide") a "non-*ayatollah*," the fifty-year-old Seyyed Ali Hoseyni Khamenei, a former Secretary-General of the Islamic Republic Party who had been elected president in 1981. Khamenei was not a *faghih* but a lower ranking cleric, a *hojat-ol-eslam.* Taking the analogy I have drawn of the *ulama* to a university faculty, we can say he was not a full professor but only an assistant professor. The choice of Khamenei forced the Constitutional Reform Council to innovate. In violation of Shia tradition, which held that government played no role in assigning clerical status, it "promoted" him and his close associate, Ali-Akbar Hashemi Rafsanjani, who moved into position to be elected president in July 1989, to the rank of *ayatollah.*

Like the Islamic Republic's first appointed president, Mehdi Bazargan, a decade earlier, Rafsanjani based his program as president on the idea that the revolution was over. Bazargan was much too early—the revolution had only just begun—but Rafsanjani thought the time had come to heal the wounds of Iran. So he forthrightly set out to emphasize enjoyment of the fruits of the revolution rather than suffering more of its violence. As he rather incongruously put it, "It was time to put away childish things." Working closely with the newly appointed Supreme Guide Khamenei, he loosened government control over the economy and even allowed the opening of a stock exchange. Taking advantage of the ending of the Iraq-Iran war, he also slashed military spending.

The public obviously approved: Iranians were tired of violence and wanted more "bread." He did too. While president for two terms, Rafsanjani would become one of Iran's richest men, but he did little to alter the harshness of the regime. He did, however, make one major policy shift: With the approval of Supreme Guide Khamenei, he undertook a remarkable campaign to halt the runaway growth of population. As Robin Wright has written, during the 1980s "millions of women complied with the theocrats' dictate to breed a new Islamic generation that would defend the revolution."[29] Population soared from about thirty-four million to about sixty-six million. Realizing that the economy could not keep up, the regime arranged that the *mujtahids* issue a *fatva* (ruling) proclaiming that Islam favored families with only two children. This allowed the government to introduce one of the world's most extensive family-planning programs, including mandatory sex education, birth control clinics, free contraception devices, and even sterilization. The government also organized thousands of women and sent them from house to house to urge family planning. As a result, population growth fell from 3.2 to 1.2 percent between 1989 and 2003.

Perhaps as impressive as the population policy was the "social justice" policy the regime pursued even during periods of severe political oppression.

In 1978, just before the revolution, almost half (47 percent) of the population was below the poverty line; that figure had dropped to less than one Iranian in five (19 percent) in 2003.

Much of this transformation was the result of higher oil prices, but the regime also found a peculiarly Iranian way to turn the traditional role and institutions of Islam into a powerful means of social uplifting. Since it would have powerful social, demographic, and political consequences and would set the basis for the elections of 2009, it must be understood.

As I have earlier pointed out, most of the functions that Westerners think of as the proper role of government—education, public health, and social welfare—had been considered by Iranians to be the responsibility of the *ulama*. But from the late nineteenth century the state began to take them over; then Reza Shah in the 1930s and Muhammad Reza Shah in the 1960s and 1970s virtually excluded the *ulama* from civic affairs. So, after the revolution, the theocracy had only a memory on which to build a new model. What the new rulers did was to modify that memory to fit a modern economy.

Most of the traditional activities of the *ulama* had been financed by "pious foundations," what are known in Islamic Arabic as *awqaf* and in Farsi as *evghaf* or *bonyads*. Traditionally such organizations were endowed and run by private citizens. Some grew quite rich so over the centuries greedy or impecunious rulers had periodically confiscated their assets, as Reza Shah did in the 1930s. Effectively, *bonyads* had ceased to exist by 1979. So they offered the incoming clerical regime little material with which to work, but it found new sources of money by confiscating the property of Muhammad Reza Shah, his courtiers, members of the old aristocracy, and those entrepreneurs who had fled Iran.

Incorporating the assets of the Shah, the largest *bonyad,* known as "The Foundation for the Oppressed and Disabled" (*Bonyad Mostazafin va Janbazan*), is now the owner of some 400 companies, with assets said to be worth $12 billion, which it uses, among other things, as a quasi-private Iranian version of the American Veterans Affairs Administration to care for 12,000 families of the combatants who were wounded in the Iraq-Iran war. Although it is the largest, it is only one of some 123 *bonyads* that produce an estimated 33 to 40 percent of Iran's Gross Domestic Product (GDP). So necessary to the Islamic Republic did the post-Khomeini presidencies regard the *bonyads* that they gave them tax exemption, special privileges in the customs for what they imported, access on concessionary terms to credit, and, when necessary, regulatory protection against competition in the private sector. The *bonyads* became the nation's largest employers, with as many as five million employees, and were providing welfare payments to several million more. Thus, as Kenneth Katzman of the Congressional Research Service told the U.S. Congress in July 2006, they are crucial in building "support for the regime among the working and lower classes."[30] As the presidential elections of June 2005 and 2009 demonstrated, their economic and social welfare programs had become essential to a vast number of Iranians. Consequently, they created a new ideological thrust—often called in the Western press "populism"—and built a massive constituency for the incumbent administration.

In addition to the *bonyad*s, each administration since the death of Ayatollah Khomeini empowered the regime's favored institutions, particularly the Revolutionary Guard and the *Basijis*. The Guard, in which the current president Mahmoud Ahmadinejad served, was awarded Iran's largest project, a $2.3 billion contract to develop Iran's South Pars gas field.

Energy is the major asset of Iran. The water-poor country contains the world's third-largest reserves of petroleum (an estimated 10 percent) and the world's second-largest (after Russia) gas reserves (an estimated 15 percent). Energy provides 80 to 90 percent of Iran's export earnings, 27 percent of the GDP, and 50 percent of the government revenues. But, curiously, Iran remained a major importer of petroleum products because its refineries could meet only 60 percent of its domestic requirements. Thus, the price of gasoline (as in America) is a major political issue. The regime could not even consider raising the price of automobile fuel if it wished to retain public support. So, by the end of the presidency of Muhammad Khatami, it was forced to spend $5 billion a year to import the gasoline it was selling at very low prices to the public.

The oil sector has been severely hit by sanctions. As Shayerah Ilias, also of the Congressional Research Service, reported in January 2009, "It is believed that millions of barrels of oil are lost annually because of damage to reservoirs and . . . aging infrastructure and old technology. . . . Structural upgrades and access to new technologies, such as natural gas injections and other enhanced oil recovery efforts, have been limited by a lack of investment, due in part to U.S. sanctions."[31] Use of Iran's natural gas has been even more restricted. "Iran has been seeking international investment to help build its natural gas sector. However, U.S. sanctions have limited Iran's access to technologies from abroad that are necessary for developing liquefied natural gas plants." The energy sector of the economy has been state-dominated for at least the last 50 years, but today "Iran is engaging in [an] effort to privatize nearly 50 state-run oil and gas companies, estimated to be worth $90 billion by 2014. . . ."

Rafsanjani wanted to go much further in reducing the role of the state in the economy and even proposed allowing foreign companies to resume major roles. These plans were strongly opposed by the large number of people who benefitted from the *bonyads*.[32] Recipients did not want their incomes cut back and managers certainly did not want foreign competition. If Rafsanjani's program was "liberalism," it was very unpopular. There were strikes by workers who had not been paid their wages but saw the managers living relatively rich lives. Worse, massive corruption was commonly attributed to Rafsanjani personally. While a senior government official, he controlled one of Iran's biggest sources of foreign exchange, the lucrative pistachio market, and put other members of his family in charge of development projects. Disposing large amounts of cash, he reached far beyond Iran and even acquired a luxury resort in Goa, India. As M. Cist commented in *The Guardian,* "a visitor from Mars would see little difference between him and the late CIA-backed Shah."[33]

When Rafsanjani's second term ended in 1997, the Council of Guardians (*Shora-ye-Neaban*) approved the candidacy of Seyyed Muhammad Khatami, who had served under Rafsanjani as minister of culture. He campaigned for a politically more open society with individual liberties guaranteed by a rule of law. The public reacted enthusiastically: Almost twice as many voters turned out as had for Rafsanjani, and he won 70 percent of their votes. He started well, but, during his tenure in office, Iran faced severe economic problems that caused him to fail to deliver on the hopes for a higher standard of living. Many people remained unemployed and sunk in poverty. Thus, during his second term, talk of corruption and failure of hopes of economic improvement continued to deflate the "moderates" while sights of social permissiveness began to infuriate the "conservatives."

By 2003, midway through Khatami's tenure in office, we are offered insights that help clarify the events leading down to the disputed election of June 2009 and the street demonstrations and suppression that followed it.

The first issue was the growing perception that the *ulama* had become materialistic and were engaged in "improper" activities. Traditional Shia doctrine, as I have pointed out, held that the *ulama* should stand aloof from government because engaging in it would corrupt them; their proper role was a sort of moral holding action while awaiting the return of the Hidden Imam, when it would be proper for them to assist him. Ayatollah Khomeini famously rejected that tradition. As he said, "Islam is politics." The *ulama* should rule. That was the message of his *Velayat-e Faghih*. So he rejected the warning of his protégé, former President Mehdi Bazargan, that the *ulama* would use the political power he gave them to become a privileged class. Indeed, they quickly became Iran's new rich and the higher up the echelon of power each man got, the more opportunities for enrichment he found. Thus it was that the "reformist" government of Khatami became tarred by the brush of such of its patrons as Rafsanjani. He "may have been the most notorious . . . but he was one of many," wrote Ray Takeyh. "Over the past 26 years, the clerical oligarchs have constructed an economy designed to operate to their direct benefit."[34] Disillusionment with "moderates" like Rafsanjani and Khatami spread as, despite the rise of oil income, increasing numbers of Iranians saw little or no improvement in their living standards—one in eight Iranians was still unemployed and nearly one in five remained below the poverty line—while their spiritual and political leaders became enormously rich.

Reacting angrily in their disappointment, students in June 2003 again poured into the streets as they had in 1979. This time their target was not a foreign embassy but the national government. They did not try to occupy anything but clogged the streets with parades, of which one was said to be five kilometers (three miles) long. As they marched, they sounded an ominous new note: "Death to Khamenei."[35] As Iran's supreme guide, the *Rahbar*, Khamenei was considered sacrosanct, so their protests were regarded as seditious, and they were set upon by gangs of *molla*-inspired thugs armed with sticks and chains. In a television address, Khamenei blamed the riots on the United States. In a sense, he was right: The students were encouraged by radio and television broadcasts, but they did not come from the American government; they came from the huge Iranian exile community, numbering more than half a million, in Los Angeles.[36] The government cracked down, but, undeterred, the rioters continued to protest.

However, their ability to protest was restricted: Neither the *Majles* nor other organs of state were open to them; the public media was controlled; speaking out endangered one's job; and everyone feared denunciation and arrest. Citizens were allowed to support one or the other of the approved public figures, but at best they represented two sides of the same coin; there were no non-regime public figures representing different policies. Even supporters of the regime were tightly controlled and vetted, and most were disbarred by the Council of Guardians. Of the hundreds who put themselves forward for election, only a few were allowed to stand.

So, toward the end of Khatami's term, the sense of disillusionment became widespread, but it was a confused sense: The "moderates," whom apparently most of the younger Iranians wished to have set the pattern of their *social* lives, were engaged in self-serving *economic* activities that many found repellent, while their most vocal opponent stood for *financial* honesty but also a tightening of *religious control* of the society. The voters manifested their disturbance at the choice they were offered in the 2005 election—either to support the financially corrupt or the socially restrictive—by abstaining. Those who voted had to choose either the well-known and "soiled" Rafsanjani, who was running again, or the then relatively unknown but apparently "clean" mayor of Tehran, Mahmoud Ahmadinejad. Probably largely supported by the poor, Mahmoud Ahmadinejad defeated Rafsanjani with 61.69 percent of the relatively light final vote.[37] Adept at landing on his feet, Rafsanjani did not lose much by his defeat at the polls: he continued his lucrative personal business activities and was rewarded by his friend the Ayatollah Khamenei with the leadership of what is potentially the most powerful organ of the government, the 86-member Assembly of Experts (*Majles-e Khobregan*), which is charged with the selection of the successor to the Supreme Guide. Since Khamenei is now 70 years old and reputedly in poor health, Rafsanjani has emerged as potentially Iran's "king maker."[38]

On taking office in 2005, Ahmadinejad further emphasized the already established welfare programs and from his first days distanced himself from Rafsanjani and Khatami: He was, as he constantly postured and proclaimed, a man of the people. He made much of his deprived childhood and was careful to live—and to be seen to live—a frugal life. His campaign worked. By early 2009, many thought he was the first president "to understand Iran's poor and working class and who seemed capable of fulfilling the revolution's promises of economic and social justice."[39]

He also staked out for himself the popular role of the defender of Iran against the threat, which virtually all Iranians perceived, of foreign, particularly American, intervention. I will discuss Iranian-American relations in the next chapter, but here I mention some of the issues that affected Iranian domestic politics. So important was the overhang of fear of America to become during Ahmadinejad's presidency and so popular was his response to it that we must pause to consider it as objectively as possible if we are to understand the Iran of today.

In the 1979 Revolution, Iranian society split into two parts both geographically and emotionally. Large numbers of Iranians fled the country to join the tens of thousands of Iranian students already in America and Europe. Almost all the expatiates were opposed to the Islamic Republic and many favored its destruction; whatever their nostalgia for Iran, which was palpable, most enjoyed their relatively free and affluent lives in the West. Those who remained in Iran were influenced by different experiences. Perhaps the most important of these experiences was the Iraq-Iran war, in which the United States aided Saddam Husain and actually engaged in armed combat against Iran. In that war, virtually a whole generation of Iranians was killed or severely wounded. Ahmadinejad's generation are the survivors of that terrible conflict.

In the years after the war, and particularly during the administration of George W. Bush, America engaged in a number of ostensibly covert but well publicized actions, on which it spent hundreds of millions of dollars, to "destabilize" the Islamic Republic. It also ringed Iran with huge military forces, openly discussed attacking the country, and proclaimed its right to do so in official documents and public addresses. It killed a number of Iranians. The most egregious episode was the shooting down in Iranian airspace of a civilian airliner, killing all 290 passengers. But there were many less publicized actions by special forces and agents. While few Americans even know of these events, Iranians constantly dwell on them.[40]

Meanwhile, riding the wave of his 2005 electoral victory, Ahmadinejad set about a wide-ranging purge of officials he had inherited from the previous two "moderate" regimes. It was such a clean sweep that his opponents accused him of a virtual coup d'état. In his first four years in office, he replaced the governors of all 30 provinces and sacked dozens of deputy ministers, many administrators of state organizations, several ambassadors and about 10,000 other government employees. In their places he put men whose formative experience was in the horrifying Iraq-Iran war.[41] As Richard Bulliet has written,[42] in that war "Iranians born between 1955 and 1970 [who] bore the brunt of the fighting . . . came disproportionately from the country's lower social strata. They passed their childhood under the shah, saw their lives transformed by the revolution and enjoyed the postwar benefits granted to veterans . . . they know in their hearts that theirs is the Greatest Generation, and for most of them Ahmadinejad is their leader and spokesman."

Thus, Ahmadinejad built a formidable organization that, while officially charged with running the government, was also able to mobilize political support for him. This move was particularly notable in that the Supreme Guide, which had once rebuked him for excessive zeal, permitted him to do so.[43] The 120,000-man Revolutionary Guard, in which Ahmadinejad had served, was already with him and he won over the (at least) three million-man *basiji* organizations—successors to the traditional *lutis* or private body guards of religious figures. The Revolutionary Guard had already become an economic powerhouse and *basijis* were rewarded in 2008 by the creation for it of the "Basij Construction Organization."[44] In short, Ahmadinejad did what many American city bosses had done: He created a powerful constituency for his administration by using government funds to subsidize popular programs and place his men where they would do his bidding and at the proper time deliver votes.

What was happening in Iranian society in the build-up to the 2009 elections can now be fairly accurately described. I suggest that the society can be thought of in three tiers, divided partly by age.

The first tier was the "old guard," those who had suffered under the Shah, made the Revolution, and who had been closely associated with Ayatollah Khomeini. They were aging and except for the *Rahbar* himself, their grip on power was loosening; following the lead of 75-year-old Ali Akbar Rafsanjani, many had settled down to enjoy the fruits of their youthful militancy. Apart from them but still beneficiaries of the revolution was a smaller group in the senior ranks of the *ulama,* some who had also been associates of Khomeini, but who had not joined the regime. They were finding it harder to support actions which their theological training had taught them to regard as wrong. Outstanding in this group today is Grand Ayatollah Hossein-Ali Montazeri. Signs are now emerging that he is not alone: Members of the lower-ranking *ulama,* particularly in the seminary city Qom, and even their students are beginning to find a new and generally critical voice.[45] Whether or not this split in the old guard will prove significant is not yet clear. It can be decisive only if its few outstanding members put themselves in a position of leadership of the young.

Foremost among those trying to do so is Mir Hossein Mousavi. (Like other names, his has several spellings in English transliteration, including Moussavi). Hardly a "liberal," Mousavi served as prime minister during the worst of the "Terror," which he did not oppose. A close associate and protégé of Ayatollah Ruhollah Khomeini, he belonged to the inner circle of the post-Revolutionary secular elite. He mobilized Iran's economy during the Iraq-Iran war from 1981 to 1989, when Khamenei was president. The two men allegedly then had a disagreement and Mousavi dropped out of public life. When he reemerged in 2008, aged 67, and decided to run for the presidency, Khamenei could have stopped him but did not; he was vetted and approved by the Council of Guardians. Coming, as Khamenei said, from "within the system,"[46] he presumably was regarded as a reliable member of the old guard who would enable the disaffected to let off steam without endangering the regime. The most that can be said with assurance of Mousavi's politics is that he wished to soften aspects of the regime, to restrain somewhat its exercise of power, and to leave open the opportunity for political evolution. A very moderate "moderate," he certainly cannot be regarded as an opponent of the regime. As a campaigner, he did not sound the call for major change. Indeed, as even his supporters admitted, he was a boring speaker,[47] without charisma, and made little effort to establish rapport with the people. He made only six campaign trips and those were confined to the larger cities. Finally, Mousavi had no party structure or even a significant campaign headquarters. As one observer put it, he was "an accidental leader, a moderate figure anointed at the last minute."[48]

As the leader of what I have suggested is the "second tier," Mahmoud Ahmadinejad stood in stark contrast. Born in 1956, 15 years after Mousavi, he was a man of the next generation. He was also active, focused, and showed a popular touch. His campaign featured highly effective videos that were widely seen, and he made some 60 campaign trips around the country to carry his candidacy to cities, towns, and even villages.[49] His message was that under his regime, the lot of the average Iranian had greatly improved and, despite what the statistics showed,[50] his audience appeared to believe him.[51] He also hammered a nationalist theme to which most Iranians instinctively responded: protection of Iran from predatory imperialists. He was raucous and insulting to his opponents—to the point that he was reprimanded by Ayatollah Khamenei[52]—but in the live television debate what he did appeared to be effective.

Probably, Ahmadinejad's main strength and Mousavi's main weakness came down to a single difference: Ahmadinejad's position was clear while Mousavi's was hedged with ambiguities. Ahmadinejad was a man of the Revolution, had long served it, fervently believed in it, and was able to put himself constantly before the public in the media while Mousavi, distinguished though his services to Iran had been, had been out of the public eye since before many of the voters were even born. And, while he supported the Islamic Republic as a concept, he was critical of it and wanted to change it in ways that must have seemed unclear to many of his supporters and dangerous to those whose livelihood was dependent upon the *bonyads* or other government programs.

This takes us to what I suggest we consider the "third tier." It is less sharply defined than the "old guard" or the Iraq-Iran war generation, but for the most part it can be considered to be made up of the younger generation. Its composition would become clear only in the aftermath of the voting, but we can gain some insight into it from polls.

Only one poll was independent. It was conducted roughly three weeks before the election by an American group, the Center for Public Opinion of the New America Foundation, commissioned by the BBC and ABC News. It predicted the result reported by the government, a 2 to 1 victory for Ahmadinejad.[53] The poll is open to question on two counts: first, it was taken before the opposition claimed there was a shift from Ahmadinejad to Mousavi and, second, a minority of those interviewed expressed a clear opinion—27 percent expressed no opinion, 15 percent refused to answer and 8 percent said they would vote for none of the candidates.[54] There were other polls, including what the *New York Times* editors called the "opposition polls," but we know little about how they were conducted. One dated June 6 showed Ahmadinejad with 53 or 54 percent and Mousavi with 35 or 36 percent. A second poll,[55] not identified, showed Ahmadinejad falling to about 40 percent and Mousavi holding about 37 percent. No poll indicated that Mousavi would win the election.

In judging the subsequent charges of vote tampering, it is significant that the son of Mousavi's ally, Ayatollah Rafsanjani, set up a western style campaign headquarters to monitor the voting. As he told *New York Times* correspondent Robert Worth, "We have 50,000 observers in these elections. . . . If anyone is barred from a ballot box, we will find out."[56] If true, this was a remarkable check on the elections, equating to more than one monitor for each ballot box.

𝒱oting took place on June 12 throughout the country with, as is usual in elections, high hopes on both sides. Iran did not have the electronic voting machines that have been so controversial in America; what it had was some 45,713 ballot boxes to accommodate the nearly 40 million registered men and women who actually voted. The average box thus contained 875 ballots. Voters were allowed to vote in any district, but since each voter's fingerprints were on his or her ballot stub there was a "paper trail" in the voting. What is in dispute is which way the "trail" pointed.

Almost immediately both the government and the followers of Mousavi claimed it pointed to their victory. The government figure was almost identical to the one Ahmadinejad polled in 2005: Of 39,165,191 votes counted (85 percent of those eligible), Ahmadinejad was credited with 24,527,516 or 62.63 percent while Mousavi was said to have received 13,216,411 or 33.75 percent.[57] The opposition did not put forward precise figures but asserted that it had won overwhelmingly and that the government had falsified the results.

Because the opposition charges were believed by millions of Iranians and most of the foreign press, they need to be examined. Among the specific charges made were that some polling stations ran out of ballots and turned voters away (*apparently true*), that the ministry of the interior had not followed legal procedures that required a three-day interval to take account of challenges (*true*).[58] Mousavi and the two other candidates lodged 646 complaints with the Council of Guardians. (*Not enough information is yet available to judge these, but the regime has admitted that some are probably justified.*) Some Iranians and foreigners went further and charged that the votes had never been counted and that the government had predetermined the outcome to be above 51 percent to avoid a run-off. (*Ayatollah Khamenei vociferously denies these charges and so far no evidence has been brought forward to substantiate them.*)[59] And there were a number of suspicions voiced: that it would have been impossible to count all the ballots before the results were officially announced. (*If the votes were counted locally, they could have been quickly tallied because there were few per box and the ballots were relatively simple, but they may have been forwarded to Tehran for counting. We still do not have solid information.*) Mousavi charged that Ahmadinejad personally or his supporters effectively bought votes by handouts. (*Almost certainly true.*) Another charge was that it was unlikely that Mousavi would have lost his home province, Azerbaijan. (*"Favorites sons" usually do well in their home territories, but, as we have seen in American politics recently, Al Gore failed to carry Tennessee and George McGovern did not carry South Dakota. It appears that Ahmadinejad was worried about this possibility and campaigned vigorously in Azerbaijan, where he had been a popular governor. He speaks the local language, Azeri Turkish, and made a point, always popular in Iran, of quoting Azari poetry in his speeches. It is notable that the independent poll had predicted Ahmadinejad would win Azerbaijan with twice Mousavi's vote.*)

Outright fraud is certainly possible as Americans know from our own experience, but much of the foreign media commentary on the Iran vote was based just on what outsiders and the opposition wished to happen rather than what they had reason to believe actually happened.[60] Americans wanted Mousavi to win so we believe he did.[61]

But, it has been asked, if the government was really so sure of the figures why did it not simply set up an independent auditor to verify them?[62] While this appears to be a logical move, it is actually unattractive even for democratic, open governments, as Americans learned during the controversy over the 2000 vote in Florida, because it implies that the official process *was* fraudulent. While, initially at least, Khamenei was willing to discuss the voting process—he did meet with Mousavi two days after the election to discuss opposition charges and arranged that the Council of Guardians offer to recount ten percent of the ballots, a move that was done, much too late, in front of television cameras on June 28[63]—he insisted that verification of the results be done by the government itself. He was not willing to consider the implicit challenge to its legitimacy that referral to an outside arbiter would raise. That, of course, is the nature of a theocracy: Its legitimacy is God-given and opposition is a sin. In Iran, Khamenei reacted in precisely this sense, saying that the system "worked."

This issue, which Khamenei regarded as a challenge to the regime, was raised to a more serious level when the angry and disappointed followers of Mir Hossein Mousavi began mass demonstrations. What I think he must have decided was that, whether peaceful or violent, demonstrations would inevitably lead to challenges to the regime itself. He made this clear in a highly publicized speech on June 19 at the great mosque of Tehran University in front of an audience of tens of thousands and to millions of others on television. Protests, he said firmly, must stop or protesters would face "bloody consequences" of their lawlessness.[64]

It is suggestive to compare the June 2009 events in Iran to those that took place 20 years before in June 1989 in Beijing's Tiananmen Square. There are, of course, many differences, but the similarities are striking: Supreme Guide Ali Khamenei in Iran and Paramount Leader Deng Xiaoping in China had both grown up in a revolutionary environment and both knew how revolutions arose from often modest beginnings. Both had seen protests bring down apparently strong governments and were determined not to see that bit of history repeated. As Jonathan Mirsky, who witnessed the Chinese events as a reporter, has written,[65] Deng Xiaoping "probably recalled" that the charge against the Guomindang government had been led by "young students like himself." Ali Khamenei had similarly been a young student agitator against the Shah. Change a few words and Khamenei would have subscribed to "Deng's words on April 25, [1989 that] the demonstrations had become 'anti-Party, anti-socialist turmoil,' a situation to be stopped at once, 'in the manner of using a sharp knife to cut through knotted hemp.'"

The great demonstrations—about a million people each—in Beijing's Tiananmen Square and Tehran's Revolution Square were the "knotted hemp." Those who were at least formally responsible for the knot, Zhao Ziyang in Beijing and Mir Hossein Mousavi in Tehran, bore strong resemblances: Both were former prime ministers, believers in single "party" authoritarianism, but within that system were "moderates" who sought enough openness to allow citizens sufficient scope to criticize but not enough to change or overthrow the political order.

Both regimes regarded the demonstrations as threats. Both decided that they must beat them down so both cracked down on those who took part. The Chinese suppression was savage and massive: The police and army killed an estimated 15,000 people, mainly students. In Iran suppression was ugly but more modest: The reported number of deaths is 20 people. The Chinese put Zhao Ziyang into house arrest until his death in 2005. We don't know what will be the fate of Mir Hossein Mousavi.

It is striking that "out of fear that history might repeat itself," the Chinese government began in June 2009 censoring the news coming from Iran; the Chinese government, like the Iranian government, has portrayed the events in Tehran as the result of agitation by the United States and other foreign powers rather than an indigenous movement.[66]

What I think the comparison of the Chinese and Iranian regimes' reaction to the events shows is that an authoritarian regime has little flexibility:

Faced with even a peaceful challenge, it fears that any sign of weakness or offer of compromise will open a fissure that will inevitably and quickly break apart its halo of legitimacy. As an act of self-preservation, it must "win."

So now, I believe, we are in position to see the nature of the conflict and to analyze the "third tier" of Iranian society.

Feeling cheated and having no other forum in which to express their anger and to overturn the official results of the election, Mousavi's supporters took to the streets. Their identity is as disputed as the results of the election. Many of the journalists who witnessed the subsequent demonstrations thought that the pro-Mousavi crowds were made up of the relatively privileged and better educated. They particularly noted that many of the surprisingly large number of women demonstrators, purposely violated dress codes. *The Independent's* experienced Middle Eastern correspondent Robert Fisk, who walked with the demonstrators disagreed, writing that "A million people marched from Revolution Square to Freedom Square with Mir Hossein Mousavi riding atop a car among them . . . this was not just the trendy, young, sunglassed ladies of north Tehran. The poor were here, too, the street workers and middle-aged ladies in full chador." While among a million people there was diversity, most observers found that the bulk of Mousavi's followers were the relatively privileged and most were young.

Everyone was struck by the strange silence of most of the marches and by the fact that there were no calls for the dismantling of the Islamic Republic. While the issues they addressed were contemporary, the media in which their protests were expressed were traditional: Like their grandparents in the 1905 revolt against the then shah, they shouted from their rooftops the Muslim chant, "*Allahu Akbar.*" Reaching far back into Iranian memory, many wore black clothing, the ancient symbol of revolution and the Shia symbol of martyrdom; as in the sequence of twentieth-century upheavals, they took to the streets as their only available forum; and when the police shot a young woman demonstrator, they echoed the 40-day mourning ritual that played so powerful a role in the 1979 revolution against Muhammad Reza Shah. The demonstrators were anxious to show their deveotion to the ideals of the regime but also to make clear their opposition to its current leadership, which most thought to be corrupt and deceitful.[67]

The demonstrations were the largest seen in Iran since the revolution. Hundreds of thousands of people marched silently in peaceful protest on Monday, June 15.[68] The mayor of Tehran said it numbered three million.

Marches continued day after day. At first, the police made no attempt to dissuade the crowds. Then, the government began to react. Police and vigilantes turned out in force and clashes became violent.[69]

Not surprisingly, given the social services programs Ahmadinejad had implemented over the previous four years, building his constituency, the regime was able to call out large number of supporters. They may be considered as the "other half" of what I have labeled the "third tier." Those on the streets were young men or even teenagers, who everyone agreed were less well educated and of more humble social status. Many were identified as *basiji*s. *New York Times* columnist Roger Cohen heard them called "chicken Basiji" (*joojeh basiji*) and described them as teenagers who had been brainwashed from youth.[70] Unrestrained by any code of discipline, they were the hooligans of the aftermath of the election.

Their acts of savagery horrified but also intimidated the protesters, whose numbers began to dwindle. They also brought into the open the deep divisions in the "first tier" between the improperly appointed *Rahbar* and the secular officers of state on the one hand and the traditional and venerated religious establishment. The leader of that establishment, Grand Ayatollah Hossein-Ali Montazeri, a *marja-e taghlid*—a figure regarded by Shiis as having the right to issue orders that had to be obeyed—ruled on June 21 that the actions of the pro-government thugs were the worst of sins, religiously forbidden (*haram*), and ordered that "every one of our religious brothers and sisters [that is the whole population] must help the nation in defending its lawful rights."[71]

So what does the future appear to hold?

To judge from the past 30 years, the fervor demonstrated by the mass demonstrations will die down but the sense of disillusionment will remain latent. The regime has built a new society in its "third tier." Even though it is split between the relatively educated and privileged on the one hand and on the other the less educated and poorer, and probably will remain so, the coming years will bring a shift in relative numbers. Already, during the demonstrations, a million young men and women pulled back to sit for examinations. As education spreads, that million will be joined not only by younger members of the same group but by entrants from the "other half."

Meanwhile, the "old guard," the first tier, will pass from the scene. Many observers believe that when Khamenei dies or steps down, he will be followed by Ali-Akbar Hashemi Rafsanjani. A crafty and skilled politician who is

thought to be not only ambitious but also personally hostile to both Ayatollah Khamenei and President Mahmoud Ahmadinejad, Rafsanjani has adroitly
positioned himself in the events centering on the June 2009 election: On the
one hand, he was a backer of the "liberals," covertly assisting the campaign of
Mir Hossein Mousavi, but, on the other hand, he portrayed himself as an
elder statesman, a man above the political fray. He has struck a note that is ap-
plauded by the demonstrators and cannot easily be denied even by the most
conservative of the *ulama*—that the regime is "in crisis." While carefully
avoiding the charge that the election, which he arranged to have monitored
by an impromptu organization he set up, was fraudulent, a charge that would
have struck at the legitimacy of the state and outraged the conservatives
whose support he would need to move to leadership, he asserted that the current line-up of authority no longer enjoy the trust of many Iranians.[72] No
other member of the upper *ulama* appears as an obvious candidate to be
supreme leader. But Rafsanjani is now 75 years old; at best he will be a tran-
sitional figure. I therefore believe it is likely that in the next few years, Iran will
experience a shift away from the theocracy toward a secular government.
Whether or not this shift will be toward a civil regime, probably one that is
culturally more open than the current regime, or toward an secular authoritarian regime, headed by such a man as Mahmoud Ahmadinejad and supported by the army and quasi-military Revolutionary Guard and Basiji
organizations, will, I think, be at least partly and probably largely determined
by what happens in the relations between Iran and the United States. To this
issue I now turn.

Six

THE UNITED STATES AND IRAN TODAY

merica's activities in Iran have included individual ventures; missionary and foundation works; governmental and government-inspired multinational and international programs dealing with the whole range of cultural, educational, and technological exchange; economic and military assistance; development and planning advice; diplomatic representation; intelligence gathering and analysis; espionage; economic sanctions; blockade; overflight; penetration of special forces; and large-scale combat. That is, in the last half of the twentieth century, American-Iranian interactions have covered virtually the whole field of international affairs. Probably no two countries have ever been more completely intertwined. As though this were not enough, the bilateral relations have been further complicated by cooperation and conflict on Iranian issues with Great Britain, the Soviet Union (and its successor, Russia), Israel, and other countries. The purpose of this chapter is to understand their current U.S.-Iranian relations. Then, in the Afterword, I will project where U.S. dealings might be leading the Iranians and foreign powers.

Before the government got involved, Americans acted in what today are known as non-governmental organizations (NGOs). In 1829, American missionary groups began to send representatives to Iran, where, as an adjunct to their religious activities, they opened schools and hospitals. As they had done in other parts of the Middle East, they brought with them a printing press with a Farsi font on which they published mainly religious tracts but also teaching materials and occasional works from the Iranian literary tradition. They encountered resistance to their actions, but generally they convinced the Iranians that, unlike the Russians and the British, they had no sinister designs on Iran. As confidence grew, so did their activities. Before Reza Shah in 1935 forbade Iranians to attend foreign schools, the American Presbyterian Mission[1] maintained 31 schools, of which the largest, in Tehran, enrolled nearly seven hundred students. Afterward their hospitals were allowed to continue to operate because Iran for some years did not have a suitable replacement.

To facilitate such private citizen contacts, in 1856, the two governments signed a "Treaty of Friendship and Commerce." As an indication of how distant the relations then were, it was negotiated and signed not in Iran or America but in the then capital of the Ottoman Empire, Constantinople, by the diplomatic representatives of the two governments. Its aim, as it proclaimed, was "establishing relations of Friendship between the two Governments, which they wish to strengthen by a Treaty of Friendship and Commerce, reciprocally advantageous and useful to the[ir] Citizens and subjects. . . ."[2] In short, the purpose was not "diplomatic" or strategic but only helped the citizens interact. This limited relationship convinced the Iranians that distant America was a benign force in the world, of which, unlike Russia and Britain, they need have no fear. That was to be a principal element in their relationship for almost a century. It was in stark contrast to the dealings of the British and Russians.

At the Peace Conference in Paris in 1919, the United States championed the right of the Iranians to be heard. As Secretary of State Robert Lansing wrote, "In Paris I asked of [British Foreign Minister] Mr. Balfour three times that the Persians have an opportunity to be heard before the Council of Foreign Ministers because of their claims and boundaries and because their territory had been a battle ground. Mr. Balfour was rather abrupt in refusing to permit them to have a hearing. It now appears that at the time I made these requests Great Britain was engaged in a secret negotiation to gain at least economic control of Persia."[3] The British action, temporarily at least, worsened Iranian regard for America.

Beginning at the end of the First World War, a different group of Americans became active in Iran. Their aim was not conversion but salvation in a different sense: The American Committee for Armenian and Syrian Relief was originally organized in 1915 to help save the Armenian community. Most of the Armenians were in what became the Turkish Republic. Hence, for the Committee, Iran was at first a side activity, although, as Acting Secretary of State Frank Polk pointed out, it did benefit from large U.S. government donations to the Red Cross. But from their original purpose, these organizations developed a broader concern and grew into the Near East Foundation, which has remained active down to the present time.

Quite different from these activities were those of other individual Americans. Instead of working for charities, they worked as employees of the Iranian government. Two men I have discussed in Chapter Four were private citizens who were hired by the *Majles* to assist in organizing and running the fiscal affairs of the government. W. Morgan Shuster acted in this capacity from 1910 to 1911, and his work was taken up by A. C. Millspaugh from 1922 to 1927. From this experience with non-governmental assistance, the government of Iran moved on a larger scale, hiring whole groups of private American citizens.

Yet another non-governmental American activity was commerce. Unlike the British, the American oil companies were not government owned or controlled. Rather, they were powerful influences on the American government; moreover, they conducted what amounted to their own foreign policy, whose principal aim was to break into the monopoly the British had established on Middle Eastern oil production. Their intervention in Iranian affairs began at the end of the First World War when Standard Oil began negotiations with the Iranian government in 1920 for a concession.

Negotiations were unsuccessful primarily because of British opposition. To the British, firmly in control of Iranian oil production, Americans were dangerous interlopers. The newly appointed American minister to Tehran advised British Foreign Minister Earl Curzon that the U.S. government was contemplating a role in the financial and economic recovery of Iran and asked what the view of the British government would be to such a move. Curzon was "rather startled" when the American "incidentally at the end of his explanation dropped in the word oil. I at once realised that he was referring to the American Standard Oil Company, and that that omnivorous organisation was endeavouring to secure a foot hold on Persian soil." In reply, Curzon warned the American minister that "the British Government could not be expected to regard with any favor . . . any attempt to introduce the Standard Oil Company in Persia."[4] It would not be until after the renamed Anglo

Iranian Oil Company (AIOC) was nationalized years later that any American companies were able "to secure a foot hold on Persian soil."

During the Second World War, America played a role formally subsidiary to that of Great Britain, but de facto it was a major independent presence in southern Iran, where it was engaged in the transshipment of hundreds of millions of tons of supplies and equipment to the Soviet Union. Altogether about thirty thousand noncombatant American soldiers served there under nominal British command. As in Japan, Korea, and other areas, the troops had generally bad relations with the Iranian civilians in their area because of reckless driving and, as the American minister in Tehran put it, "drunkenness and rowdyism." One of the most popular changes Reza Shah had promulgated in the 1930s was to make all foreigners subject to Iranian law, thus ending the "capitulations." However, during the war Reza Shah was deposed, and Iran was occupied by the Soviet Union and Great Britain. So, being part of an occupation force, the Americans were protected by a de facto extraterritoriality, and their contact with the Iranian government was minimal.

Then, in 1942, apparently partly in response to these difficult relations, President Franklin Roosevelt declared that Iran was eligible, as "vital to the defense of the United States,"[5] for aid under "Lend Lease." When he attended the Tehran Conference from November 28 to December 1, 1943, with Prime Minister Winston Churchill and Marshal Josef Stalin, President Roosevelt saw little of the country. He stayed at the Russian embassy and rarely ventured out. The attention of the three leaders was, of course, on the war in Europe, but, partly at the insistence of Roosevelt, they affirmed their intention to guarantee the sovereign independence of Iran. They also said that they "realised that the war has caused special economic difficulties for Iran, and they are agreed that they will continue to make available to the Government of Iran such economic aid as may be possible. . . ." As a practical matter, given the situation in both England and Russia, that meant American assistance, and, given the nature of the American economy, that intention gave rise to an Iranian-American trade agreement.

Shortly after his brief exposure to Iran, President Roosevelt was quoted as saying that he was thinking of "using Iran as an example of what we could do with an unselfish American policy" to make Iran a "model for what economic and technical assistance could do throughout the underdeveloped world."[6] Secretary of State Cordell Hull then narrowed Roosevelt's focus to Iran but broadened the scope of American policy to include political support when he wrote to the president, "Since this country [America] has a vital interest in the fulfillment of the principles of the Atlantic Charter and the establishment of foundations for lasting peace throughout the world, it is to the advantage of the United States to exert itself to see that Iran's integrity and independence are maintained and that she becomes prosperous and stable."[7]

American officials realized that Iran needed more than food. So they sent a mission to help train the Iranian army, of which an American general was made "intendant general." A police mission of 30 officers, successor to the Swedish police mission of the First World War, under an American chief also was sent to train the Iranian national police. Both of these activities under various acronyms continued for the next 30 years. In addition, various other "experts" were requested by the Iranian government.[8]

The first major American action, however, was aimed in a different direction and would increasingly dominate American-Iranian relations: In June 1947, the U.S. government made a loan of $25 million to enable Iran to buy surplus or used American military equipment, and arms shipments began to arrive in Iran in March 1949. In the years to follow, they would reach enormous quantities and costs.

Meanwhile, another crucial and long-term aspect of American-Iranian relations was being developed by U.S. Ambassador George Allen, more or less on his own. He paid little attention to the *Majles,* which he and most Americans regarded as a boisterous and irresponsible gathering, rather than anything they could understand as a parliament. Neither he nor his successors paid attention to the vast religious establishment of the *ulama.* Rather, Allen set out to achieve a close relationship with the Shah. He played tennis with the Shah, and their two families met for dinner every Monday night, and, as James Bill writes, "As Ambassador Allen tightened his relationship with the shah, American policy slowly moved in support of autocracy in Iran."[9]

Allen did not understand the subtle policy of Prime Minister Ahmad Ghavam, who played the Russians' desire for an oil concession against their military support for the two breakaway "republics" of Mahabad and Qazvin, causing them to lose both objectives. It was a masterful policy that infuriated the Russians but convinced Allen that Ghavam was a communist. So Allen advised the Shah that he had "finally reached the conclusion that he [the Shah] should force *Ghavam* out and should make him leave the country or put him in jail if he caused trouble." Allen's was probably the first official

American intervention in Iranian domestic politics and by no means the least unenlightened. But it signaled the new American preoccupation with communism.

In his inaugural address of January 20, 1949, President Harry S. Truman called for a "bold new program" to assist the developing world. From October 1950, the U.S. government began to assist Iran with grants under Truman's "Point Four" program.[10] As with subsequent aid efforts, each administration stressed the anti-Soviet or anti-communist aspects of its generosity; in the accepted wisdom of Washington politics, this was the only way to get the Congress to appropriate the needed funds.

So the mindset of Ambassador Allen fairly represented the thrust of American policy. Because all the problems of decolonization, underdevelopment, and poverty were at least exacerbated, if not actually caused, by the Soviet Union, it followed that evolving Third World countries must be enabled to uplift their economies—that was the purpose behind Point Four— but also that anti-communist governments of whatever political persuasion must be encouraged and supported. To that end, Muhammad Reza Shah was encouraged to visit the United States. He made a whirlwind tour in November–December 1949 and everywhere was given an extraordinary welcome. A handsome and glamorous young man, he immediately became a popular "star." All over the country, he was wined and dined, and he was given 21-gun salutes during visits to Annapolis and West Point. For the public, as for the government, over the next 30 years, the Shah was Iran, and Iran was the Shah.

America also reached out to Iran in other ways. The most important two were private. The Iranian government engaged the Morrison Knudson International firm to survey the Iranian economy to lay the basis for a major planning effort by Overseas Consultants Inc. These two studies formed the basis for the first of a series of Seven Year Development Plans that reshaped and uplifted the Iranian society and economy.

In 1950, American oil companies were buying roughly 40 percent—some 240 million barrels—of the production of AIOC. So the United States realized that it had a significant interest in Iran. American and European industry was heavily dependent on Iranian oil, but the danger that it might be disrupted was seen to be "clear and present" because the Iranians increasingly thought they were being treated unfairly while the British refused to consider any alteration in the terms of their 1935 concession. As the two sides pulled further apart, the Truman administration decided it had to try to stave off a major confrontation. In a letter to the Iranian prime minister, Truman asserted, incorrectly, that the British had accepted the principle of nationalization.[11]

On the British side, first the Conservative and subsequently the Labour governments and the management and board of directors of AIOC refused all efforts to reach an accommodation. They argued that they were performing correctly under a valid contract and stated that, as a matter of principle, they would not negotiate. Perhaps more practically, having emerged from the Second World War in desperate financial condition, the British government needed the profits it made from selling cheap Iranian oil.

On the Iranian side, Prime Minister Mossadegh replied that Truman was wrong—the British had not accepted the principle of nationalization.[12] He was right. He also argued that at the time when the concession was awarded, the Iranian parliament had no say in drafting its terms, and many believed that it was concluded as a result of bribery or threat. Not only Mossadegh but the *Majles* and virtually the entire Iranian public believed that Iran was being cheated by AIOC and its majority owner, the British government (which attributed what it took mainly to taxes). The figures, when eventually they became known, bore them out. For example, in the one year of 1950, AIOC earned £200 million, of which Iran received only £16 million.[13] Intelligent Iranians realized that unless they could change the terms of the concession, they would be perpetually relegated to the underdeveloped world.

This was the objective issue that divided the two sides, but the emotional underpinning went far deeper. Britain regarded Iran as a country of "Asian" people, weak, corrupt, decadent, and childish: The only arguments the Iranians understood were bribes and force. From long experience with colonials, British officers knew how to handle them. Meddling by ill-informed and incompetent Americans would make things worse. Indeed, the American oil company operating in Saudi Arabia, ARAMCO, had precipitated the crisis: By offering to split profits "fifty-fifty" with Saudi Arabia, it incited the Iranians. The British had always regarded the Americans as naïve; now they felt betrayed. So they dug in their heels.

The Iranian view was the mirror image of the British view: Britain was a selfish, grasping, evil imperialist power that ran roughshod over Iranian rights and aspirations. It had been doing so since long before the current crisis. It had divided Iran with the Russians twice in the previous half century, had helped to subvert the Iranian constitution, and had used its money and wiles to corrupt Shahs and their officials. Britain was the major obstacle to achievement of the Iranian national objectives.

In short, there was not much of a basis for an accommodation. A military clash seemed more likely. Indeed, the British were already planning to land forces at Abadan to secure the refinery and had "persuaded" the Iranian naval commander in the area to put up little or no resistance.

As Truman's Secretary of State Dean Acheson watched the British edging toward military action against Iran, he tried to warn them off. When he got reports that "British troops [were] moved to bases in the Near East and warships [had] appeared off Abadan," he called in British Ambassador Sir Oliver Franks and told him that "[o]nly on invitation of the Iranian Government, or Soviet military intervention, or a Communist *coup d'état* in Teheran [*sic*], or to evacuate British nationals in danger of attack could we support the use of military force."[14] When Franks reported Acheson's warning to London, Prime Minister Clement Attlee told the Cabinet that, in view of American opposition, it would not be "expedient to use force to maintain the British staff at Abadan."[15]

As they heard more from the British, the Americans were uniformly appalled by their attitude. When Averell Harriman, a senior statesman with vast business experience, returned from a mission of inquiry on behalf of the State Department—during which, as he pointed out, he spent more time than the "total combined time of the board of directors of AIOC"—he said "he never in his entire experience had known of a company where absentee management was so malignant."[16] Acheson put it even more graphically as he watched the crisis unfold: Commenting on British stubbornness, he wrote on a Churchillian model: "Never had so few lost so much so stupidly and so fast."[17] The British would not even allow the Iranians, who after all were 20 percent owners of AIOC, to examine the company's account books. The British had good reason: The accounts would have justified the Iranian anger. Not only was AIOC taking the lion's share of the profits, but the British government was charging taxes on the rest.

It was clear that if a major showdown, and possibly a British invasion, was to be avoided, the U.S. government would have to take the lead in effecting a workable accommodation.

Thus it was that America began the most sustained diplomatic encounter it had ever had with Iran. In this effort, Assistant Secretary of State George

McGhee became the link between the British and the Iranians. He met with the AIOC board and the Foreign Office officials and held virtually continuous discussions—as he later told me[18] they aggregated over 75 hours—with Iranian Prime Minister Muhammad Mossadegh. Together, McGhee and Mossadegh hammered out a deal that would have cost Britain practically nothing, would have assured it of incredibly cheap (just over $1 a barrel) oil for 15 years, but would have enabled Mossadegh to return to Iran without having "lost face" or given in to great power pressure. In short, it would have resolved the crisis peacefully. However, despite the best American efforts, the British refused to consider the proposal. As they put it, they stood on principle: Iran had no right to nationalize the company. Neither the U.S. government nor the International Court of Justice agreed. Although AIOC was largely British-government-owned, it was after all a company, and its concession was not a treaty between sovereign states. Provided that Iran paid compensation, which it offered to do, the U.S. government, backed by the International Court, held that it had the right to nationalize the company.

The British were almost as angry at America as at Iran. Indeed, some American officials feared that the very basis of Anglo-American relations, which was obviously more important to America than Iran, was endangered. And the danger of a serious breach in Anglo-American relations stretched beyond the immediate crisis. If American oil companies, which for decades had been excluded from the area dominated by the British, took advantage of the British failure, which in their own economic interests they could be assumed to try to do, the whole Western alliance might be jeopardized. Thus, one of McGhee's tasks, despite his strong personal feeling that the problem had been created by the British, was to ensure that the American companies did not move into Iran to replace AIOC. It was not an easy task, and having to work out self-denying arrangements to protect Britain's selfish and short-sighted policy infuriated all the senior American officials.

As important as it was, however, oil was not the only concern, even for Britain. For America, it was not even the main concern. America had already plunged into the Cold War with the Soviet Union. Both the U.S. and British governments believed that like a loose rug the map of the "Free World" was slipping from under their feet. Or, as some also put it with increasing alarm, they saw "dominos" falling everywhere.[19] They looked with increasing alarm at Europe: Large communist parties were active in Italy and France, half of Germany and the rest of Eastern Europe had been

178

turned into Soviet satellites, and Greece was torn by civil war. The situation did not appear better in Southeast Asia and the Pacific: Major insurgencies challenged pro-Western governments in the Philippines and Indochina, and a new Soviet satellite had emerged in Korea. Africa was destabilized by postcolonial turmoil, and Britain's position in the Middle East was under attack. Danger was everywhere. The Soviet Union, like its tsarist ancestor a century before, was seen to be poised to plunge into South Asia through a weak and divided Iran. Mossadegh's hand on Iran's helm appeared to Western leaders to be at best unsteady. Some even thought he was a secret supporter of communism.

But oil posed the immediate danger. Iran had precipitated the crisis, and Britain refused to consider sensible means of ending it. Going their own way, the British sent 14 warships of the Royal Navy to the Gulf and threatened to bombard Iran or even to invade it; they froze Iran's deposits in England and instituted a drastic program of sanctions that prevented Iran from selling its oil abroad or importing goods. Meanwhile, AIOC withdrew its fleet of tankers, shut down its refinery, and put together a cartel of oil companies that agreed to boycott Iranian oil. When the Iranians tried to break the blockade, using a Panamanian oil tanker, the British forced it into Aden, where the oil was seized by the British court at AIOC's request.

These actions were meant to harm Iran, and they did: They resulted in massive unemployment and severe privation. This was truly what Shuster had written about 30 years earlier in his book, *The Strangling of Persia*.

British threats and pressure weren't working. Oil wasn't flowing. The Iranian government enjoyed great popular approval and appeared unlikely to collapse. The American government was worried that the crisis would go on and perhaps get totally out of control. As Secretary of State Acheson later wrote, "Within our government my own colleagues in the State Department and in the Treasury and Defense had come to the conclusion that the British were so obstructive and determined on a rule-or-ruin policy in Iran that we must strike out on an independent policy. . . ."[20] The British had one to suggest: overthrow the Mossadegh government. The Central Intelligence Agency (CIA) liked the idea, but President Truman rejected it. So, Allen Dulles, then head of the CIA, told his staff they should wait for the change of the administration after the elections; then his brother, John Foster Dulles, would be

Secretary of State, and the attitude in Washington would have changed.[21] He was right. It did. When that happened with the advent of the Eisenhower administration, the British played their trump card.

The trump card in 1952 was fear of the Soviet Union. The way to get America to take over Britain's imperial role in the then prevalent atmosphere of the Cold War was to raise the specter of communism. That was what the senior British Secret Intelligence (MI6) officer for the Middle East, Colonel C. M. Woodhouse, did. As he put it, "Not wishing to be accused of trying to use the Americans to pull British chestnuts out of the fire, I decided to emphasize the Communist threat to Iran rather than the need to recover control of the oil industry."

Woodhouse was able to convince the new Secretary of State, John Foster Dulles, that Iran was a "domino" about to fall into the Soviet Union. Dulles needed little convincing; he saw the Soviet hand in every problem throughout the world. In a meeting of the National Security Council (NSC) on March 4, 1953, "Mr. Dulles pointed out that if Iran succumbed to the Communists there was little doubt that in short order the other areas of the Middle East, with some sixty percent of the world's oil reserves, would fall into Communist control." So he arranged for his brother, Allen Dulles, then head of the CIA, to appoint the grandson of President Theodore Roosevelt, Kermit Roosevelt, to overthrow Mossadegh.

Kermit Roosevelt realized what Woodhouse later admitted—the proposed coup had little if anything to do with the Russian threat to Iran. In his account of the coup, Roosevelt wrote, "The original proposal for AJAX [or TP-Ajax, both of which were used as code words for the coup] came from British Intelligence after all efforts to get Mossadegh to reverse his nationalization of the Anglo-Iranian Oil Company (AIOC) had failed. The British motivation was simply to recover the AIOC oil concession." Roosevelt never mentions Woodhouse's role, but he commented that the British "from burning desire more than judgment, were all for the operation."

What happened next is still partly obscure because key parts of the story are differently related by British, American, and Iranian participants and observers while others are still held as secret.[22] Moreover, the CIA says that many of the documents were destroyed. But the coup so seared the memory of Iranians and is so formative of subsequent events in Iran, right down to today, and so crucial for an understanding of subsequent Iranian-American relations that it must be understood. I focus on the major results—destruction of the moderate political forces in Iran, accentuation of the tradition of autocracy, opening of the way for the extremists, and creation of the legacy of anti-American sentiment so evident today. These issues need to be ventilated, but I leave aside the organizational and conspiratorial aspects of the CIA-MI6 espionage venture except where they impacted the wider issues.

To understand the profound effect on Iranians of all classes and persuasions of the American role in the action, it should be borne in mind that Iranians had, for nearly a century, unrealistically to be sure, regarded America as a country "above politics" to which they turned when threatened by Russia and Britain. As the attack on their elected government was about to begin, President-elect Dwight Eisenhower gave further substance to this myth. On January 10, 1953, he wrote to Prime Minister Mossadegh, "I hope you will accept my assurances that I have in no way compromised our position of impartiality in this matter [the oil dispute] and that no individual has attempted to prejudice me in the matter. This leads me to observe that I hope our future relationships will be completely free of any suspicion, but on the contrary will be characterized by confidence and trust inspired by frankness and friendliness."[23] It was not until the end of May that Mossadegh replied. In that letter, he pointed out that, from the beginning of the crisis, "the Iranian Government was prepared to pay the value of the former Company's properties in Iran in such amount as might be determined by the International Court of Justice [and that] The British Government, hoping to regain its old position, has in effect ignored all of these proposals."[24]

What Mossadegh did not know was that the die had already been cast. On April 4, the CIA approved a fund of $1 million to get started on a program to overthrow Mossadegh's government. Then, on behalf of the CIA and MI6, Kermit Roosevelt began a program of "black" propaganda, in which he and his team spread counterfeit materials purporting to show that Mossadegh and the members of the National Front were communist agents intent on destroying Islam. In addition to propaganda, the team arranged to have at least one building blown up and for the act to be blamed on alleged communist or Russian agents. As this propaganda and subversive assault gained momentum, Roosevelt sneaked into Iran, obviously hugely enjoying his team's fake names and code words in a sort of replay of the nineteenth-century "Great Game" and giving a foretaste of the "James Bond" novels that Ian Fleming began to write at the same time.[25] In Iran, working out of the American embassy, he made contact with a senior army general, Fazollah Zahedi, and Ayatollah Abol-Qasem Kashani. Both were men of at least questionable reputation. Zahedi was a well-known speculator in foodgrains, and not only did Kashani have a long record of conspiracy, surprising as that may be for a man in his position, but even more surprising he was in negotiations with the communist Tudeh Party to be their candidate for prime minister.[26] To these and various other prospective facilitators of the coup, the agents eventually passed out about $5 million in bribes and expenses.

One of the major problems the CIA team faced was that the Shah proved to be a weak reed on which to lean. As the secret history shows, the CIA "had almost complete contempt for the man . . . whom it derided as a vacillating coward."[27] The Shah panicked and fled the country on August 16, 1953. Someone in the CIA in Washington, presumably Allen Dulles, "cabled Tehran, urging Mr. Roosevelt, the station chief, to leave immediately." But Roosevelt was undeterred. He was determined to "win" with or without the Shah. As he bribed, cajoled, and threatened his way deeper into the plot, many people sensed that something was afoot. As the rumors of strange goings-on circulated, Mossadegh began to take defensive police measures.

What began to unfold then seems to have been a series of accidents. The first was that Mossadegh thought that what now could be identified as an attempted coup had failed, and he pulled back the loyal forces he had deployed at key points around Tehran. The second is that Mossadegh's erstwhile principal clerical supporter and secret CIA agent, Ayatollah Abol-Qasem Kashani, organized a mob, made up of the thugs (*lutis*) clerics often used as their private armies, to attack Mossadegh's house. They almost caught the prime minister, who escaped over a garden wall. For this act, although it had failed, Kashani later received a "gift" from the CIA of $10,000. But the key element in the plot was that the Royal Guard, whose members had prudently gone to ground, recovered their spirit and managed to get hold of a single tank, with which they threatened the *Majles* and seized that essential asset in a coup, the radio station. There, the CIA put on the air General Fazollah Zahedi, who had been in hiding, to announce that the "communist" government of Mossadegh had been overthrown and the monarchy was restored. His announcement apparently turned the tide as key people rushed to join the winning side.

As the official history makes clear, the coup somewhat resembles a "Keystone Kops" comedy except that it had deadly serious immediate and long-range results. Mossadegh was overthrown—to be put into house arrest, where he remained for the next 14 years until his death in 1967—while the Shah was returned to Iran and reinstalled in power. Once there, the Shah put Roosevelt's Iranian collaborators in positions of command: General Zahedi became prime minister, and hundreds of other *Majles* appointees and other officials were replaced by "loyalists" throughout the bureaucracy.

Later events would show that the American coup produced results that were highly detrimental to American interests and to Iran. It and the subsequent repressive policies of the Shah caused a collapse of the National Front, which was Iran's best hope for a liberal, pluralist democracy—neither monarchist nor communist. Thus, the coup encouraged the Shah's despotism and drove his opponents into revolution. It also poisoned Iranian-American relations for the next half century. As Mark Gasiorowski wrote, it "made the United States a key target of the Iranian revolution."[28] It also fixed on the Shah the image that Iranians of all classes believed—that he was a puppet of America. That he owed his throne to America and had put his hand into America's pocket could not be disguised. He struggled for years against that image. But the way he did so would accentuate the long-term tradition of Iranian autocracy. Only, he believed, by magnifying the monarchy could he rise above his perceived weakness and dependence. Thus, ironically, and certainly without fully realizing the long-term effects of its policy, the American government accentuated trends evident already in earlier dynasties that would prepare the way for the autocracy of Ayatollah Ruhollah Khomeini and his successor Ayatollah Ali Khamenei.

The overthrow of Mossadegh had made possible a solution to the oil crisis, which was the aim of British policy. The solution was not quite what the British had sought, but it was, in principle, both acceptable and simple: The National Iranian Oil Company would own the oil fields and production facilities, which is what Mossadegh had advocated, but production and marketing would be handled by a consortium of foreign companies, of which the renamed British company, British Petroleum, would be the dominant party, with American companies given a minority share of 40 percent.[29]

With that troublesome issue—defined as ownership of the export of oil by the British and the blocking of a trend toward communism by the Americans—settled, the Eisenhower administration devoted most of its efforts to strengthening the Shah's position. The major assistance was in the form of money—roughly $1 billion divided between military and economic programs in the following decade—but money was not all. The United States encouraged the Iranian government—that is, effectively the Shah—to join the interlinking system it had established of regional security pacts, through the Baghdad Pact in 1955 and its successor CENTO after the Iraqi coup in 1958, which tied into SEATO and ultimately into NATO. A stream of American officials, including Vice President and Mrs. Richard Nixon, and delegations of congressmen made highly publicized visits to Iran, and the Shah and his queen created a glamorous "presence" throughout America in a second two-month-long tour. Visits followed in profusion in both directions and were capped by the visit in December 1959 of President Eisenhower.

In line with its basic philosophy, the Eisenhower administration encouraged private businesses and foundations to establish a presence in Iran. As a result, several American banks set up joint ventures with Iranian banks; a major construction and development company headed by the men who had played major roles in the Tennessee Valley Authority (TVA) joined with the Plan Organization (the *Sazeman-e Barnameh*) to develop a whole province in the southwest of Iran; and various existing and newly formed foundations undertook work similar to the original missionaries in education and public health. All of these groups developed emotional interests in Iran; almost uniformly they were dazzled by the royal court and felt privileged to be entertained by the Shah; most also developed a shared financial interest in the success of American-Iranian relations; and nearly all became lobbyists for the regime.

As the Eisenhower administration ended, signs of disillusionment were becoming prevalent in Iran. The glamour of the court was more persuasive to Americans than to Iranians; many of the figures around the court were involved in whispered-about if not openly publicized scandals; intrigues, always a feature of Iranian society, were crippling even major development projects; and the Shah, after a period of triumph over Mossadegh and the National Front, had become fearful, especially after assassination attempts, and increasingly relied on repression. Dulles, the "true believer," had died, and the State Department even had to deny a newspaper article alleging a change of American policy in January 1960. In a letter to Walt Rostow, then in the NSC and later the chairman of the Policy Planning Council, Princeton Professor T. Cuyler Young had warned that the Shah's regime "is considered by most aware and articulate Iranians reactionary, corrupt, and a tool of Western (and especially Anglo-American) imperialism."[30]

So it was that, as the Kennedy administration came into office, some of the new appointees began to think that the regime was in trouble. The president felt that the problems that had arisen from the overthrow of Mossadegh had largely been covered over rather than addressed and that, despite the fears in Iran that the regime of the Shah was a puppet of America, the reality was that the State Department and other agencies, particularly the CIA, had become virtual adjuncts of that regime. Kennedy made no secret of his disdain for the State Department and demanded fresh thinking on Iran, among other issues inherited from the Eisenhower administration. So, at his insistence, the "Iran Task Force" was created to review the situation and recommend what should be done about American policy.[31]

The Iran Task Force was deeply divided. Secretary of State Dean Rusk and Assistant Secretary Talbot resented the intrusion of the White House and argued that relations with Iran were the best that could be hoped for. The two representatives of the White House and I argued that the very success of the economic development programs had created distortions that made some form of upset likely in the near term and inevitable over the longer term. Our arguments came down to two issues. The first issue was that, although statistically the economy was growing rapidly, the benefits of growth were not spread throughout the society so that the rich got much richer and, harmed by inflation, the urban poor often did not benefit while the rural poor actually lost ground. The second and more controversial issue was the Shah's refusal to allow any sharing of power. I thought it was obvious that economic growth unmatched by political growth frustrated even those—indeed especially those—who had gained the most economically. But having overthrown Mossadegh and crushed the National Front, the Shah regarded the religious establishment, as he told me, as a "bunch of lice-ridden, dirty old men" and the remaining secular Left as communist agents. Anyone who opposed him was simply a subversive and should be exiled, imprisoned, or hanged. In short, there was no one with whom to share power. This attitude would lead eventually to the 1979 revolution. The task force debated these issues and also considered the Shah's insatiable desire for more and more elaborate military equipment. But because of the attitude of Secretary Rusk and Assistant Secretary Talbot, little was done about either issue. Thereafter, the U.S. government restricted its advice to a more or less administrative issue: It urged

THE UNITED STATES AND IRAN TODAY   *185*

that the Shah pick up where William Morgan Shuster and Arthur C.
Millspaugh had left off: to get the government finances under control.

Those of us who were disturbed by events in Iran had little material with
which to develop our arguments. The reports we were receiving in Washington rarely reflected serious exchanges of views between our ambassador and
the Shah or the ministers. They were virtually all of the "He said to me and I
replied . . ." variety, with little analysis or even opinion. It seemed to me that
our ambassador was so inhibited by protocol that he never had a real conversation, particularly with the Shah. But the ambassador was intent that no
other American official have one either. Thus, although I met with the Shah
on a number of occasions, it was not until I left government in 1965 that, as
a private citizen, I had a really frank and free discussion with him.[32]

The Shah often said to visitors that America was improperly forcing him
into actions he did not want to take and into positions that were dangerous
for his regime. It particularly irritated him, he told every American he saw,
that the U.S. government kept trying to get him to cut back his armed forces
and had forced him to appoint a "reforming" prime minister.[33] Because I was
partly responsible for advising modesty in his military program and knew
that we had not chosen his prime minister, I used both themes to probe the
nature of our relationship. Our exchange in 1967, after I had left government
service, went as follows[34]:

After we had shaken hands, I said, "Your majesty, I understand that you
have identified me as your principal enemy in America."

"That's right. I have," he replied.

"Then I think we have a great deal to talk about," I said.

"So do I," he rejoined. That began a conversation that lasted about two
hours. He fired the first shot. "Why," he asked rhetorically, "do you think you
have the right . . . no, you have no right . . . why do you think you have the
wisdom to tell me how large an army I should have or how much I should
spend on it?"

"Your Majesty," I replied, "let us avoid the issue of wisdom. We Americans have little of that. But I think it is fair to say that we have the right because you wanted us to pay for it."

"That," he nodded, "is a fair and just answer."

I went on to say that if he questioned our opinions and decisions on
arms, it might be worth probing a particular case. Rather than a current issue,
on which I might not be informed and on which he might wish to demand

more than he really expected, I suggested that we consider his requests for 1961. He had then wanted, I pointed out, to build a lavishly equipped armed force to protect Iran against the Soviet Union. There was no way America could give Iran that—because we did not ourselves have such a conventional force. Nor could Iran build or sustain it. That being the case, Iran's security ultimately depended on America. Recognizing this fact, I admitted openly that I had opposed his purchase of large amounts of military equipment. Such purchases would have been provocative, expensive, and irrelevant.

I went on to outline what I assumed he already knew—that the Soviet air order of battle on Iran's northern frontier then consisted of three regiments of fighter bombers, in addition to massive numbers of support aircraft. To counter these, Iran had asked the U.S. government for only about three squadrons of jet fighters. Clearly, in themselves, these puny forces could not deter, much less defeat, such a massive force as the Russians deployed.

"Yes," he agreed. He understood that, but "clearly you cannot expect me to trust you."

"No," I agreed. "In your place, I would not have blindly trusted America either. Consequently, the United States had developed for Iran, as for Berlin, the concept of the 'trip wire' as a quasi-automatic trigger to activate an American response. Under this arrangement, Iranian forces had to be large enough to force upon an invader a level of onslaught that would be 'unacceptable' to Iran's defender, the United States. Over the exact dimensions of this trip wire," I admitted, "men of goodwill might disagree, but that was the bottom line on the American security commitment to Iran."

"As to the second reason then advanced by your government to our embassy for a large infusion of military hardware, that you feared invasion from Afghanistan," I twitted him, "this does neither you nor your military planners credit."

He burst out laughing and said, "Well, I had to try to find arguments."

I thought bitterly how seriously our embassy had taken this ploy, how urgently our ambassador had reported it to Washington, and how much time I had wasted to counter it.

The Shah then returned to the words "trip wire," which he appeared not to have heard before. I was astonished if that were true because I knew that our military attachés and the CIA station chief—as well as salesmen from the "military-industrial complex" and even some members of the U.S. Congress—were constantly talking with him about the Soviet danger to Iran.

I did not discuss this at that time, but during the Kennedy administration, the U.S. government spoke with two contrary voices. At least some of those concerned with Iranian affairs—and the Shah knew I was one of them—urged him to rein in his voracious appetite for military equipment. However, American military attachés, arms merchants, and visiting members of Congress encouraged the Shah to buy more. The Shah chose more. He thought of military power as quite distinct from economic, social, and intellectual capacity. For him, military power meant both the size of his forces— he multiplied the army of his father by ten to some 400,000 men—and the sophistication of their equipment. He loved military technology. A joke was told at the time that, whereas some men got their thrills from reading "girlie" magazines, the Shah got his from reading defense industry brochures on military aircraft. As his ambassador to Great Britain quipped, he was obsessed "with everything that flies and fires. . . ."[35] I can attest to that from personal experience. In one of our earlier meetings, he had surprised me by rattling off the performance characteristics at different altitudes of the Russian Mig–23, which was just then being sold to Egypt.

During the Kennedy administration, arms supply was already too large for Iran's needs; then, during the Johnson administration, it accelerated, and in the Nixon administration, it became a feeding frenzy. The Shah believed, and Americans encouraged him to believe, that he could match the Soviet Union in military power. To that end, Secretary of State Henry Kissinger arranged for the Defense Department to facilitate the sale to Iran of about $10 billion worth of its latest models of aircraft, naval ships, tanks, and other pieces of equipment[36] and to help Iran start on a nuclear weapons program.[37] (It is perhaps the supreme irony of Iranian-American relations that had the Shah survived another few years, the Islamic Republic would have inherited the nuclear weapons for which we today find their possible quest so frightening.) Then, under the Carter administration, despite President Carter's attempt to go back to the restraint that I among others had tried to encourage during the Kennedy administration, the pace of procurement actually increased. When the revolution occurred in 1979, Iran had placed orders for an additional $12 billion worth of arms. So the Shah set out to do, at nearly ruinous cost, what Iran could not possibly do—to match the Soviet Union.

Back to our private meeting in 1967: The Shah turned from the military to the economic issues. "Why," he asked, "do you believe that my economic development plan is a danger to my regime?"

Politely, but mincing no words, I said that economic development was not itself at issue. Neither he nor we had a choice about modernization. It was happening and would continue. The choice was not development or no development but the political response to it. The range of choice was demonstrated by England and France during the Industrial Revolution. England invited the new industrialists into "the club" while France tried to exclude them. England got rich while France suffered a bloody revolution. "It is essentially simple," I said. "Economic and social development combined with political autocracy makes for revolution."

I thought he winced, but to my surprise, he only commented that he had read an article I had written on the subject for the American journal *Foreign Affairs*.[38] I was surprised that he had read the article, but as the prime minister later told me, he had distributed it to his own "Task Force." Whatever their reaction, it did not sway him or affect his policies.

He then changed the topic to what was then to him a sensitive issue.

"But you Americans . . . you Americans," he went on, "you went too far by trying to protect a particular prime minister and to make him your man. That I could not tolerate."

In reply, I reminded him that I had been a member of the Iran Task Force—he nodded, saying, "Yes, I knew you were"—at the time the appointment was being made, and I said, "Your Majesty, you and I know we did not select the prime minister. You did that. All that we did was to urge, once he was in office, that you allow him to move toward institutional rather than personal rule."

In fact, the Task Force had urged only a modest administrative reform, as I have mentioned, just to follow what Shuster and Millspaugh had urged decades before, whereas as I admitted to him, "I had wanted to push for a much deeper political reform. That, as I believed then and still believe, was to America's advantage, to Iran's advantage, and to your advantage."

The Shah then became quite emotional and said, "No, many of your people tried to tell us exactly what to do. You Americans must learn that you cannot rule the world."

I nodded and said that the ancient Greeks were right: "The gods do punish hubris."

The Shah gazed off in the distance, apparently pondering that analogy, but then turned back to the Iranian-American relationship. "What right do you have to try to force me or any other leader to accept your system?"

I granted his implied criticism but said that, in the final analysis, what really mattered was what worked in his country. Whether it was just (as at least some Americans thought) for people to govern themselves or irresponsible (as he thought) was arguable but not essential for him in evaluating his policies.

"Yes," he agreed, "that is true."

We had pushed him, I continued, toward institutional reform with the assessment that he had made himself the linchpin of the existing system. If he were killed—and he had nearly been assassinated a few days before—or overthrown, the whole political system, indeed the whole "social contract" between the Iranian government and society, would disintegrate into chaos. (That, of course, is exactly what happened in the later revolution.) Hence, institutional reform was in the interest of Iran and America, and indeed in his own interest.

"Yes," he said, suddenly becoming very agitated physically. He stood up and waved his arms. I had never seen him do anything like that before, and I watched, I am sure, with my mouth agape. He then almost shouted, "When my father was worried about death . . . when I was 20 . . . no, I was then 21 . . . he told me that he was concerned that I would have to rule a country without institutions. I was furious and took his words as a slight, as an insult that I was not capable. It is only after all these years that I understand what he meant."

It was getting late, and the Shah made what I took to be a signal that our conversation was over. "Well," he said, "I cannot say that I agree with you, but this is the first time that anyone from your government has spoken to me as an adult."

I laughed and replied, "Perhaps, your Majesty, that is because I am no longer in the government."

"Yes," he ended our talk. "When I heard that you had resigned, I was glad."

So, reflecting on our talk and my years of analyzing Iranian-American relations, I concluded that intervening in the wrong way, as we did in overthrowing the duly elected government of Prime Minister Muhammad Mossadegh and catering to the Shah's predilections as we did on arms supply, distorted Iranian-American relations and convinced the Shah that he had a sort of blank check from America. The one set in motion and the other carried along the events leading up to the 1979 revolution. At least partly they were beyond the Shah's control. From his entire career, as I have pointed out, it was evident that he would seek someone to play the role in his life that his father Reza Shah had played. On his own, he would be unable to make up his mind on how to face the challenges to his regime. He turned to America, in effect *in loco parentis,* to tell him what to do. In my view, America could not and should not have attempted to do so. But the fact was that, at least in large part, America had assumed that task.

Also, arguably by 1978, it was already too late to do anything to stave off the revolution. America had taken the first leap forward into chaos in 1953 with the overthrow of Mossadegh; the Shah had taken the next by the destruction of the political center. Successive American administrations had taken no stand or even played deleterious roles in his policies. This is not to say that we could or should have forced any policy or any choice of prime minister on the Shah. But we could have (and in my view should have) linked our positive steps—that is, what we gave or sold him—to opening the Iranian political process in parallel to the economic development program. Had we done so, I believe it is probable that Iran could have evolved toward an open, democratic, reasonable, and peaceful society. In fact, for the most part, we did the opposite. We, along with the Shah, are complicit in the revolution. At the very minimum, we should have met what I believe was his desire for open and frank discussion. But, I think it is fair to say that in all the years from the overthrow of Prime Minister Mossadegh in 1953 up to the 1979 revolution, there was no effective *official* intellectual exchange at the most crucial points of the Iranian-American relationship.

I discussed the eight-year destructive Iraq-Iran war in Chapter Five. It, of course, came after the fall of the Shah, when our relations with the Islamic Republic of Iran were always tense and usually hostile. Here, I briefly mention only that aspect that directly involved America.

As "Third World" wars always are, the Iraq-Iran war was a bonanza for arms dealers and countries that sought to use arms as a way of enhancing their influence: America used Israel as the conduit for the supply of hundreds of millions of dollars' worth of arms to the Iranian regular army while the Russians and Chinese supplied the *Pasdaran-e Enghelab* with its equipment. The French supplied a part of the more sophisticated equipment required by the Iraqi army while the Russians provided tanks, armored fighting vehicles, and artillery. Half a dozen other countries supplied arms to both sides, as did America with its most sophisticated intelligence, satellite battlefield images, which it provided to Iran in 1986 and Iraq in 1988.

Unlike the other powers, the United States also engaged in the war. In 1987, America "reflagged" Kuwaiti and other oil tankers seeking to break the Iranian blockade in the Gulf, stationed there what a congressional study termed "the largest armada deployed since the height of the Vietnam war," and maneuvered "as if our objective was to goad Iran into a war with us." The U.S. government nearly succeeded in causing that war. The U.S. naval forces destroyed about half of the Iranian fleet in the Gulf in 1988 in what was described as "the biggest sea battle since World War II."[39] In a particularly tragic incident, the USN guided missile cruiser *Vincennes,* operating within Iranian waters, shot down an Iran Air civilian passenger plane, killing all 290 passengers, in July 1988.[40]

Those activities were, of course, external to Iran, but America also sought "regime change" within Iran. Starting in 1982, the CIA was funding émigré dissident organizations such as "the Front for the Liberation of Iran" in Paris, headed by former Prime Minister Ali Amini, and two paramilitary groups in Turkey, of which one was headed by the Shah's former army chief.[41] Thus, having begun with a policy in 1981 of supplying Iran with weapons, the Reagan administration had come to fear that Iran might actually win its war against Iraq; so, to compensate, it "tilted," as the popular expression then put it, toward support for Iraq.

When the revolution against the Shah's regime occurred in 1979, one of its many ugly acts was an attack on the American embassy, in which the staff members were taken hostage. I related in Chapter Five the long and futile attempts by both Iranian government officials, including the then prime minister, Mehdi Bazargan, and Americans to negotiate the release of the Americans. As I recounted, none of the negotiations worked, and for his part in the attempt, Bazargan fell from power and fled the country. Here I relate the consequence of the diplomatic failure. It wasn't only the group around Bazargan and later his successor, Abol-Hasan Bani-Sadr, that was attacked; President Carter was also attacked. Everyone expected Carter to "do something" to get the hostages out. He was increasingly charged by his Republican critics as being indecisive, weak, and incompetent. Why couldn't big, powerful America control little, weak Iran? Carter began to be blamed for everything happening in Iran. Worse, although he certainly knew better, former Secretary of State Henry Kissinger, a staunch supporter of the Shah, led a chorus in attacking Carter with the charge that he had "lost" Iran, just as earlier critics had charged Roosevelt and Truman for having "lost" China. This charge was not only personally humiliating for Carter but also politically dangerous as the elections approached. The hostage crisis riveted the American public to their television sets as nothing had since the Vietnam War. Political analysts were already predicting that it would determine the presidential contest.

The hostage crisis was thus intensely dangerous to both the Iranian and the American political leadership.

To add to its impact, the hostage crisis proved not to be the "only show in town." All around the world, events seemed to show the American position in the world deteriorating as its friends and even its own installations and personnel came under attack. On November 20—just two weeks after the seizure of the American embassy in Tehran—a fanatical and armed group of Iranians occupied the Great Mosque in Mecca, the holy center of the country singled out as America's longtime ally. The next day, allegedly because somehow they thought that America was responsible for the attack in Mecca, a mob invaded the U.S. embassy in Islamabad, Pakistan. Then on December 2, a similar attack was carried out in Tripoli, Libya. In the most serious action of all, on December 27, the Soviet Union invaded Afghanistan. That, ironically, caused an attack on the Russian embassy in Tehran. So at least America was not the only object of fury in Tehran, but it was read by some critics of the Carter administration as a sign that the Russians saw American prestige, power, and will be to faltering.

As all these events were happening, where was Carter? Why had he let all this happen? Why didn't he *do* something? Those questions resonated through the American media.

Carter was furious and frustrated. He had no good options and little information. His advisers were divided. As one of his staff quoted him in his foul mood, he

wanted to "get our people out of Iran and break relations. Fuck 'em." . . . [U]nder no circumstances would he consider extraditing the shah. . . . [The crisis was,] he said, one of the most difficult problems the government faced

since he had been in the White House. American citizens had been captured, and there appeared to be no desire on the Iranian side to negotiate. . . . We faced the prospect, he said, of the hostages being killed one at a
time, or perhaps all of them. The honor and integrity of the country demanded some form of punitive action if that should occur.[42]

Emissaries, some encouraged and others on their own, tried to act as intermediaries. None got very far. The facts "on the ground," as I have described
them, made it difficult for any Iranian except perhaps Khomeini to risk getting involved. Those who briefly tried paid a great, sometimes the supreme,
price for their indiscretion. As Captain Sick comments, "The Carter administration and the U.S. public were poorly equipped to comprehend the nature
of the fury and hatred they saw each evening boiling out of Tehran [on tele-
vision]. That comprehension gap was of more than academic concern. It had
a profound effect on the formulation and conduct of U.S. policy throughout
the crisis."[43]

The United States then appealed to the International Court, which ruled
unanimously in its favor, but Iran rejected the decision. To increase pressure
on Iran, the U.S. navy moved a carrier task force within striking distance of
Iran. Consideration was given to mining Iranian harbors, bombing oil installations, and even larger actions. None seemed suitable, and all were
deemed likely to get the hostages killed. So a different approach was approved.

When President Jimmy Carter concluded that Ayatollah Ruhollah Khomeini would not allow his government to negotiate, even attacking his own foreign minister, Ibrahim Yazdi, who had been one of his closest aides during his
exile in Paris, for suggesting a way out, and that there was little or no hope of
getting the hostages released, he decided to allow the American military to attempt a rescue operation. It was an extraordinary gamble, and it failed, but
it was nonetheless a remarkable effort.

The plan involved sending some 90 American soldiers in six giant transport aircraft to a spot in the Iranian desert about three hundred miles southeast of Tehran. There they were to meet eight large helicopters, which
meanwhile had flown from an aircraft carrier in the Indian Ocean. The troops
would then board the helicopters and fly to an abandoned airstrip just outside
Tehran, where they were to be met by a number of cars and trucks supplied

by undisclosed agents in Iran and driven during the early hours to the embassy compound. There, armed with stun guns, they would overwhelm the guards and put the hostages on the helicopters, which, meanwhile, would have flown in and landed on the embassy grounds. From there they would be whisked back to the waiting transport planes and flown out of Iran.

To succeed, the venture required an unlikely set of circumstances—reasonable weather, perfectly functioning equipment, no alarm systems, empty streets, sleepy guards, all the hostages in one location, good luck, and absolute secrecy. Whether it ever had much of a chance is doubtful, but it failed before that question could have been answered. Weather conditions and faulty equipment caused it to be aborted at the desert landing. Worse, one of the helicopters collided with a transport and burned to death eight of the would-be rescuers.

The Iranians were furious. Ayatollah Ruhollah Khomeini threatened to have the hostages killed if America tried another "silly maneuver" and said that President Carter had "lost his mind."

So what to do about them? President Carter had the NSC set up a group to plan a new rescue effort and tried to reopen negotiations with the Iranian government. Meanwhile, unbeknownst to him or anyone in the U.S. government, it appears that a separate, as-yet-unofficial "rescue" attempt was being organized. Although it has, so far at least, not been proved, there is substantial evidence that members of Ronald Reagan's election team, led by William J. Casey, who would become head of the CIA, and allegedly including George H. W. Bush, who would become Reagan's vice president, began a series of meetings in Madrid in July 1980 and subsequently in Paris with secret representatives of Ayatollah Ruhollah Khomeini.

This is a thesis developed by Captain Gary Sick, who, as I have pointed out, was the Iran specialist on the NSC.[44] He comments that "the story is tangled and murky, and it may never be fully revealed," but that it has a compelling logic: On the Iranian side, in addition to the hatred Khomeini had developed against Carter, the Iranian government had been trying to get its overseas funds unblocked and to acquire spare parts it urgently needed for its military forces. The frontier clashes that led to Iraq's invasion of Iran on September 22 added to the urgency. On the American side, it was clear that Carter was failing to get the hostages released. If he did not do so, he would almost certainly lose the presidential election, but, if he did, he probably would win. Captain Sick believes that these factors formed the basis of a deal:

Casey promised that, if he was elected, Reagan would return the blocked assets and supply the requested equipment and supplies but that Iran must release the hostages to him, not to Carter.

A wild card was added by Israel. At least two Israeli agents got involved in the discussions to enable Israel, as it had been trying to do for some time, to develop a market for military equipment in Iran. It is known that Israel, during the time that Captain Sick believes the discussions were taking place, did send at least one shipment of arms to Iran. At this time also, the Carter administration was discussing the possibility of using arms supply to get the hostages released. Sick notes that, in the middle of these discussions, the Iranians told the U.S. government that it was no longer interested in acquiring American arms from the Carter administration.

Although some aspects of this scenario cannot be proved or disproved, the end of the story is public knowledge. As Captain Sick wrote, the Iranians released the remaining 52 hostages in January 1981 "exactly five minutes after Mr. Reagan took the oath of office," and hundreds of millions of dollars' worth of "arms started to flow to Iran via Israel only a few days after the inauguration." He says, further, that "events suggest that the arms-for-hostage deal that in the twilight of the Reagan presidency became known as the Iran-contra affair,"[45] instead of being, as it is often thought, a deviation was in fact the reemergence of a policy that began even before the Reagan-Bush administration took office. It would continue long afterward.

The administrations of George H. W. Bush and Bill Clinton focused on Iraq and paid relatively little attention to Iran.[46] However, during their administrations, a concerted propaganda campaign against Iran began to be mounted by a group calling themselves the neoconservatives. They argued that Iran was a danger to America because it was working secretly to fabricate a nuclear weapon and was a danger to Israel because it was encouraging the Lebanese Shia Hezbollah movement. Working as advisers to the White House, the Defense Department, and the CIA and also as commentators in the media and "strategists" in a number of policy institutes and foundations, they advocated an attack on Iran as well as on Iraq. They had some success during the Clinton administration when in 1995 President Clinton imposed oil and trade sanctions on Iran for alleged encouragement of terrorism, but in March 2000 Clinton's Secretary of State, Madeleine Albright, announced the lifting of the sanctions and called for a new start in Iranian-American relations. Subsequently, in September she held a ministerial-level meeting with the Iranians, the first in 21 years. It began to seem that an accommodation with Iran might be possible. Before any further moves were made, however, the Clinton administration ended with the Republican electoral victory that put George W. Bush in the White House.

Thus, in 2001 hard-liners controlled the governments of both the United States and the Islamic Republic of Iran. In America, they were new arrivals, but in Tehran, they had dominated the government for years. Activists who had grown up in the *komitehs,* the *Sazeman-e Basij,* and the *Pasdaran-e En-ghelab* were inspired and led by the conservative wing of the ruling *ulama.* At the top of the regime was the dour Ayatollah Ali Khamenei, who became the supreme guide (*Ayatollah al-Ozma* or *Rahbar*) at the death of Ayatollah Khomenei in 1989. Like many of the leading members of the religious establishment, Khamenei had spent years in prison, where he endured torture by Muhammad Reza Shah's political police, SAVAK. Also, like many of his colleagues, he emerged from that background bitterly opposed to those he regarded as the patrons of the Shah and the instructors of SAVAK, the Americans and the Israelis.[47] Thus, as we have seen, he had joined with other religious leaders to make it impossible for those Iranians like Mehdi Bazargan and Abol-Hasan Bani-Sadr who favored restoration of relations with America to remain in office. As one senior Iranian official ruefully remarked to me, "We have our 'hawks' too."

In America, the neoconservatives had begun to exercise influence in the administration of George H. W. Bush. Then, after a period of "exile" during the Clinton administration, they moved in January 2001 into senior positions in the White House (where they were strongly supported by Vice President Dick Cheney) and the Department of Defense (where they were similarly encouraged by Secretary Donald Rumsfeld). Having virtually taken over at least the foreign policy and security organs of government, they began to advocate an aggressive policy toward Iran.[48]

During the Bush administration, the neoconservatives, who probably numbered less than a hundred men and women, were so influential that the thrust of their program and their means of action must be explained.

The members of this group shared three characteristics: First, they were strongly influenced by the political philosopher Leo Strauss, who led them to believe that they were an elite who could remake the world in a new image if they pushed a unified program; second, they were also influenced by the leading "big bomb" strategist of nuclear war, Albert Wohlstetter, who argued that the only thing in world affairs that really counted was power; finally, almost all of them were Jewish and had close ties with the Israeli hard Right, for whose leaders some had worked.

In the years before the Bush administration, the neoconservatives had prepared their way by forming committees, drafting policy papers, and building a network of their members in universities, businesses, foundations, and think tanks. The most visible of these were the American Israel Public Affairs Committee (AIPAC), the American Enterprise Institute (AEI), the Washington Institute for Near East Policy (WINEP), the Jewish Institute for National Security Affairs (JINSA), and the Middle East Forum. The directors and fellows of these groups often held positions in several of them, and their programs overlapped. Influential members of the group also were active in the Brookings Institution (where the Saban Center for Middle East Policy was created for them), the Johns Hopkins School of Advanced International Studies (headed by one of their leaders, Paul Wolfowitz), the RAND Corporation, the Hudson Institute, and the Council on Foreign Relations. Individual neoconservatives also became columnists for *The Washington Post, The New York Times,* and other newspapers; they had their own journal in *The Weekly Standard;* and they adopted Fox News as their television outlet. Hardly a month passed without a well-publicized conference on Israel, Iraq, and Iran, and their lobbying activities in Congress became legendary.

Well-funded, dedicated, and smart, the neoconservatives for years had worked closely with the president's newly appointed senior officials and moved into government with them. In the Defense Department, Paul Wolfowitz, Douglas Feith, and Steven Cambone were given the top positions while in the White House Lewis Libby became chief of staff to the vice president. Because Bush had no experience in or knowledge of world affairs, he adopted them as his brain trust, and they provided a ready-made program that they had forecast in such papers as the 1992 "Defense Policy Guidance," the 1996 "Clean Break" paper, and the 2000 "Project for a New American Century." These earlier démarches formed the basis for the subsequent official U.S. National Defense Strategy papers issued by the Bush administration.

As their Iraq policies were implemented, the neoconservatives turned their attention to Iran, which they argued was a major danger to America (and Israel) and also was "on the point of collapse and just needed a push from America and Israel to do so." As one of their leading members, Michael Ledeen, told the April 30, 2003, meeting of JINSA, "the time for diplomacy is at an end; it is time for a free Iran. . . ." In short, the neoconservatives made "regime change" in Iran a central thrust of U.S. government policy. If America was reluctant, they also urged their close associates in the Israeli government to take up the task independently with the arms the neoconservatives helped Israel purchase from the United States.[49] Throughout the Bush administration, they constantly urged an attack on Iran and today, even out of office, are still doing so.[50]

Meanwhile, beginning in 2001, despite the advocacy by hawks in both Washington and Tehran for a policy of confrontation, the Iranian government was assisting the United States in its campaign against the Taliban in Afghanistan and in the establishment there of an American-designated government.[51] To this end, Iran deported numbers of suspected al-Qaida operatives and convinced Afghan warlords to support American activities.[52] It also employed about twenty thousand troops and police, sustaining almost as many casualties as America suffered in Iraq, trying to interdict the drug trade.[53] In these actions, Iran made major contributions to the achievement of America's objectives in its Afghan campaign.

Despite these activities, President Bush identified Iran as a part of what he called "the Axis of Evil" in his January 29, 2002, State of the Union address. Bush's terminology, which apparently was coined by a neoconservative,[54] set the style of American-Iranian relations during the rest of his administration. No attempt was made to establish contact with the Iranians. Indeed, American officials were ordered not to do so. Even the U.S. ambassador to Iraq, Zalmay Khalilzad, himself a neoconservative, required a presidential exemption to deal with the Iranian ambassador in Baghdad.[55] When the Iranian government asked the Swiss ambassador in Tehran to convey a conciliatory offer to Washington, which he did, the Bush administration angrily complained to the Swiss foreign ministry that its ambassador had exceeded his authority.[56]

More significant was the impact of Bush's "Axis of Evil" denunciation on Iranian policy. The president's language focused the attention of Iranian leaders on what they came to see as the two lessons inherent in the address. The first lesson derived from the American treatment of Iraq, which did *not* have a nuclear weapon: Iraq was effectively destroyed as an independent state.

Iranians thought that they were next on the list.[57] Not having a nuclear bomb, they believed, put them in mortal danger.

The second lesson they drew was almost as important: It was that *once a country actually gets a nuclear weapon, it is safe.* No state will attack a country that can retaliate by inflicting "unacceptable" damage on the attacker. North Korea, which did have a bomb, was not attacked but was offered an aid program. The history of the nuclear age shows that once a country gets the bomb, it is quickly accepted by the other nuclear powers as a "member of the club."[58] India provides recent proof of this: Although it secretly acquired the weapon and did not join the Nuclear Non-Proliferation Treaty (as Iran did), the Bush administration said, in effect, "We will make an exception—as we have done for Israel, which also has not joined Nuclear Non-Proliferation Treaty—and share with you our nuclear technology."[59]

What is the Iranian government doing about these insights? We know that Muhammad Reza Shah, with American help, was moving to acquire nuclear weapons in the 1970s and that Ayatollah Ruhollah Khomeini stopped the program as "un-Islamic" after 1979. Inspection after inspection has tried to find out what has been happening since. The U.S. National Intelligence Council found in 2005 that it was likely that Iran had begun to move toward creating at least the capacity to build a weapon, but in November 2007, the Council issued a National Intelligence Estimate (NIE)[60] in which the 16 federal intelligence agencies declared "with high confidence"—that is, as the publication explains, "the judgments are based on high-quality information [making] it possible to render a solid judgment"—that Iran had halted its nuclear weapons program four years before: "We judge with high confidence," the NIE continued, "that in fall 2003, Tehran halted its nuclear weapons program. . . . We judge with high confidence that Iran will not be technically capable of producing and reprocessing enough plutonium for a weapon before about 2015."[61]

These shifts raise the fundamental question, "Why would Iran want a nuclear weapon?"

Because such a huge investment of the industrial, monetary, and intellectual resources of a country is required to build, maintain, and protect a nuclear weapons program, we can probably brush aside such real but relatively trivial answers as national prestige. I think the only compelling answer is national survival. That is the answer shown by an analysis of the policies of each of the world's nuclear powers: Russia had to have nuclear weapons because America had them; China, because of Russia; India and Pakistan, because of each other; Israel, because of fear of the Arab states. In short, a nuclear weapon is the ultimate deterrent to attack. If this is the "bottom line," whom would Iran seek to deter?

The answer, I believe, is the United States and/or Israel acting with American permission and American weapons.

So the second question is, "Is the Iranian fear reasonable?"

The answer has two elements—what the Bush administration and Israel have been saying and what the United States has been doing. First, consider the statements.

For most of the last eight years, the White House, the Department of Defense, and the State Department, not to mention influential members of Congress and the media, have been discussing, mostly favorably, an attack on Iran. Phrases such as "all options are on the table" echo down the years. The official U.S. National Defense Strategy of 2005 and successive years, which grew out of the early neoconservative papers cited above, proclaims that

> America is a nation at war . . . [and] will defeat adversaries at the time, place, and in the manner of our choosing . . . [rather than employing a] reactive or defensive approach. . . . Therefore, we must confront challenges earlier and more comprehensively, before they are allowed to mature. . . . In all cases, we will seek to seize the initiative and dictate the tempo, timing, and direction of military operations.

In other words, this strategy justifies preemptive military strikes at the order of the American president. These threats were aimed specifically at Iran. Advance planning was under way in April 2007 at the Pentagon for a full-scale war with Iran in a war game called TIRANNT.[62] Laying out a "three day blitz plan" for Iran, President Bush warned in September 2007 that "the US would act before it is too late."[63]

Air Force General Thomas McInerney (Rtd.) described the potential "shock and awe" campaign against Iran in the neoconservative journal *The Weekly Standard*.[64] His description is so detailed that it appears to have come from planning documents and was certainly read by the Iranians. It ends with the statement that "destruction of Iran's military force structure would create the opportunity for regime change as well. . . ."

The statements of the Israeli government have been, and remain, even more bellicose. Reaffirming previous and frequently repeated statements, incoming Israeli Prime Minister Benjamin Netanyahu said he told President Barack Obama in April 2009 that "either America stops Iran['s nuclear program] or Israel will."[65]

The second element of the answer to why Iranians would be tempted to acquire a nuclear weapon capacity is what the Bush administration actually did. It includes the following: positioning about half of the U.S. navy along Iran's frontier; aiming hundreds of cruise missiles at its nuclear sites, factories, military camps, and cities; putting on standby alert hundreds of aircraft at bases surrounding Iran in Qatar, Iraq, Turkey, Uzbekistan, Afghanistan, and the Indian Ocean and priming other aircraft to deliver bombs directly from the continental United States[66]; sending to the Persian Gulf amphibious assault ships, equipped with helicopters and fast hovercraft to be ready to "insert" troops within hours of a decision to attack[67]; infiltrating covert agents and special forces into Iran[68]; and finally, overflying Iran with drone aircraft to gather intelligence and "also [to be] employed as a tool for intimidation."[69] In 2007, Congress funded a $400 million Presidential Finding "designed to destabilize the country's religious leadership." Then, just before the end of his second term, President Bush "embraced more intensive covert operations aimed at Iran . . . to undermine electrical systems, computer system and other networks on which Iran relies."[70] Apparently, until April 2006, the administration was planning to use nuclear weapons in an attack on Iran.[71]

These activities not only posed a threat to the Iranians but also deeply disturbed America's military commanders. The Chairman of the Joint Chiefs of Staff, General Peter Pace, USMC, was reported to have led a virtual revolt against the plan.[72] Out of government, 22 former high-ranking military and civilian officials in August 2006 wrote to urge the president to negotiate rather than to bomb.[73] And the senior officer in the Central Command, Admiral William J. Fallon, USN, "was one of a group of senior military officers . . . who were alarmed in late 2006 by indications that Bush and Vice-President Dick Cheney were contemplating a possible attack on Iran."[74] The neoconservatives urged that Fallon be replaced by General David Petraeus, and he was.

The Iranians must have observed that these various actions were not just the work of a perhaps "rogue" president but also had considerable support in Congress. In some cases, indeed, Congress was more bellicose than the administration. To show that Democrats were not "soft" on Iran, HR 362 of October 9, 2008, strongly pushed with lobbying by AIPAC, proposed a blockade on Iran. As Colonel Sam Gardiner, USA (Rtd.), pointed out, "blockade is not a step short of war; it is war." The resolution's proposer (and presumed author), Representative Barney Frank, later admitted, "I agree that this should not be our policy and I regret the fact that I did not read this resolution more carefully."[75]

The Bush administration also used Israel to frighten Iran. It leaked documents to the media warning that Israel was on the brink of an attack.[76] More important, the administration furnished Israel with the means: fighter-bombers (the F–16i and the F–15i) with sufficient range to reach at least some Iranian sites and with the munitions (the GBU–28 and the more powerful GBU–39 "bunker-buster" bombs) designed for just the sort of attack planned against Iran.[77] Apparently, the administration also allowed Israeli commandos to operate inside Iran from bases in U.S.-occupied Iraq.[78] In January 2007, Israel publicized its determination not to "tolerate Iran going nuclear" and briefed correspondents on "two fast assault squadrons based in the Negev desert and in Tel Nof, south of Tel Aviv [that were] already training for the attack." It said that some of the planes would be prepared to drop nuclear weapons.[79] Then, in June 2008, Israel put on an impressive display of its ability to use American fighter-bombers to attack Iran.[80] But, following the release of the November 2007 NIE denying that Iran had a nuclear weapon program, President Bush told the Israelis that the United States would not support a military strike by them.[81]

However, the Israelis continue to assert their determination to act whether or not the U.S. government approves. "In an interview with Jeffrey Goldberg of the *Atlantic,* incoming Israeli Prime Minister Benjamin Netanyahu claimed to have told President Barack Obama that either America stops Iran or Israel will. . . . So once again, in spite of President Obama's best efforts, the military option was put back on the table and the atmosphere for dealing with Iran was turned into 'Do as we say—or else.' . . . The message of Israeli hawks has been that it can only afford to give diplomacy 'a few months . . . otherwise Israel will take military action.'"[82] Several events in the last few days and weeks appear to translate these words into visible preparation for military action. "'The message to Iran is that the threat is not just words,' one senior defence official told *The Times.* . . . 'We would not make the threat [against Iran] without the force to back it. There has been a recent move, a number of on-the-ground preparations, that indicate Israel's willingness to act,' said another official from Israel's intelligence community."[83]

The Bush administration also attempted to use the United Nations, long despised by the neoconservatives, in its campaign against Iran. There, two approaches were attempted: On the one side, the International Atomic Energy Agency managed a limited program of inspections; on the other side, the Security Council voted for sanctions in December 2006, which the United States enforced by freezing Iranian overseas assets,[84] and in March 2007 the Security Council voted unanimously to strengthen sanctions.

Despite this unpromising atmosphere, Iran has made periodic gestures for negotiations. In May 2003, Iran sent a secret "grand bargain" proposal to the United States in which it "talks about ensuring 'full transparency' and other measures to assure the U.S. that it will not develop nuclear weapons." Meetings were scheduled, but the Bush administration decided not to attend.[85] Then, following the American elections in November 2008, Iranian President Mahmoud Ahmadinejad sent a "clear signal that he would like to see some kind of relationship between Iran and the United States—if there are 'fundamental and fair' changes in Washington."[86] Even Ahmadinejad, himself regarded as a hawk, had to contend with more extreme hawks in his own camp: Ayatollah Ahmad Janati, the powerful chairman of the Guardian Council, denounced attempts at rapprochement with the United States.[87]

In a remarkable new venture, on the occasion of the Iranian New Year, *No Ruz,* March 20, 2009, President Barack Obama videotaped a "message to the Iranian people and leaders," saying, "My administration is now committed to diplomacy that addresses the full range of issues before us, and to pursuing constructive ties. . . . This process will not be advanced by threats. We seek instead engagement that is honest and grounded in mutual respect." On his message, *The New York Times* columnist Roger Cohen commented,[88] "With his bold message to Iran's leaders, President Obama achieved four things essential to any rapprochement. He abandoned regime change as an American goal. He shelved the so-called military option. He buried a carrot-and-stick approach viewed with contempt by Iranians as fit only for donkeys. And he placed Iran's nuclear program within 'the full range of issues before us.'"[89]

As expected, the Iranian leaders were suspicious. Ayatollah Ali Khamenei was not moved. Addressing a huge crowd in the shrine city of Mashad, he said that Americans "chant the slogan of change, but . . . we haven't seen any change. . . . [M]ake it clear to us what has changed."[90] Nevertheless, the process seems to have begun. A few days later, on April 13, 2009, President Obama made a major concession: He dropped the Bush administration's insistence that Iran stop its centrifuges before talks could begin.

I now turn to how we can evaluate the prospects for the future.

AFTERWORD

s I have written in the Foreword, I think that the primary reason for learning about another culture is humane: Our world would be a dreary, drab place if we were ignorant of the richness and diversity of the ways of life that have evolved from the endowments of history and geography. Here I want to turn to more urgent reasons: avoiding destructive war and moving toward security. So, while I have anchored my account in the past, I now look forward to the future.

In recent years, Americans have developed two methods of predicting the flow of international relations. Both are flawed; indeed, both have occasionally misled us into danger. The first of these is the adaptation mathematicians have made of the German Army General Staff's *kriegspiel,* the "war game." Essentially the war game sets out to show how the opponent will respond to an escalating series of "moves." It assumes that he will be guided by a balance sheet of potential profit and loss. If he does not add them up accurately, we say he has "miscalculated." We view the foreigner as a sort of accountant—culturally disembodied, mathematically precise, and governed by logic. In short, we posit in him precisely those qualities that do not shape our own actions. So when we apply the lessons to "grand strategy" in our culturally diverse world, war games are nearly always misleading.

I offer an example unrelated to Iran. In the aftermath of the Cuban Missile Crisis (during which I was a member of the "Crisis Management Committee"), I was ordered to participate in a sort of replay, a war game designed to press the events toward, but not quite to, nuclear war. My colleagues on "Red Team" were some of America's most senior military, intelligence, and foreign affairs officers, and we drew upon the most sensitive information the U.S. government had on the Soviet Union.

The game focused on an escalating crisis at the end of which we were informed that "Blue Team" had obliterated a Russian city. How should we respond? Do nothing? Retaliate by obliterating a U.S. city? Or go to general war? After careful consideration, we opted for general war, firing all our missiles with thousands of nuclear weapons to attempt to wipe out all American retaliatory capacity.

The "umpire," Thomas Schelling, an MIT mathematician and author of *The Strategy of Conflict,* called a halt to the game, saying that we had "misplayed," and called a general meeting in the War Room of the Pentagon for what would have been, in real life, literally a postmortem. He opened by saying that if we were right, the United States would have to give up the theory of deterrence. Why had we acted in this way?

In response, we showed that we went to general war because we had to. If the leader of Red Team had done nothing, he almost certainly would have been regarded as a traitor and overthrown by his own military commanders; had he played tit-for-tat, obliterating, say, Dallas, what could an American president have done? He could not have just turned the other cheek. So, despite the catastrophe for both *nations,* neither *government* could have stopped the fateful process. In short, whatever the "interest of state," the "interest of government" compelled actions that were not governed by the same category of logic. No war game had predicted this outcome. Indeed, for the previous decade, all predicted, as did Schelling, exactly the opposite: The Russians would back off in the face of threat or even attack. We did not then know how very close we had come to total world annihilation in the real-life Cuban Missile Crisis and how much had depended on sheer luck[1]—and on the bravery or foolhardiness of Nikita Khrushchev.[2]

To supplement or correct the war game, the United States has developed a second means of predicting the future, the "National Intelligence Estimate" (NIE). The flaw in the NIE is perhaps less than that in the war game but is nonetheless serious. It depends on assembling "facts." That is, it takes the vast input of statements, acts, and capabilities of the adversary and from them makes an "appreciation" describing what the adversary is doing and, drawing from this appreciation, what he is likely to do. What is often deficient in this approach is that no assemblage of facts can ever be complete. Even more important is that it cannot account for all the emotions, religious beliefs, fears, memories, and even ignorance of the opponent. The NIEs produced on Iran in 2005 and 2007 came up with contrary results.

The failures of the war game and the NIE approaches to world affairs are particularly evident in the attempt to understand Iran. It is virtually impossible for Americans to know exactly how the current Iranian regime views its options and makes its decisions. Governments rarely document the process—as I learned in my government service—and certainly do not share their thoughts with others. As two well-informed former senior American officials with long experience on Iranian affairs have pointed out, "Of all the black holes in America's foreign relations few have been darker than Iran."[3] So what can we do?

I offer two interconnected answers. The first, as I have laid out, is a different sort of "appreciation": It is the attempt to view the formation of contemporary Iranian mores, beliefs, and attitudes from the whole range of the Iranians' experience. To do that requires an emotional leap in which outsiders will fall short but which will get us closer to understanding the influences, fears, and motivations that are not always or even often what foreigners would see as "logical" but which in sum define Iranians. In short, this is the approach with which I began, inspired by Herodotus' attempt to do the same more than two thousand years ago.

The second answer I now offer resurrects or redefines the mechanisms by which we have attempted to understand Iranian reactions to our policy. It arises from my own experience as a sometime policy planner and diplomat. It really comes down to a very simple notion: To understand what someone is likely to do, it always helps to try to put oneself in his position, to look at events from his perspective, to try to see what he sees, to make the effort to understand what he wants or fears, and within the context of his experience to guess how—or whether—both of us can find a way toward a viable accommodation. So, based on what I have learned, I want to bring forward a view of recent events that an Iranian acting as I used to act for the U.S. government would probably recommend to his government.

As I have shown, Iran has lost much of its territory to foreign powers, but Iranians do not appear to have any ambitions to acquire assets or territory beyond their present-day frontiers. There is no evidence of current military or political expansionism. However, its government naturally supports allies. So its influence is felt in Iraq and Lebanon. Nor is it religiously aggressive: Shia Islam is eschatological but not messianic. Its government is a theocracy that seeks to shape its society within a pattern of Islamic law, but it is also influenced by its desire to create conditions in which the Iranians can live in safety, prosperity, and, above all, dignity. This is an area of growth.

Viewing the record of the past half century, the Iranian regime believes that the major danger to its aspirations and even to its survival is America and what it regards as America's surrogate, Israel.

Certainly, in recent years, as I have recounted in Chapter Six, the record shows that the United States and Israel had planned to attack Iran, abort its nuclear program, and "regime change" it. Iranians share a negative view of the United States based on the overthrow of the first elected Iranian government, under Prime Minister Muhammad Mossadegh, by the CIA in 1953; America's support for the Iraqi invasion of Iran in 1981; and the shooting down of an Iranian passenger plane over the Gulf in 1988. President Obama has repudiated actions of these kinds, but Iranians wonder if he really speaks for America. They note that in 2008 millions of Americans voted for Senator John McCain, whom Iranians heard sing the words "Bomb bomb bomb, bomb bomb Iran" to the tune of a Beach Boys song.[4] Americans might have found it funny, but Iranians didn't laugh. There were too many serious statements saying essentially the same thing. Iranians believe America's statements and see themselves surrounded by U.S. warships, overflown by U.S. aircraft, and infiltrated by American and Israeli agents. As Iran's Supreme Guide Ayatollah Ali Khamenei has written to President Obama, he likes what he hears but is not convinced that the words represent "change in which he can believe." So, as a matter of prudence, Khamenei will not quickly let down his guard.

His "guard" is Iran's ability to make an attack unattractive or impossible. I believe Khamenei would see his means of action like this:

1. *To make espionage impossible.* The price for doing this is the imposition on Iran of stern ideological and security control: purging suspected dissidents and placing *mullas* in virtually every neighborhood to keep watch on the people as ideological police. In short, circumstances favor the Iranian hard-liners from the religious establishment. Probably Khamenei favors such a policy as a matter of principle, but his personal experiences—having suffered six arrests, torture, and imprisonment by the Shah's political police, whom he believes were trained by the CIA and the Mossad—must have shaped his emotions.

2. *To create a "capacity" for guerrilla war that could survive an American or Israeli attack.* Iranians would be as unlikely to welcome a foreign invader as the anti-Castro Cubans were during the American attacks on Cuba at the Bay of Pigs in 1961 and the anti-Saddam Iraqis were during the 2003 U.S. invasion. In Iraq, after the army shattered in "shock and awe," there was no prepared resistance, but the campaign there cost America more than 4,200 dead, several hundred thousand wounded or partially incapacitated, and nearly $1 trillion. An attack on Iran would cost America far more because Iran (unlike Iraq) has trained and equipped about 150,000 Revolutionary Guards and even more *Sazeman-e Basijs* for guerrilla warfare. At sea, Iran now has nearly a thousand missile-armed speedboats scattered among more than seven hundred little ports along the Persian Gulf. They could be used in kamikaze-type attacks and would certainly do great damage to attacking forces.[5]

3. *To cultivate trading partners, friends, and allies abroad.* Both China and India depend heavily on Iranian energy exports. Iran has the capacity to interdict or at least slow down the 25 percent of the world's energy that is conveyed down the Gulf; even if Iran did not itself act, a conflict would jeopardize attempts by the entire world to work its way out of the current recession. Apart from energy, the whole Muslim world would see an American—and, even more so, an Israeli—attack on Iran as an attack on Islam. More broadly, such an attack would conjure dark memories of imperialism. In sum, the costs to the United States of an attack on Iran, as the Bush administration reluctantly and belatedly concluded, would be enormous—indeed, "unacceptable."

4. *To acquire the ultimate defense.* The United States, Russia, Britain, France, China, India, Pakistan, and Israel all agree that the ultimate defense is the threat of retaliation: Once a country acquires a nuclear weapon and the capacity to deliver it, it is immune to attack. Thus, I believe, it would be ahistorical and illogical for Iran not to be acquiring at least the capacity to manufacture a nuclear weapon.

The Iranian government, of course, realizes that the period of acquisition—when other states believe a country is trying to acquire nuclear weapons but has not yet succeeded—is a time of great danger. The Bush administration repeatedly threatened and prepared forces to carry out a "shock and awe" aerial attack and an invasion to stop Iran's nuclear program; Israel still says it can and will stop any move toward a nuclear weapon.[6] The Iranian regime has denied seeking such a weapon and has said that its program is solely for peaceful purposes. The November 2007 NIE affirmed that. However, even if it was and remains true, at some point I believe that threats will convince the Iranians to weaponize. Already in March 2008, the International Atomic Energy Agency (IAEA) reported evidence that is "not consistent with any application other than the development of a nuclear weapon."[7] If this is correct, how could Iran implement its policy safely?

The answer is "just as the existing nuclear powers have done." Iran would have to act secretly and in subtle ways. In the present circumstances, with frequent inspections, China and Vietnam provide a feasible model: They alternated offers to negotiate with moves to build power. That was what Mao Zedong called "talk talk fight fight." Such a policy is congenial to Iranians. Dissimulation (*taqiyyah*) is a traditional Shia protective mode. Throughout their history, when Iranians were faced with great danger, they pretended to beliefs they did not hold. Such tactics today would give them the option, when in danger of attack, of agreeing to nuclear restraint and, when danger recedes, of moving ahead to acquire at least one nuclear weapon and the means to deliver it. The means to deliver a weapon has been in hand for five or six years. The Shihab–3 missile has a range of nearly a thousand miles. Estimates vary on the length of the acquisition period of a nuclear bomb.[8] That is the period of danger, so a smart policy for Iran during the period could be "translated" from Mao's slogan to "offer to talk, offer to talk, spin centrifuges, spin centrifuges." I think that is probably a fair description of Iranian government actions in the last few years.[9]

What restraints are there, or could there be, on such a policy? It is almost certain that threat is not among them.[10] The more Iran feels threatened, the more incentive it has to push its nuclear program toward the acquisition of a weapon. Nor have sanctions worked.[11] Particularly against a less organized and therefore less fragile economy, sanctions have little leverage. They were tried by the British against Iran in the 1950s without result.

So now I will lay out what steps I think could avoid armed conflict, satisfy the Iranian government's desire for security and recognition, and meet the demands of the Western powers for a lessening or an avoidance of the nuclear danger.

The bottom line is for Iran to get a satisfactory security guarantee. As even senior American generals have pointed out, "Iran cannot accept long term restraints on its fuel-cycle activity as part of a settlement without a security guarantee."[12] So what does a "security guarantee" mean? There are three basic steps.

The first step is that the United States must renounce its assertion of the right to attack Iran preemptively and, as the 2005 "National Security Paper of the United States" puts it, "at the time, place, and in the manner of our choosing."[13] As long as this remains a valid statement of American policy, and it is reaffirmed in later documents, the Iranian government would be foolish not to acquire a nuclear weapon.

President Obama has indicated that he intends to drop the doctrine of preemptive strikes. When his intention becomes official policy, the first step will have been taken.

The second step is to get an internationally guaranteed statement recognizing Iran's sovereign independence and certifying that no other state, particularly the United States and Israel, will be allowed to attack it.

Such guarantees have often been made among states, but in and of themselves they have rarely prevented war. They are necessary but not sufficient.

So *the third step* is to create a nuclear-free Middle East. Movement toward this step must be taken in a phased manner. It could begin with a decision by the United States to pull back its enormous nuclear armed forces from Iran's frontier. More complex, of course, is what to do about Israel. Getting Israel to join in a nuclear stand-down will require sweeping compensatory agreements and sophisticated international negotiation. But the essential element is clear: "Imbalance" is what has successively motivated other nuclear powers: Russia had to have the bomb because America had it; China, because of Russia; India and Pakistan, because of each other. This attitude was clearly articulated by the then head of India's nuclear program to justify his nation's acquisition of the bomb. He said, essentially, that there can't be a license for Europeans and a prohibition for Asians. Iran will not give up its quest unless at least Israel reciprocates.

Is nuclear disarmament a feasible, even if a long- or middle-term, objective?

I think it is. Cutting back and then abolishing nuclear weapon inventories is in *everyone's* interest. The simple fact is that nuclear weapons anywhere are a danger to people everywhere. From my experience in the Cuban Missile Crisis, I speak with some assurance of this fact. Of course, it will be difficult to persuade Israel, which has a huge nuclear inventory, but even Israel has a logical reason to join in this effort. In its own interest, it must face the fact that, whether or not Iran decides to get nuclear weapons, other neighboring countries soon will.[14] So while having nuclear weapons, arguably, was a source of security for Israel in the past, retaining them today is becoming a source of insecurity. Moreover, giving them up would remove the major danger the Israelis have identified: A conventionally armed Iran poses no threat to Israel, and a conventionally armed Israel poses no threat to Iran. Both could benefit from regional security guarantees that would naturally be incorporated in a move toward a nuclear-weapon-free Middle East.

Within a nuclear-weapon-free Middle East, there would be nothing to stop Iran and other countries from benefiting from the intellectual, industrial, and energy-saving aspects of nuclear technology, and, within a balanced system, Iran would not find it humiliating to take up the various proposals[15] to have other powers and the IAEA monitor its activities and safeguard its fuel.

The Iranians, I believe, could be induced to move in this direction before it is too late. Their motivation is that such a move would be in their national interest. The Supreme guide Ayatollah Ali Khamenei is said to seek "an Iran that is scientifically and technologically advanced enough to be self-sufficient, self-sufficient enough to be economically independent, and economically independent enough to be politically independent."[16] All Iranians are tired of living under the gun. The ruling *ulama* have shown that they want to continue enjoying the perquisites of wealth, and millions of young working-class Iranians want their government to meet their desire for a richer, fuller life.[17]

If security guarantees are supplemented with more open international trade—for example, enabling Iran to join the World Trade Organization (a move that the United States has blocked), to have better access to capital for investment, and to get the advanced technology it needs to improve oil extraction and to liquefy natural gas—Iran's government will have achieved a true "victory."

In conclusion, on the basis of my study of Iranian history and mores and my experience in international negotiation and policy planning, I believe that the incoming Obama administration has a "window of opportunity" that even a man as hostile to America as President Mahmoud Ahmadinejad cannot afford to try to close. Indeed, even he has at least spoken in favor of what he calls "real changes." In a recent television address, he said, "The Iranian nation welcomes a hand extended to it should it really and truly be based on honesty, justice and respect."[18] And there are faint signs that the Supreme guide Ayatollah Ali Khamenei is "tilting" in the direction of some form of accommodation. These are good omens.

However, we should be realistic: The path toward peace will not be easy, and our progress along it will be slow and probably will be hampered by frequent missteps. We and the Iranians will be looking over our shoulders: the Iranians at America's overthrow of their government in 1953, our support for Saddam Hussein in his attack on Iran, and the long-simmering—often boiling—threats and actions of recent years; we Americans at the ugly hostage affair, the terrorist attack on American Marines in Lebanon, and our assertion that Iran helped to kill our soldiers in Iraq.

Both countries will have to contend with prejudice and ignorance. Both countries will be emotional and quick to fault the other. But let us reflect on a positive step we have already taken in the right direction: We are both participating in the program to abolish a whole category of lethal substances that are almost as evil as nuclear arms, chemical weapons.[19] That might be the first step in building our confidence in each other's peaceful aims.

None of us can afford not to try.

NOTES

A FEW WORDS ON WORDS

1. A convenient diagram of the languages is given by Philip E. Ross, "Hard Words," in *Scientific American*, April 1, 1991.

CHAPTER ONE: BECOMING IRANIAN

1. M. L. West, *Indo-European Poetry and Myth* (Oxford: Oxford University Press, 2007). Also see Wendy Doniger's review of this remarkable book in the *London Review of Books*, April 10, 2008, and Luigi Luca Cavalli-Sforza, *Genes, Peoples, and Languages* (New York: Farrar, Straus & Giroux, 2000).

2. Quotations and translations from the *Avesta* and other Zoroastrian writings are drawn from Professor Mary Boyce's *Textual Sources for the Study of Zoroastrianism* (Manchester: Manchester University Press, 1984) and *Zoroastrians: Their Religious Beliefs and Practices* (London: Routledge & Kegan Paul, 1979), as well as from Ehsan Yarshater, "Iranian Common Beliefs and World-View," in *The Cambridge History of Iran*, vol. 3, part 1, ed. Ehsan Yarshater (Cambridge: Cambridge University Press, 1983).

3. A remarkable 1925 documentary film, *Grass: A Nation's Battle for Life*, on the Bakhtiari nomads shows this yearly progress. Lois Beck has written an account of one family in *Nomad: A Year in the Life of a Qashqa'i Tribesman in Iran* (Berkeley: University of California Press, 1991).

4. Ehsan Yarshater, "Introduction," in *The Cambridge History of Iran*, vol. 3, part 1.

5. In the national myth of Iran, the *Shahnameh*, we are given a picture of Alexander cradling the dying Persian king in his arms, weeping, rending his garments, pouring dust on his crown, and offering to restore his kingdom to him. The king replies, "We are from the same stock, the same root, the same people," and he asks Alexander to marry his daughter. "When the Persians saw how Sekandar [Alexander] honored [the Persian Shah] Dara and mourned for him, they offered the young king their homage and loyalty."

6. A. D. H. Bivar, "The Political History of Iran under the Arsacids," in *The Cambridge History of Iran*, vol. 3, part 1.

7. The texts are given in Nina Garsoïan, "Byzantium and the Sasanians," in *The Cambridge History of Iran*, vol. 3, part 1.

8. Many editions of Firdowsi's epic have appeared. It was often illustrated by the greatest of the Persian and Indian artists. To commemorate what he proclaimed to be the 2,500th anniversary of the Persian Empire by Cyrus the Great, Muhammad Reza Shah in 1971 commissioned an edition of the magnificent miniatures painted for one of the most famous of the remaining manuscripts of Firdowsi's poem. Another manuscript, prepared

for Shah Tahmasp around 1550 and containing 258 paintings, has been dismembered and sold in pieces. Many translations of Firdowsi's work have been made. An excellent, mainly prose, translation has been done by Dick Davis in *Shahnameh: The Persian Book of Kings* (New York: Viking Penguin, 2007). In two senses, Firdowsi's work was conservative: First, it gathered together and so preserved myths and legends from all over the Persian world—not just from Iran as we know it today but also from areas that are no longer today considered Iranian; second, it was written in a deliberately archaic language, rather than in the language used in Firdowsi's own time. (Firdowsi was thus adopting a psychological approach similar to that of the committees charged by King James with making his rendition of the Bible: Both achieved some of their emotional impact from the deliberate use of the unfamiliar expression.)

9. Known to English readers in the brilliant translation or adaptation of Edward FitzGerald, about which the nineteenth-century American poet James Russell Lowell aptly wrote:

> *These pearls of thought in Persian gulfs were bred,*
> *Each softly lucent as a rounded moon;*
> *The diver Omar plucked them from their bed,*
> *FitzGerald strung them on an English thread.*

10. A more detailed summary of the horrifying effects of the invasion is given by Professor I. P. Petrushevsky of the then Leningrad University in "The Socio-Economic Condition of Iran under the Il-Khans," in *The Cambridge History of Iran*, vol. 5, ed. J. A. Boyle (Cambridge: Cambridge University Press, 1968); H. R. Roemer, "Timur in Iran," in *The Cambridge History of Iran*, vol. 6, ed. Laurence Lockhart (Cambridge: Cambridge University Press, 1986).

CHAPTER TWO: BEING IRANIAN

1. From the time of the Prophet Muhammad, a number of religious-political-military leaders arose in times of crisis in Muslim societies, virtually all of whom insisted that they were going back to the pure religion. From the Arabic word for "return" (*salafa*), the movements they created and led are usually termed *salafiyah*. They include the Libyan Sanusi, the Egyptian Muslim Brotherhood, the Sudanese Mahdiyah, the Salafiyah in Algeria and Morocco, the Ahmadiyah in India, the Jamaat-i Islami in Pakistan, and the Sarekat Islam in Indonesia. Comparable movements were formed in medieval Europe by the Bogomils in Byzantium, the Cathars in what became France, the Lutherans in northern Europe, and the Puritans who spread from England to Holland and America.

2. Coined by the Turks, the term was apparently meant to deride them, much as American soldiers in Iraq have used the term *raghead* to mock Iraqis who wore the *kifiyah*.

3. H. R. Roemer, "The Safavid Period," in *The Cambridge History of Iran*, vol. 6.

4. "The voyage of M. Anthony Jenkinson through Russia, and over the Caspian sea into Persia, Anno 1561"; "The fift voiage into Persia made by M. Thomas Banister, and master Geofrey Ducket, Agents for the Moscovie companie, begun from England in the yeere 1568, and continuinng to the yeere 1574, following. Written by P.I. from the mouth of M. Lionel Plumtree"; and "Further Observations concerning the state of Persia, taken in the foresayd fift voyage into those partes, and written by M. Geofrey Ducket, one of the Agents emploied in the same." The latter includes the note "Of the name of the Sophy

of Persia, & why he is called the Shaugh, and of other customes." *Voyages*, ed. Richard Hakluyt (London: Dent, 1907, reprinted 1973), vol. 2, 121. Spelling as in the original.

5. "P.I. from the mouth of M. Lionel Plumtree: Observations of the Sophy of Persia, and of the Religion of the Persians," in *Voyages*, ed. Richard Hakluyt (London: Dent, 1907, reprinted 1973), vol. 2, 121. Spelling as in the original.

6. *Travels of Venetians in Persia* (London: Hakluyt Society, 1873), 206; quoted in Roger Savory, *Iran under the Safavids* (Cambridge: Cambridge University Press, 1980), 24.

7. In Turkish, the language of the Iranian warriors and of the court, *Qurban oldïghïm pirüm mürshidim.*

8. Kukimo Yamamoto, *The Oral Background of Persian Epics* (Leiden: Brill, 2004).

9. Abolqasem Ferdowsi, *Shanameh: The Persian Book of Kings*, trans. Dick Davis (New York: Viking Penguin, 2006), "The Beginning of the War between Iran and Turan," 110–111.

10. Hakluyt, *Voyages*, vol. 2, 126.

11. H. E. Wulff ("Qanats of Iran" in *Scientific American*, April 1968) mentions that the Assyrian King Sargon II observed them in seventh-century BC Iran. His son adopted the Iranian system to give water to the Assyrian capital at Nineveh. In turn, Darius of Persia introduced the system to Egypt about 518 BC. The system never went out of use. In 1960, Wulff found that there were still some 22,000 *qanats* in Iran comprising more than 170,000 miles of underground aqueducts.

12. *Travels in Persia*, quoted in Laurence Lockhart, *Persian Cities* (London: Luzac, 1960), 5.

13. In a land of little water, gardens were the luxuries of the rich and powerful and had to be protected against marauding goats and hungry people. So the Persians called them *pairidaeza*, which meant a garden or park "surrounded by a wall." Hearing the name, Alexander the Great's thirsty soldiers thought them true paradises and so coined the Greek word *paradeisos*, from which the English word derives.

14. The quotations are from Julie Scott Meisami, "Allegorical Gardens in the Persian Poetic Tradition," *International Journal of Middle Eastern Studies* 17, no. 2 (May 1985): 1–232.

15. In Isfahan, there was a Jewish quarter known as the Yahudiyeh like the famous *campo gheto* or iron foundries of Venice, from which the word *ghetto* derives, and a Christian quarter or suburb called Julfa, where the Armenian Christians lived.

16. Reported in 1568 by Richard Willes, "From the Mouth of M. Lionel Plumtree," in Hakluyt, *Voyages*, vol. 2, 123.

17. "A compendious and briefe declaration of the journey of M. Anth. Jenkinson, from the famous citie of London into the land of Persia . . . ," Hakluyt, *Voyages*, vol. 2, 27.

18. H. R. Roemer, "The Safavid Period," in *The Cambridge History of Iran*, vol. 6, 272.

CHAPTER THREE: SHAHS, *ULAMA*, AND WESTERN POWERS

1. Abdur-Rahman Ibn Khaldun has been described as the "father, or one of the fathers, of modern social science and cultural history." In the attention he paid to ways in which small social groups coalesce and interact, he was a harbinger of the French *Annales* historical school; the English historian Eric Hobsbawm remarked, "I take my stand with that great and neglected philosopher of history," and sees his analysis analogous to Marx's emphasis on the social and economic basis of events; and Arnold Toynbee lauded his study of history as "undoubtedly the greatest work of its kind that has ever yet been created by any mind in any time or place." The translations and interpretations are my own.

2. As Laurence Lockhart found (*The Fall of the Safavi Dynasty and the Afghan Occupation of Persia* [Cambridge: Cambridge University Press, 1958], p. 137), "This broath was to be prepared in bowls each which was to contain two legs of a he-goat, boiled with 325 pea-pods in water over which a virgin had repeated the Muhammadan profession of faith 325 times."

3. Louis-André Clairac, *Histoire de Perse depuis le Commencement de ce Siècle* (Paris, 1750); quoted in Lockhart, *Fall,* 172.

4. Lockhart, *Fall,* 169.

5. Peter Avery, "Nadir Shah and the Afshardid Legacy," in *The Cambridge History of Iran,* vol. 7, ed. Peter Avery, Gavin Hambly, and Charles Melville (Cambridge: Cambridge University Press, 1991), 3.

6. The title is difficult to translate because what it meant varied over time. John Perry (*Karim Khan Zand, A History of Iran, 1747–1779* [Chicago: University of Chicago Press, 1979], 215) suggests "deputy" or even "attorney" and remarked that it implied army command. The closest historical parallels, I have suggested, are the Japanese *shogun* (which also, literally, means "commander of the troops"). In Western history, the grandfather of Charlemagne, Charles Martel, affected a similar role under the title *maior domus,* or "mayor of the palace." As Perry remarks, "Karim had to dispense with the personal divine right of the Safavid monarch, theoretically vested in his puppet king, and was not prepared to risk the opprobrium that would follow if he usurped the throne as Nader had. . . . Thus he presented himself as an intermediary between the people and a purely symbolic monarchy." That was a role that none of his successors would assume.

7. Gavin R. G. Hambly, "Agha Muhammad Khan and the Establishment of the Qajar Dynasty," in *Cambridge History of Iran,* vol. 7, 125.

8. Bogdanov Artemi, *Memoirs* (London, 1822); quoted in Hambly, "Agha Muhammad Khan," 128.

9. Although this sense of guilt and the public displays of atonement are two of the most striking features of the practice of Shiism, reported by all Western visitors over the last several centuries, they are by no means unique to Islam. Various Christian groups, such as the "Brothers of the Cross," "Penitents," and others, whipped and tortured themselves in public displays of guilt much as Shia flagellants do. Passion plays have been performed since the Middle Ages in Europe and are still being performed. Perhaps the most famous is that of Oberammergau, which still draws thousands of visitors each year. Of course, the concept of martyrdom is as much a feature of Christianity as it is of Shia Islam.

10. In classical Arabic, the "technical" language of the Iranian Shia hierarchy, the word has a variety of meanings, from the simple "absent" through "beyond mental perception," "a mystery," and what is "undiscoverable except by Divine Revelation." God is described as the "knower of the hidden or secret things." In its basic form, the word can also be used for an eclipse.

11. *A History of Persia,* vol. 2 (London, 1815; reprinted by Elibron Classics, 2005), 314–316.

12. The Arabic word is typically vague, ranging from *lord* to *freed slave;* the classical meaning involved "support" in some fashion. In medieval Arabic, it came to mean a helper to either a ruler or a community.

13. The word is difficult to translate. It literally means "a sign of God," a miracle. It also conveys the sense of "refuge" and "compassion."

14. As I later discuss, in our own times, it would lead to the revolution that overthrew Muhammad Reza Shah. As the man who inspired the revolution, the Grand Ayatollah

Khomeini wrote in his treatise, *Velayat-i Faqih* (*The Rule of the Religious Jurist*), "Islam is opposed to the very notion of monarchy."

15. A number of intrepid travelers visited Iran before. The first Russian was a horse trader named Afannasii Nikitin in 1470, and the first Portuguese was Pedro da Covilhã, whom the Portuguese government sent on a mission in 1487 to spy on the ports on the Red Sea and the Indian Ocean. His report was largely responsible for the success of the Portuguese seafaring missions a few years later. See Laurence Lockhart, "European Contacts with Persia, 1350–1736," in *The Cambridge History of Iran*, vol. 6, 373ff.

16. Sir Jean Chardin, a Huguenot jeweler, arrived in Iran in 1665 and spent ten years there. See his *Travels in Persia, 1673–1677* (London: Argonaut Press, 1927; reproduced by Dover Press, 1988).

17. For the longer term, this may be regarded as the origin of the tragic Chechen war of our times. Tolstoy recounts a part of the early conflict in his novel *Haji Murat*. The Russian campaign was the first modern attempt to defoliate a land to deprive the guerrillas of sanctuary; the Chechens did not give up, so the Russians would eventually deploy about a quarter of a million troops there—many times more troops than the British ever employed in the conquest and rule of their vast Indian empire—and would suffer tens of thousands of casualties. In the final phases of their counterinsurgency, the Russians drove more than a million people across the frontier into the Ottoman Empire and replaced them with Russians, Cossacks, and Armenians. For opposite ends of the Caucasus campaign, see J. N. Baddeley, *The Russian Conquest of the Caucasus* (London, 1908); Anatol Lieven, *Chechnya: Tombstone of Russian Power* (New Haven: Yale University Press, 1998); Charles King, *The Ghost of Freedom: A History of the Caucasus* (Oxford: Oxford University Press, 2008); and Robert F. Baumann, *Russian-Soviet Unconventional Wars in the Caucasus, Central Asia, and Afghanistan* (Leavenworth, Ks: U.S. Army Command and General Staff Institute, 1993).

18. Emotional episodes of this kind have inflamed the revolutions of colonial America (the 1770 Boston Massacre), the French Revolution (the 1789 storming of the Bastille), the 1905 Russian Revolution (the "Bloody Sunday" or Gapon affair), and the February 1917 Russian Revolution (the "bread riots").

19. Having traveled that route in 1962 before the building of highways when it was relatively unchanged since the previous century, I can attest that the British had little to fear. No only was it far from India—over fifteen hundred miles and weeks of rough riding—but the logistics of moving an army also would have been a nightmare.

20. The Reuter oil venture was liquidated after having failed to find oil, while the Imperial Bank prospered and later became known as the British Bank of the Middle East.

21. Charles Issawi (*The Economic History of Iran, 1800—1914,* Publications of the Center for Middle Eastern Studies, Number 8, William R. Polk, General Editor [Chicago: University of Chicago Press, 1971], p. 23) reports that by 1918, "there were in Europe about 500 Iranian students, 200 of whom were in France, 34 in England, 9 in Germany."

22. As in Protestantism, a number of movements set out to purge later "corruptions" and to go back to what was believed to be original doctrine; in the nineteenth and early twentieth centuries, they were in part attempts to protect socially accepted ways of life from foreign ideas or even from imperialism. Thus, movements, collectively known as *salafiyah* (which can be translated as something like "back to basics"), included the Muslim Brotherhood in Egypt, the Sudan, and elsewhere; the Sanusi movement of Libya; the Mahdiyah in the Sudan; the Salafiyah movements in Morocco and Algeria; the Ahmadiyah in India; the Jamaᵃat-i Islami in Pakistan; and the Sarekat

Islam in Indonesia. Shia Islam was affected by comparable movements in Iran, Lebanon, and elsewhere.

CHAPTER FOUR: FROM POLITICAL REVOLUTION THROUGH SOCIAL REVOLUTION TO VIOLENT REVOLUTION

1.   E. G. Browne, *The Persian Revolution of 1905–1909* (Cambridge: Cambridge University Press, 1910), 112–113. Browne, who held the chair of Persian at Cambridge, was unusually well informed on contemporary Iran, having spent a year visiting all the major locations and getting to know many of the key figures in the revolutionary movement, which he described in *A Year amongst the Persians* (London: A. C. Black, 1893), and had an extraordinary grasp of Iranian culture, which he recounted in his massive *A Literary History of Persia* (London: T. Fisher Unwin, 1902). At a time in which few Europeans were more than condescending toward Iran, Browne wrote, "That in this world diversity, not uniformity, is the higher law and the more desirable state . . . [and if foreigners and foreign things destroy its culture] no material prosperity, no amount of railways, mines, goals, gas, or drainage can compensate the world, spiritually and intellectually, for the loss of Persia."

2.   Although this custom appeared quaint to Western observers, it was by no means unique to Iran. Among the Arab nomads, it was customary for a person seeking protection to grasp the tent ropes of a tribesman, who was then obliged to protect him. Places of sanctuary were well known among the Arabs (*harams*), the ancient Hebrews (tabernacles), and the Greeks and Romans (temples and even groves) and throughout Europe (churches) until, at least, the end of the eighteenth century. In medieval England, there were about two dozen places into which the king's officials were not allowed to enter in pursuit of an outlaw.

3.   Because many of them were *ulama* who had spent years studying Arabic, they would have known that the basic meaning of the word *adal* is "balance," used for adjusting saddlebags so that one side does not pull down the other. Thus, by assembling in the *Adalatkhanan*, the people would "balance" the rule of the Shah and his government. The concept was different from the Western "parliament," a place where men were allowed to talk, and from the Arabic word that came into Iranian politics, *majlis*, a place where people sat together. Thus, without pressing the point too far, the original demand of the group was moderation. It would later become more strident.

4.   Mangol Bayat, *Iran's First Revolution: Shiism and the Constitutional Revolution of 1905–1909* (Oxford: Oxford University Press, 1991), 125–129. The quotation on page 91, based on contemporary Iranian sources, is also drawn from Bayat. Ironically, particularly in view of Russian activities over the next several years, the Russian acting foreign minister told the British ambassador in August 1908 that "there were signs that the Shah was inclined to evade his engagements, and was drifting, encouraged by evil counselors, into a reactionary policy which, if pushed far, would probably be disastrous to him personally and embarrassing to the British and Russian governments." Sir A. Nicolson, F.O. 371/727, 6057/6057/09/38, reprinted in G. P. Gooch and Harold Temperley, *British Document on the Origins of the War, 1898–1914, Vol. X, Part I, The Near and Middle East on the Eve of War* (London: HMSO, 1936), 725.

5.   William R. Polk, *The Birth of America* (New York: HarperCollins, 2006), 274.

6.   Brown, *The Persian Revolution of 1905–1909*, 121.

7.   Sir A. Nicolson, December 30, 1909, F.O. 371/976, 159/159/10/38; quoted in Gooch and Temperley, *British Document on the Origins of the War*, 733.

8. On the eve of the First World War, the Royal Navy began converting its ships to oil from coal. Under the influence of Admiral of the Fleet Lord Fisher, the then First Lord of the Admiralty, Winston Churchill, pushed an agreement that in May 1914 gave the British government control of the company. As the British statesman Lord Curzon later said of the First World War, "the Allies floated to victory on a wave of oil." He and others in the British government believed that those who controlled oil would rule the world. Britain would retain the concession for Iranian oil until 1967, when the Iranian government, after two earlier attempts, finally nationalized the company.

9. Sir G. Buchanan to Sir Edward Grey, St. Petersburgh, July 11, 1911. Reprinted in Gooch and Temperley, *British Document on the Origins of the War*, 768.

10. The Russian government on November 17, 1911, informed the British government of its move in a dispatch (in French), published in Gooch and Temperley, *British Document on the Origins of the War*, 826–827. The dispatch of the British ambassador to Tehran is given in the next two pages.

11. The book was published in 1912 by Appleton Century Croft, the New York publishing house, of which Shuster became president after leaving Iran. Details of his career were reported to the British government by the British minister in Washington in February 1911. See Gooch and Temperley, *British Document on the Origins of the War*, 761.

12. Wassmus cast his appeal to the Iranians in Islamic terms, urging them to "give yourselves to the Holy Cause." It fell on deaf ears. On his mission, see Peter Hopkirk, *On Secret Service East of Constantinople* (London: John Murray, 1994), 111.

13. Lenin had bitterly attacked then Russian Prime Minister Alexander Kerensky in July 1917 for trying to conceal the Russian participation in secret treaties dealing with the "frankly predatory character . . . concerning the partition of Persia [and hiding Russian actions] which for several centuries has robbed and oppressed more peoples than all other tyrants and despots." Quoted in Bertram D. Wolfe, *Three Who Made a Revolution* (New York: Dial Press, 1948), 402.

14. Earl Curzon says that he alerted Colonel House to the British position and asked him to inform President Wilson. On September 12, 1919, Ambassador John Davis confirmed the Curzon-House conversation but advised Curzon that Wilson was unhappy at the British action. The British also took steps to get the would-be Iranian delegates recalled. Earl Curzon to Mr. Lindsay (Washington), August 18, 1919, No. 477 118250/150/34; quoted in *Documents on British Foreign Policy, 1919–1939*, ed. E. L. Woodward and Rohan Butler (London: HMSO, 1952), 1135.

15. As President Wilson's secretary and amanuensis, Ray Stannard Baker, wrote, "Persia was, indeed, one of the small nations early at Paris appealing to the President for the right of self-determination." *Woodrow Wilson and World Settlement, Written from His Unpublished and Personal Material* (New York: Doubleday, Page & Co., 1922), 51.

16. Copy of a letter dated August 9, 1919, from the British minister in Tehran, Sir Percy Cox, to the senior Iranian officials; quoted in Woodward and Butler, *Documents on British Foreign Policy*, 1141–1142. The quotation from Viscount Grey in Washington is on page 1205, dated October 18, 1919.

17. J. M. Balfour (quoted by Joseph Upton in *The History of Modern Iran: An Interpretation* [Cambridge: Harvard Middle Eastern Monograph Series, 1960]) estimated in *Recent Happenings in Persia* (London: William Blackwood & Sons, 1922) that about two million people died and charged that the famine was manipulated by "those in high authority."

18. I have relied on Cyrus Ghani's account of his early life in *Iran and the Rise of Reza Shah: From Qajar Collapse to Pahlavi Power* (London: I. B. Tauris, 1998), 161ff, and on Nikki

R. Keddie's *Qajar Iran and the Rise of Reza Khan, 1896–1925* (Los Angeles: The UCLA G. E. von Grunebaum Center for Near Eastern Studies and Mazda Publishers, 1999).

19. It is difficult for outsiders from secure, independent countries to understand the emotion generated by such symbols. Much later, in 1956, when President Nasser of Egypt nationalized the Suez Canal, Egyptians were delighted, but what they found even more exciting was his ending the British domination of the theretofore all-English club on the island in the middle of the Nile, where even the king of Egypt had not been admitted. In India, similar all-English clubs dominated the social scene to the humiliation of Indians of all classes. Even maharajas were not admitted. In Iran, in the oil company ministate of Abadan, similar British social clubs excluded all Iranians.

20. Ironically, Millspaugh was to have the last laugh. He would return in 1943, following the fall and exile of Reza, to take up, more or less, where he had left off his work on the Iranian economy. He described his experience in Iran in *The American Task in Persia* (New York: Century, 1925) and *Americans in Persia* (Washington, DC: Brookings Institution, 1946).

21. Gavin R. G. Hambly, "The Pahlavi Autocracy: Riza Shah, 1921–1941," *The Cambridge History of Iran*, vol. 7, 226, 228–229.

22. Although an investigation made at the request of the Iranian government by the International Labour Office, *Labour Conditions in the Oil Industry* (Geneva: ILO, 1950), credited the AIOC with making praiseworthy attempts to both nationalize the labor force and upgrade it through training for workers and subsidizing education in Iran and abroad.

23. I have spelled out this analysis more completely in "The Middle East: Analyzing Social Change," *Bulletin of the Atomic Scientists* 23 (January 1967): 12ff.

24. Quoted in Michael P. Zirinsky, "Imperial Power and Dictatorship: Britain and the Rise of Reza Shah," *International Journal of Middle Eastern Studies* 24 (November 1992): 639. The following quotation of German Ambassador W. von Blücher is his account of a meeting with Reza Shah in 1931 from his *Zietenwende in Iran: Erlebnisse und Beobachtungen* (Berlin, 1949), quoted and translated by Joseph Upton, *The History of Modern Iran*, 150–151.

25. The Russians threatened Prime Minister Ahmad Ghavam for his delaying tactics, saying that they constituted a "return to the policy of enmity toward and discrimination against the Soviet Union," but deputies in the *Majles* attacked the proposed concession as "the worst agreement in the past hundred years of Iranian history." See George Lenczowski, *Russian and the West in Iran* (Ithaca: Cornell University Press, 1949), 309–310.

26. As Richard W. Cottam wrote, "Many of the nationalist and tribal leaders were executed or imprisoned, the Kurdish printing press was destroyed and books in Kurdish were burned, and the old ban against the teaching of Kurdish was reimposed. Political activity gradually resumed in these areas, but strictly within the Iranian framework." *Nationalism in Iran* (Pittsburgh: University of Pittsburgh Press, 1964), 73–74. His comments were partly based on Archie Roosevelt Jr.'s article "The Kurdish Republic of Mahabad," *The Middle East Journal* 1 (July 1947): 247ff. Roosevelt was one of only four Americans to visit Mahabad during the one year of the republic's existence.

27. More detailed figures are given in Jahangir Amuzegar and Ali Fekrat, *Iran: Economic Development under Dualistic Conditions* (Chicago: Publications of the Center for Middle Eastern Studies, William R. Polk, General Editor, University of Chicago Press, 1971), 16ff.

28.   U.S. Assistant Secretary of State George McGhee tried to get the British Foreign Office and AIOC at least to allow Iran, which was a 20 percent owner of AIOC, to see its books. Both refused the American government's request. See Dean Acheson, *Present at the Creation* (New York: W. W. Norton, 1969), 649. Secretary of State Acheson commented, "Never had so few lost so much so stupidly and so fast."

29.   Amuzegar and Fekrat, *Iran: Economic Development under Dualistic Conditions,* 30.

30.   Gary Sick, *All Fall Down: America's Fateful Encounter with Iran* (New York: Random House and London: I. B. Tauris, 1985), 7.

31.   I discuss this more fully later. The source of this comment is the official, still classified, history written by Donald M. Wilber, *The Overthrow of Premier Mossadeq of Iran, November 1952–August 1953.* It was leaked to *The New York Times* in 2000 and published half a century later as *Regime Change in Iran* (Nottingham, England, 2006).

32.   Department of State Report on Human Rights in Iran to the House Committee on International Relations, December 31, 1976, reproduced in *The United States and Iran: A Documentary History,* ed. Yonan Alexander and Allan Nanes (Frederick, MD: University Publications of America, 1980), 432. Also see Ervand Abrahamian, *Tortured Confessions* (Berkeley: University of California Press, 1999), 83ff.

33.   As the British MI6 agent who was instrumental in the reinstatement of the Shah later wrote, "It is easy to see Operation Book [the name the British gave to the operation that Americans called AJAX to overthrow Mossadegh] as the first step toward the Iranian catastrophe of 1979. What we did not foresee was that the Shah would gather new strength and use it so tyrannically. . . ." See C. M. Woodhouse, *Something Ventured* (London: Granada, 1982), 131.

34.   Ervand Abrahamian, *Iran between Two Revolutions* (Princeton: Princeton University Press, 1982). Chapter 9 substantiates and elaborates much of the following information; much of it comes directly from the "AID Data Books" that were gathered by U.S. government aid organizations shortly after President Truman's "Point Four" aid program began and was later elaborated by the United States Agency for International Development.

35.   *Kashf al-Asrar.* Except for this book, Khomeini was not active in Iranian politics until about 1962, and then probably because he shared with the regime its fear of communism.

36.   The way these events impacted on his followers is brilliantly recounted by Professor Roy Mottahedeh in his book *The Mantle of the Prophet: Religion and Politics in Iran* (London: Chatto & Windus, 1986), 189ff.

37.   As Shaul Bakhash noted, "To bring down prices, the government launched a campaign against the business community. Established industrialists were hauled off to jail or sent into exile. Some 10,000 inexperienced students were recruited to check on prices in shops and the bazaar. Some 250,000 shopkeepers were fined, 23,000 traders banned from their home towns, and 8,000 shopkeepers were jailed." *The Reign of the Ayatollahs: Iran and the Islamic Revolution* (London: I. B. Tauris and New York: Basic Books, 1985), 13.

38.   "Economic Development, 1921–1979," *Cambridge History of Iran,* vol. 7.

39.   In my judgment, the best included Roy Mottahedeh, *The Mantle of the Prophet: Religion and Politics in Iran* (London: Chatto & Windus, 1986); Ervand Abrahamian, *Iran between Two Revolutions* (Princeton: Princeton University Press, 1982) and *A History of Modern Iran* (Cambridge: Cambridge University Press, 2008); Shaul Bakhash, *The Reign of the Ayatollahs: Iran and the Islamic Revolution* (London: I. B. Tauris, 1985); and Nikki

Keddie, "Is Shi'ism Revolutionary?" In *The Iranian Revolution and the Islamic Republic*, ed. N. Keddie and Eric Hooglund (Syracuse: Syracuse University Press, 1986).

40.   *Hukumat-e Islami ya Velayat-e Faghih* or *The Rule of the Islamic Jurist*.

41.   Sick, *All Fall Down*, 91–92.

42.   "Iran and the Black and Red Reactionaries," editorial in *Ettelaat* (January 7, 1978); noted in Ervand Abrahamian, *A History of Modern Iran* (Cambridge: Cambridge University Press, 2008), 158.

43.   Corruption was on a monumental scale. The Shah used the Pahlavi Foundation as a funnel through which funds provided by various government departments were passed to family members, selected government officials, and even American officials. As Fred J. Cook documented ("The Billion-Dollar Mystery," *The Nation* [April 12, 1965]), on the basis of court and bank records and both Senate and congressional committee hearings, in the one year of 1962, "some $159 million in American aid funds and Iran oil royalties (those royalties supposed to have been used to supplement American aid) had been deposited in the numbered bank account of the Pahlavi Foundation in Switzerland." Not only Iranians were beneficiaries. Mr. Cook lists American officials and prominent Americans whose favor was thought to be valuable who received checks from the foundation for $1 million each. He also furnishes a copy of the Union de Banques Suisses statement for the Pahlavi Foundation that lists Loy Henderson (American ambassador to Iran during the coup against Mossadegh), Selden Chapin (Henderson's successor as ambassador from 1954 to 1958), and George V. Allen (who was Assistant Secretary of State for the Near East at the same time). Each is listed as having received $1 million.

44.   The text, from the Foreign Broadcast Information Service, is quoted in Sick, *All Fall Down*, 75–76.

45.   Ambassador Sullivan met with the Shah on December 26, at which time the Shah asked what the United States wanted him to do. The quotation was the reply that Sullivan says he gave. See Sick, *All Fall Down*, 124–125.

46.   Sick, *All Fall Down*, 110.

47.   According to Henry Kissinger in 1976. See *The United States and Iran: A Documentary History*, ed. Yonan Alexander and Allan Nanes (Frederick, MD: University Publications of America, 1980), 402.

CHAPTER FIVE: THE REVOLUTIONARY REGIME

1.   Shaul Bakhash gives a convincing portrait of him in *The Reign of the Ayatollahs: Iran and the Islamic Revolution* (London: I. B. Tauris, 1985), 54ff.

2.   Crane Brinton, *The Anatomy of Revolution* (New York: Prentice-Hall, 1938; Vintage Books, 1957), 80.

3.   Captain Gary Sick, USN (Rtd.), who was the NSC officer most closely involved, has written a chronology of the events in *All Fall Down*. He was present at the meeting with the president. I have generally relied on his account for the American side of the hostage crisis. As Sick reports, already on March 6, the deputy director of the NSC warned President Carter that a "guerrilla group could retaliate against the remaining Americans and [refuse] to release them until the shah was extradited."

4.   Bakhash, in *The Reign of the Ayatollahs* (81ff), recounts the deliberations. The principal task of the Assembly is to choose the successor to the supreme guide. It is the group that selected Ayatollah Khamenei to replace Khomeini. Because Khamenei is now 88, the Assembly will play a key role in Iranian affairs again in the near future.

5. In Iranian Shia custom, a leading *mujtahid* could be recognized as a *marja-e taghlid* only by one who had already attained that status. Shariatmadari was one of the select few. By "awarding" it to Khomeini, he saved Khomeini's life because executing a *marja-e taghlid* was regarded as a mortal sin, and the Shah could not afford to do it. Ironically, Shariatmadari was later implicated in a plot against Khomeini, and Khomeini condemned him to internal exile in Qom, where he languished until his death in 1986.

6. Ervand Abrahamian (*A History of Modern Iran* [Cambridge: Cambridge University Press, 2008], 163ff) provides a chart showing how power was formally divided among offices and officials.

7. When Russia invaded Afghanistan, there would be an attack on the Soviet embassy also.

8. In one of those replays that history sometimes provides, Herodotus tells us of an early violation of diplomatic immunity. When Xerxes sent Persian envoys to Sparta and Athens to negotiate a ceasefire, the Spartans killed them, and the Athenians threw them "into a pit like criminals." To try to make amends, the Spartans sent two volunteers to atone with their lives for what Sparta had done. Xerxes, says Herodotus, "with truly noble generosity replied that he would not behave like the Spartans, who by murdering the ambassadors of a foreign power had broken the law which all the world holds sacred." For the widespread practice of diplomatic immunity, see my *Neighbors and Strangers: The Fundamentals of Foreign Affairs* (Chicago: University of Chicago Press, 1997), 233ff.

9. Several of the original planners of the attack on the embassy were interviewed by Mark Bowden in "Among the Hostage Takers," *The Atlantic Monthly* (December 2004), 72ff. According to him, they had planned only to "subdue and confine member of the American mission for perhaps a day or two, but they had no intention of holding them for any length of time. They made no preparations for doing so."

10. When the first attack on the embassy occurred in February 1979, most of the embassy files were shipped back to Washington, leaving behind only "working" papers. For unknown reasons, the vast collections of papers for which the American government is famous were returned to Tehran. The second attack was so unexpected and sudden that, as Gary Sick pointed out, "a very large quantity of classified information fell into the hands of the student militants . . . [who] made a great show of laboriously piecing together shredded documents, but most of the embassy files were taken intact." Sick, *All Fall Down,* 190–191.

11. Even in America, when the members of the SDS attacked the University of Chicago and the Adlai Stevenson Institute, of which I was then president, two of the founders of the SDS who were associated with the Institute fled in panic, saying to me, "These people are crazy. They may burn the building down and kill everyone in it." The Institute had no secret files and no relationship to any government, nor was Chicago in the midst of revolution, but from that experience I can imagine that men such as Bazargan feared for their lives.

12. Sick, *All Fall Down,* 195ff.

13. Sick, *All Fall Down,* 225.

14. Bakhash, *The Reign of the Ayatollahs,* 92ff.

15. Bakhash, *The Reign of the Ayatollahs,* 97.

16. A report of his statement was printed in *Middle East Research and Information Project* (*Merip Reports*) in June 1980 and is reproduced in Bakhash, *The Reign of the Ayatollahs,* 100–101.

17. Quoted from *Bamdad* (an independent newspaper that was suspended and then bombed in 1980) in Bakhash, *The Reign of the Ayatollahs,* 101; and *Iran Times* (April 17 and July 17, 1981) in Bakhash, *The Reign of the Ayatollahs,* 141.

18.   I have mentioned various comparisons with the French and Russian revolutions. Bani-Sadr's call for order and security and for economic recovery—and the reception to them on the part of the people—bears some resemblance to the Soviet government's decision to slow down the revolution in what was called the New Economic Policy. As in Iran, it was followed by a new plunge into revolutionary turmoil.

19.   As he told Flora Lewis (*The New York Times,* August 3, 1987) from his Paris exile.

20.   Palme was murdered on a street outside a theater in Stockholm three years later. The assassin was never identified.

21.   Elaine Sciolino, "Iran to Lift House Arrest for Dissident after 5 Years," *The New York Times,* January 28, 2003. A few days later, Ms. Sciolino reported (*The New York Times,* February 1, 2003) that perhaps bruised, but undaunted, "the invisible man of Qum has returned to the battlefield of Islamic politics." He called for all political prisoners to be released and for secret courts to be abolished. Although firm in his opposition to American policy, he also said, "Chanting death to this and this is not the way to run a country. We have lost our prestige in the world."

22.   I have documented it in *Violent Politics: A History of Insurgency, Terrorism and Guerrilla War, From the American Revolution to Iraq* (New York: HarperCollins, 2007, 2008).

23.   Reuters reported the bomb blast on July 5, saying that 72 leading political figures were killed (*The New York Times,* July 6, 1981). The identities of the victims noted earlier are given, without indication of source, by Bakhash, *The Reign of the Ayatollahs,* 219.

24.   Bakhash (*The Reign of the Ayatollahs,* 218–222), drawing on figures published in *Iran Times* and a personal communication to him from Amnesty International, dated July 6, 1982. The quotations from the Revolutionary Prosecutor General and the chief of the Tehran Revolutionary Court are also drawn from *Iran Times.*

25.   Abrahamian, *A History,* 181, and documented, insofar as possible, in his *Tortured Confessions: Prisons and Public Recantations in Modern Iran* (Berkeley: University of California Press, 1999).

26.   David Segal, "The Iran-Iraq War: A Military Analysis," *Foreign Affairs* (Summer 1988): 946ff.

27.   Nazila Fathi, "An Old Letter Casts Doubts on Iran's Goal for Uranium," *The New York Times,* October 5, 2006.

28.   Shariatmadari had ruled that Khomeini's "descent" into politics was not religiously legal; he was subsequently disgraced, allegedly tortured and forced to "recant" for alleged involvement in a plot against Khomeini. Montazeri had also denounced the Khomeini regime, allegedly writing a bitter letter to Khomeini in which he said "your prisons are far worse than those of the Shah and his SAVAK." To Khomeini's acute embarrassment, his statements had found their way to the foreign press. As Youssef M. Ibrahim wrote, "In letters to Ayatollah Khomeini and in messages to the public on television and on the radio, he [Montazeri] repeatedly denounced corruption and tyranny in the regime." *The New York Times,* April 2, 1989. Elaine Sciolino wrote of the result of his statements in "Montazeri, Khomeini's Designated Successor in Iran, Quits under Pressure," *The New York Times,* March 29, 1989. "In a letter to Ayatollah Khomeini, his ousted successor made it clear that he had been forced to withdraw." In a clear warning to Montazeri, Khomeini replied, "I advise you cleanse your household of unsuitable individuals and seriously prevent the comings and goings of the opponents of the system who pretend to be in favor of Islam and the Islamic republic."

29.   "Iran's New Revolution," *Foreign Affairs* (January/February 2000).

30. The CIA believed it to have fallen an additional 1 percent by 2007. Shayerah Ilias, "Iran's Economic Conditions: U.S. Policy Issues," Congressional Research Report, January 15, 2009. The figures here and the quotes below are drawn from Ilias and Katzman.

31. World Bank Report No. 25848-IRN, "Iran: Medium Term Framework for Transition," April 30, 2003; quoted by Kenneth Katzman, Specialist on Middle Eastern Affairs of the Congressional Research Service, in testimony before the Congressional Joint Economic Committee on July 25, 2006.

32. M. Cist, "Empowering the Iranian Regime," *The Guardian*, July 25, 2008.

33. When the Shah fled Iran for the second time, he and his immediate family left behind assets worth billions of dollars; he also had a huge portfolio of investments abroad.

34. "The Fatal Flaw in Iran's Regime: Corrupt Clerics," *International Herald Tribune*, August 3, 2005.

35. Neil MacFarquhar witnessed one set of riots outside Tehran University where students chanted "death to Khamenei." "Students Roil Iranian Capital in 3rd Night of Protests," *The New York Times*, June 13, 2003.

36. On the 25 Persian-language radio and television stations in Los Angeles and their broadcasts to Iran, see Christopher de Bellaigue, "Getting Iran Wrong," in *The Struggle for Iran* (New York: New York Review Books, 2007), 172.

37. Michael Slackman, "Iran Front-Runner [Rafsanjani] Faces Skepticism and Mockery," *International Herald Tribune*, June 23, 2005; the figure for Ahmadinejad's vote is drawn from Flynt Leverett and Hillary Mann Leverett, ("Ahmadinejad won. Get over it." *Politico*, June 15, 2009). As the dissident Iranian journalist Akbar Ganji has charged, the "moderates" were actually hardliners: "Under Rafsanjani [1989–1997], the Intelligence and Security Ministry routinely assassinated opposition figures in Iran and abroad, and the torture of political prisoners continued unabated. Soon after Khatami was elected, the Intelligence and Security Ministry killed a number of dissidents . . . [and] those of us who wrote about these continuing injustices were thrown in jail."

38. *The Guardian*, June 26, 2006.

39. Robert F. Worth, "A Struggle for the Legacy of the Iranian Revolution," *New York Times*, January 1, 2009 and "Riots expose a rift in Iran that will be hard to heal," June 22, 2009.

40. Flynt Leverett & Hillary Mann Leverett, "Have We Already Lost Iran?" *New York Times*, Op Ed, May, 24, 2009.

41. Simon Tisdall and Ewen MacAskill, "Iran in Turmoil as President's Purge Deepens," *The Guardian*, November 18, 2005.

42. "Cultures clash in Tehran," Op Ed in the *International Herald Tribune*, June 18, 2009.

43. Neil MacFarquhar, "Security forces seen offering unified front," *The International Herald Tribune*, June 24, 2009 and "Crackdown across Iran shows power of new elite," *The International Herald Tribune*, June 26, 2009.

44. Akbar Ganji, "The Latter-Day Sultan," *Foreign Affairs*, November/December 2008, 58.

45. Katherine Butler, "Attack of the clerics threatens Ahmadinejad's election hopes," *Independent*, June 10, 2009, She reports that when Rafsanjani wrote to Ayatollah Khamenei asking him to intervene in the review of the election, he was joined by 14 leading clerics from Qom. On Montazeri see Najmeh Bozorgmehr, "Iran crackdown intensifies," *Financial Times*, June 25, 2009 and Warren P. Strobel and Jonathan S. Landay, "Iran's senior ayatollah slams election, confirming split," *McClatchy Newspapers*, June 16, 2009.

46. Ian Black, "Frail but fierce, Iran's supreme leader Khamenei answers his critics," *The Guardian*, June 19, 2009, "Khamenei made much of how all the candidates came from 'within the system.'"

47. Robert F. Worth, "The Accidental Opposition Leader," *New York Times*, January 19, 2009.

48. Ibid.

49. Esam al-Amin, "What Actually Happened in the Iranian Presidential Election?" *Counterpunch*, June 22, 2009.

50. The Central Bank figure for inflation in 2008 is 23.6 percent and unemployment increased during Ahmadinejad's first term from 10.5 to 17 percent. The International Monetary Fund reports that growth slowed from 8 percent in 2007 to 3.2 percent in 2009. Robert F. Worth, "How is Iran doing? Candidates disagree," *International Herald Tribune*, June 11, 2009.

51. Flynt Leverett and Hillary Mann Leverett, "Ahmadinejad won. Get over it."

52. Robert Tait, "Iran's supreme leader blasts Ahmadinejad for corruption claims," *Guardian*, 4 June 2009.

53. Reported in *Washington Post* article of June 15, 2009.

54. Jon Cohen, "About those Iran Polls," *Washington Post*, June 15, 2009.

55. Renard Sexton, "Polling and Voting in Iran's Friday Election," *FiveThirtyEight: Politics Done Right* (www.fivethirtyeight.com), June 12, 2009.

56. "Bitter rivalry shapes Iran's election," *International Herald Tribune*, June 11, 2009.

57. Juan Cole, "Iran Election Numbers Don't Add Up," *Alternet*, June 14, 2009.

58. Farzad Agah, "Iran's Ayatollah under threat?" *Aljazeera.net*, June 19, 2009. "After the votes have been counted and the winner announced by the interior ministry, the Guardians have the responsibility to endorse the result within 10 days if there are no complains from the defeated candidates."

59. Flynt Leverett, Hillary Mann Leverett and Seyed Mohammad Marandi ("Will Iran be President Obama's Iraq?" June 24, 2009) maintain that: "there is no hard evidence of electoral fraud—which even some Mousavi campaign aides privately acknowledge."

60. Everyone had an opinion. Everyone was an expert. As Esam al-Amin, "What Actually Happened in the Iranian Presidential Election?" wrote, "Since the June 12 Iranian presidential elections, Iran 'experts' have mushroomed like bacteria in a Petri dish." His opinion was that "It is highly unlikely that there was a huge conspiracy involving tens of thousands of teachers, professionals and civil servants that somehow remained totally hidden and unexposed."

61. James Petras, "Iranian Elections: the 'Stolen Elections' Hoax," *Salon*, June 19, 2009, writes that "What is astonishing about the West's universal condemnation of the [Iranian] electoral outcome as fraudulent is that not a single shred of evidence in either written or observational form has been presented either before or a week after the vote count. During the entire electoral campaign, no credible (or even dubious) charge of voter tampering was raised." Professor Juan Cole, a highly respected specialist on Middle Eastern affairs, disagreed in "Iran Election Numbers Don't Add Up." And *The New York Times* columnist, Roger Cohen quoted Ayatollah Hossein Ali Montazeri saying that "no wise person in their right mind can believe" the election result. "City of whispers," *New York Times*, June 20, 2009.

62. Mark Levine, "Iran on the brink?" *Aljazeera.net*, June 17, 2009. "If the official tally was in fact broadly accurate, then they will likely be more willing to agree not just to a recount, but even to a run-off election, if that is what it takes to pacify the angry protesters."

63. Najmeh Bozorgmehr, "Iran reconfirms Ahmadi-Nejad victory," *Financial Times*, June 29, 2009.

64. Peter Popham, "The Ayatollah speaks—and the protesters are warned," *The Independent*, June 20, 2009.

65. "China's Dictators at Work: the Secret Story," a review of *Prisoner of the State: The Secret Journal of Zhao Ziyang, New York Review of Books,* July 2, 2009.
66. Authoritarian Regimes Censor News from Iran," *Washington Post,* June 27, 2009.
67. As Robert Fisk wrote ("Fear has gone in a land that has tasted freedom," *The Independent,* June 17, 2009), "this is not a revolution to overthrow the Islamic Republic."
68. Robert F. Worth & Nazila Fathi, "Ayatollah calls for inquiry into vote result," *International Herald Tribune,* June 16, 2009 and Nazila Fathi and Alan Cowell, "Tehran crowds number hundreds of thousands," *International Herald Tribune,* June 19, 2009.
69. Neil MacFarquhar, "Vigilantes emerge into light of day: shadowy group tracks protesters and begins to demonstrate its power," *International Herald Tribune,* June 21–22, 2009, Nazila Fathi and Alan Cowell, "Iran Guards flex muscle on a day of uncertainty," *International Herald Tribune,* June 23, 2009, Nazila Fathi and Alan Cowell, "Clashes continue in Tehran as leaders hold firm on vote," *International Herald Tribune,* June 25, 2009 and Najmeh Bozorgmehr, "Iran crackdown intensifies," *Financial Times,* June 25, 2009.
70. Roger Cohen, "Iran's children of tomorrow," *International Herald Tribune,* June 23, 2009.
71. Muhammad Sahimi, "Grand Ayatollah Declares 3 Days of National Mourning," *Nieman Reports* (of Harvard University), June 21, 2009.
72. Robert F. Worth and Alan Cowell, "Police use tear gas in new Iran protests," *Global Edition of the New York Times,* July 18, 2009; Ian Black and Saeed Kamali Dehghan, "Clashes in Tehran as Hashemi Rafsanjani warns regime," *Guardian,* July 17, 2009; Najmeh Bozorgmehr, "Rafsanjani says Iran is 'in crisis,'" *Financial Times,* July 17, 2009; "Rafsanjani: Iran in crisis," *Al Jazeera,* July 17, 2009. The government moved to put upward of a hundred protesters, including a former vice-president, a deputy speaker of the *Majles,* and other senior officials on trial, charging them with attacking government installations, creating terror, contact with hostile groups and violence against police and the public, reporting for foreign media, and distributing materials against the "holy regime." *Al Jazeera,* August 1, 2009 and *Haaretz,* August 1, 2009.

CHAPTER SIX: THE UNITED STATES AND IRAN TODAY

1. The papers of the American Board of Commissioners for Foreign Missions are on deposit in the Houghton Library, Harvard University. They consist primarily of letters, of which I have used mainly the earlier ones.
2. The text is given in Yonan Alexander and Allan Nanes, eds., *The United States and Iran: A Documentary History* (Frederick, MD: University Publications of America, 1980), 2ff. This treaty was replaced in 1928 by another, more commercial agreement.
3. Washington, August 20, 1919, Alexander and Nanes, *The United States and Iran,* 23. The following quotation is from Secretary Lansing to Ambassador John Davis in London, dated October 4, 1919. Alexander and Nanes, *The United States and Iran,* 25–27. The reference to Acting Secretary Frank Polk is given in Alexander and Nanes, *The United States and Iran,* 21.
4. Earl Curzon to Sir Percy Cox, 191069/150/34, April 10, 1920; reprinted in Rohan Butler, J. P. T. Bury, and M. E. Lambert, *Documents on British Foreign Policy, 1919–1939, First Series, Volume XIII* (London: HMSO, 1963), 466–467.
5. Roosevelt to Edward Stettinius, Washington, March 10, 1942; Alexander and Nanes, *The United States and Iran,* 91.
6. Jahangir Amuzegar, *Technical Assistance in Theory and Practice: The Case of Iran* (New York: Frederick A. Praeger, 1966), 122. Although I can find no indication of the source

of Roosevelt's remarks, it seems likely that he was picking up from a perceptive analysis of the USSR, Great Britain, and the United States in Iran by John Jeregan dated January 23, 1943. Alexander and Nanes, *The United States and Iran*, 91ff.

7. August 16, 1943; reprinted in Alexander and Nanes, *The United States and Iran*, 103–104.

8. Memorandum of conversation with the Iranian minister by John Jernegan, May 8, 1942; reprinted in Alexander and Nanes, *The United States and Iran*, 108–109, and discussed in James A. Bill, *The Eagle and the Lion* (New Haven: Yale University Press, 1988), 19.

9. Bill, *The Eagle and the Lion*, 39.

10. The State Department announced the first Point Four project in Iran on October 19, 1950. It was described as "an integrated health, agriculture, and education project for improving living conditions in rural villages" and was budgeted at $500,000 for the first year. Alexander and Nanes, *The United States and Iran*, 211–212.

11. This was the gist of President Truman's letter to Prime Minister Mossadegh on July 8, 1951. Truman emphasized "our sympathetic interest in this country in Iran's desire to control its natural resources." Reprinted in Alexander and Nanes, *The United States and Iran*, 218–219.

12. Letter from Prime Minister Mossadegh to President Truman, July 11, 1951; reprinted in Alexander and Nanes, *The United States and Iran*, 219–220.

13. Bill, *The Eagle and the Lion*, 63 and 74, quoting a lecture by Richard Funkhauser, "The Problem of Near Eastern Oil," at the National War College on December 4, 1951.

14. Dean Acheson, *Present at the Creation* (New York: W. W. Norton, 1969), 653.

15. Mark J. Gasiorowski in "The 1953 Coup d'Etat in Iran," *International Journal of Middle Eastern Studies* 19, no. 3 (August 1987): 264. His account is based on Cabinet records, State Department records, and interviews with an unnamed retired MI6 officer who had been in a position to know.

16. Funkhauser, 170; quoted in Bill, *The Eagle and the Lion*, 74.

17. Acheson, *Present at the Creation*, 650.

18. We served together in 1961 on the Policy Planning Council of the U.S. Department of State.

19. The domino metaphor, which would so affect America's view of world affairs and particularly the Greek and Vietnamese insurgencies, was first urged on Winston Churchill in 1945 by South African Prime Minister General Jan Christiaan Smuts. See my book, *Violent Politics* (New York: HarperCollins, 2007 and 2008), 99.

20. Acheson, *Present at the Creation*, 868.

21. Kermit Roosevelt, quoted in an article by Robert Scheer in *The Los Angeles Times*, March 29, 1979; reprinted in Bill, *The Eagle and the Lion*, 85. The Republicans' use of the anticipation of the change of administration was echoed in the 1979–1980 hostage crisis, as I discuss shortly.

22. Woodhouse tells his version of the beginning events in *Something Ventured* (London: Granada, 1982). Kermit Roosevelt tells his version in *Counter Coup: The Struggle for the Control of Iran* (New York: McGraw Hill, 1979). The official and still classified history was written by Donald M. Wilber, *The Overthrow of Premier Mossadeq of Iran, November 1952–August 1953*, as a training manual for CIA officers. Mr. Wilbur's account was turned over to *The New York Times* in 2000 and was summarized by James Risen in an article called "Secrets of History: The C.I.A. in Iran" on April 16, 2000. *The Times* subsequently made it available at http://www.nytimes.com/library/world/mideast/041600 iran-cia=index.html. It has been published as *Regime Change in Iran* (Nottingham, UK: Spokesman, 2006). The episode was also discussed by Mark J. Gasiorowski in "The 1953

Coup d'Etat in Iran," *International Journal of Middle Eastern Studies* 19, no. 3 (August 1987), and in his book, *Mohammad Mosaddeq and the 1953 Coup in Iran* (Syracuse: Syracuse University Press, 2004), and by Stephen Kinzer in *All the Shah's Men* (Hoboken, NJ: John Wiley & Sons, 2003). In addition, I have had the opportunity to discuss the events with a number of Iranians and Americans, including Kermit Roosevelt, and so I could fill in a few points not otherwise known.

23.   His letter is reproduced in Alexander and Nanes, *The United States and Iran*, 231–232.

24.   Mossadegh's letter of May 28, 1953, which he regarded as a reply to Eisenhower's January letter, is reproduced in Alexander and Nanes, *The United States and Iran*, 231–232.

25.   While Roosevelt and I never discussed his role in the coup, I got to know him years later when we served on the board of directors of the Middle East Institute; so I believe I have some judgment of his personality.

26.   Both the most senior Iranian army officer, General Fazollah Zahedi, and the religious leader, Ayatollah Abol-Qasem Kashani, were regarded by the British during the Second World War as pro-German. Ambassador Sir Reader Bullard, *The Camels Must Go* (London: Faber and Faber, 1961), 250. Indeed, Zahedi had been "arrested" and hustled out of Iran by Brigadier Fitzroy Maclean. As Maclean describes him, "Zahedi was known to be one of the worst grain-hoarders in the country [and] secret sources showed that he was planning a general rising against the Allied occupation force." [He was, the British consul said, also] "a man of unpleasant personal habits. . . ." *Eastern Approaches* (London: Jonathan Cape, 1949), 214–215. More immediate and surprising is that it did not bother the American officials that Kashani was known to be intriguing with the communist Tudeh. Gasiorowski gives a list of relevant documents in his article "The 1953 Coup d'Etat in Iran," 281, footnote 28. It was Kashani and Zahedi on whom Roosevelt had to rely.

27.   James Risen, "Secrets of History: The C.I.A. in Iran—A Special Report: How a Plot Convulsed Iran in '53 (and in '79)," *New York Times*, April 16, 2000. "The document shows that the agency had almost complete contempt for the man it was empowering, Shah Mohammed Reza Pahlevi, whom it derided as a vacillating coward."

28.   Gasiorowski, "The 1953 Coup d'Etat in Iran," 261.

29.   The five major American companies claimed the whole American stake, but the group of independent companies demanded in. They lobbied the State Department, arguing that they had gone along with the boycott of Iranian oil and deserved to be paid for their cooperation. The State Department got the majors to reduce their share by 5 percent, which was divided among the independents. The British successor to AIOC (which became known as British Petroleum) got 40 percent, while Shell got 14 percent, and Compagnie Française des Petroles got the final 6 percent.

30.   The State Department's denial is reproduced in Alexander and Nanes, *The United States and Iran*, 315. An internal document written by John Bowling painted a rather different view: that the Shah was hanging onto power with rigged elections and repression. Bowling's appreciation basically agreed with Cuyler Young's. Rostow later told me of Young's letter, but I have read an extract of it only in Bill, *The Eagle and the Lion*, 135.

31.   The Iran Task Force was established in the State Department under the chairmanship of Assistant Secretary for Near Eastern Affairs Philips-Talbot; the White House sent Deputy Director of the National Security Council Robert Komer and Deputy Director of the Bureau of the Budget Kenneth Hansen (who had directed the Ford Foundation advisory group to the Economic Bureau of the Plan Organization), and I represented the Policy Planning Council. About 15 other members were from the Department of Defense, the CIA, AID, the Treasury, and other agencies.

32. The first meeting I had with the Shah was at an Iranian ski lodge. The Shah was not in court uniform and appeared very relaxed. On the way to that meeting, Ambassador Julius Holmes spent the entire time of our drive briefing me on the protocol of our entering and leaving his presence. So insistent was he on form rather than the substance of our discussion that finally the Shah interrupted the ambassador to suggest that he allow us just to talk.

33. It was curious that the Shah repeated this charge often because he arranged that the Pahlavi Foundation give the man in question, Ali Amini, a gift of $2 million, paid in Switzerland on February 5, 1962. The Shah clearly had Amini's number. The transaction was noted in the statement of the Pahlavi Foundation from the Union de Banques Suisse of Geneva and is reproduced in Fred J. Cook, "The Billion Dollar Mystery," *The Nation*, April 12, 1965.

34. I wrote down my remarks and those of the Shah immediately after our meeting, and I believe them to be accurate.

35. Parviz Radji, *In the Service of the Peacock Throne: The Diaries of the Shah's Last Ambassador to London* (London: Hamish Hamilton, 1983), 228. This was not new. The American ambassador reported in 1949 that the Shah's "position amounts to an obsession." In those early days, it was tanks for which as the head of the military mission wrote "the military justification [at] this time [is] non-existent." The two dispatches are reproduced in Alexander and Nanes, *The United States and Iran*, 198 and 199.

36. Statement of Joseph Sisco on June 10, 1975; reproduced in Alexander and Nanes, *The United States and Iran*, 400ff.

37. The agreement, signed on March 5, 1957, called only for support for "civil uses of atomic energy" but also involved provision of technical information that could lead to weapons production." The agreement is reproduced in Alexander and Nanes, *The United States and Iran*, 290ff.

38. "The Nature of Modernization," *Foreign Affairs*, October 1965.

39. Captain Gary Sick, USN (Rtd.), "Failure and Danger in the Gulf," *The New York Times*, July 6, 1988; and Ronald O'Rourke, "Gulf Ops," *Proceedings of the U.S. Naval Institute*, May 1989.

40. *The Boston Globe*, September 16, 1989. Initial accounts of the incident, blaming the pilot, proved to be false, as the ship's commander later admitted. Compensation was offered. *The Boston Globe*, July 22, 1992.

41. Stephen R. Shalom, "The United States and the Iran-Iraq War," http://www.zmag.org/zmag/articles/ShalomIranIraq.html.

42. Sick, "Failure and Danger in the Gulf," 205–216; quotations and comments were during the first days of meetings in the Cabinet, in the NSC, and in the special Crisis Management Committee. One idea discussed involved revoking the visas of the thousands of current and lapsed Iranian students legally or illegally in the United States. Vice President Walter Mondale shot down this suggestion, saying that "it would be folly for a great nation to respond to this kind of situation by 'kicking out a few sad-ass students.'"

43. Sick, "Failure and Danger in the Gulf," 221. From my own experience in the Policy Planning Council and in the White House, I had ample proof of this comment.

44. Gary Sick made an exhaustive study of the necessarily sketchy but surprisingly voluminous materials on what would have been an illegal activity and conducted hundreds of interviews with participants and observers. He published his findings in an op-ed piece in *The New York Times* on April 15, 1991, and subsequently in *October Surprise* (New York: Crown, 1991). Shaul Bakhash, writing long before Sick, takes a different view: He

thought that the Iranians moved because the hostages had served their purpose, quoting the Iranian chief negotiator saying that they were "like a fruit from which all the juice has been squeezed out." He also believed that the Iranians moved so swiftly when Ronald Reagan became president because they were worried that the Republicans might actually attack Iran. (See Shaul Bakhash, *The Reign of the Ayatollahs: Iran and the Islamic Revolution* [London: I. B. Tauris, 1985], 149–150). I find Sick's account persuasive.

45. The Iran-contra affair was the subject of an investigation by independent counsel Lawrence E. Walsh, whose final report was published August 4, 1993, by the U.S. Court of Appeals. Fourteen members of the Reagan administration were indicted, of whom eleven were convicted only to be pardoned during the administration of George H. W. Bush, who was mentioned as a possible participant in the illegal negotiations. Theodore Draper, *A Very Thin Line: The Iran Contra Affairs* (New York: Hill & Wang, 1991), gives somewhat more information on the Iranians involved. They included men who would play major roles in the 2009 elections and riots: Ali Khamenei, Ali Akbar Hashemi Rafsanjani, and Mir Hossein Mousavi. Rafsanjani had been willing to work with the Americans but Mousavi was quoted as saying "negotiations with the United States in the light of its crimes against the Islamic Revolution will never take place."

46. I have dealt with the Iraq issue fully in my book *Understanding Iraq* (New York: HarperCollins, 2005 and 2006) and in the book I wrote with Senator George McGovern, *Out of Iraq: A Practical Plan for Withdrawal Now* (New York: Simon & Schuster, 2006), so I will not duplicate here materials that are available there.

47. Karim Sadjadpour's *Reading Khamenei: The World View of Iran's Most Powerful Leader* (Washington, DC: The Carnegie Endowment for International Peace, 2008) is an excellent analytical biography of Ayatollah Ali Khamenei.

48. Meeting with Paul Wolfowitz and a team of his advisers, then Secretary of Defense Donald Rumsfeld was heard to say, "Link Iraq to Iran. Iran is the concern." David Barstow, "Behind Analysts, the Pentagon's Hidden Hand," *The New York Times*, April 20, 2008. For further information, see William R. Polk, *Violent Politics* (New York: HarperCollins, 2007 and 2008), 202ff.

49. I have discussed the neoconservatives and their programs in more detail in a series of essays that are available on my Web site, www.williampolk.com.

50. See, for example, Norman Podhoretz's article "Stopping Iran: Why the Case for Military Action Still Stands," *Commentary*, February 2009.

51. Max Rodenbeck, "The Iran Mystery Case," *The New York Review of Books*, January 15, 2009.

52. Flynt Leverett and Hillary Mann Leverett, "Opportunity Knocked," *National Interest Online*, July 23, 2008.

53. Antonio Maria Costa, "The New Golden Triangle," *International Herald Tribune*, December 1, 2006. "Iran has deployed almost 20,000 antinarcotic police and border guards along its 1,845 kilometer border with Afghanistan and Pakistan—the world's most active opium smuggling route. Twenty-eight mountain passes have been blocked by huge concrete structures. Hundreds of kilometers of trenches—four meters wide and four meters deep—have been dug to stop drug caravans eluding patrols. Towers and barbed wire stretch as far as the eyes can see."

54. Who coined the phrase is disputed. Both David Frum and Michael Gerson claimed credit.

55. Personal communication.

56. Guy Dinmore, "US Stalls over Iran Talks Offer," *Financial Times*, March 17, 2004.

57. Julian Borger, "Soft-Spoken Line from Washington May Terrify Tehran," *The Guardian,* January 29, 2009. "While mixed messages emanated from the Bush administration, only one was clearly received in Tehran—that Iran was next on the Axis of Evil list after Iraq. . . . The lesson of the Iraq invasion for the Iranian leadership was that Saddam lost his job and then his life not because he might have had weapons of mass destruction but because he had none. North Korea, the third member of the axis, which had nuclear bombs, was treated with much greater respect." Also see James Fallows, "Will Iran Be Next?" *Atlantic Monthly,* December 2004.

58. Brian Jones, "Nuclear Blindness," *The London Review of Books,* June 22, 2006. Also see James Fallows, "Will Iran Be Next?"

59. Former President Jimmy Carter, "India Deal Puts World at Risk," *International Herald Tribune,* September 12, 2008; and Peter Baker, "Congress Approves U.S. Nuclear Trade with India," *International Herald Tribune,* October 3, 2008.

60. It is unusual for an NIE to be published. Since this one undercut the policies of the Bush administration, publication was particularly surprising. William Pfaff wrote on his Web site on December 5, 2007, that the NIE was delayed for some months and that there was a "ferocious battle to change or suppress it . . . by the president's and Dick Cheney's men, as well as by the surviving neo-conservatives in the policy apparatus."

61. Issued by the Office of the Director of National Intelligence (DNI). The report contradicted some aspects of a May 2005 NIE on Iran's nuclear program. The fact that the DNI decided to publish the NIE seemed to indicate a growing worry by the intelligence agencies that the United States was sliding toward war with Iran.

62. William M. Arkin, "The Pentagon Preps for Iran," *The Washington Post,* April 16, 2007.

63. Sarah Baxter, "Pentagon 'Three-Day Blitz' Plan for Iran," *The Sunday Times,* September 2, 2007.

64. Thomas McInerney, "Target Iran," *The Weekly Standard,* April 26, 2006.

65. Trita Parsi, "Israel Is Bluffing . . . ," *AlterNet, Huffington Post,* April 13, 2009.

66. Tariq Ali, "Why Has the US Manufactured a Crisis over Iran?" *The Guardian,* May 4, 2006.

67. "US Strike Group Transits Suez Canal," *The Jerusalem Post,* January 30, 2007. "A 7 ship group with 2,200 Marines and sailors led by the assault ship USS *Bataan* is on the way to the Gulf where the US 5th fleet was comprised of 50 warships before this new group arrived. The aircraft carrier USS *Stennis* is joining the *Eisenhower* and the *Bataan* will join the other amphibious assault ship, the USS *Boxer,* which is already there."

68. Seymour Hersh, "Preparing the Battlefield," *The New Yorker,* July 7 and 14, 2008.

69. Dafna Linzer, "U.S. Uses Drones to Probe Iran for Arms," *International Herald Tribune,* February 13, 2005.

70. David E. Sanger, "U.S. Rejected Aid for Israeli Raid on Iranian Nuclear Site," *The New York Times,* January 10, 2009.

71. Seymour Hersh, "Last Stand," *The New Yorker,* July 10 and 17, 2009.

72. Hersh, "Last Stand."

73. "From News Reports," *International Herald Tribune,* August 18, 2006. "Twenty-two former high-ranking military officers and retired diplomats urged President George W. Bush on Thursday to open discussions immediately. . . ."

74. Gareth Porter, "Dissenting Views Made Fallon's Fall Inevitable," *IPS,* March 11, 2008. Admiral Fallon was quoted as saying, "There are several of us trying to put the crazies back in the box." That was an apparent reference to the opposition of the Joint Chiefs of Staff to an attack on Iran. A long interview and article on him appeared in Thomas Barnett, "The Man between War and Peace," *Esquire,* March–April 2008.

75.   Maya Schenwar, "In Reversal Democrats Shelve Iran Resolution," *Truthout*, October 9, 2008.

76.   "Iran Returns to the Global Stage," *Stratfor*, November 10, 2008.

77.   *Haaretz*, September 14, 2008.

78.   Colonel Sam Gardiner, USAF (Rtd.), "The End of the 'Summer of Diplomacy,'" The Century Foundation, 2006.

79.   *The Sunday Times*, January 7, 2007.

80.   Michael Gordon and Eric Schmitt, "An Israeli Dry Run for Raid against Iran?" *International Herald Tribune*, June 21–22, 2008. More than a hundred F–16i and F–15i fighter-bombers participated over the eastern Mediterranean and Greece, flying the exact range of flight to the Natanz nuclear facility, 1,400 kilometers (868 miles).

81.   Jonathan Steel, "Israel Asked US for Green Light to Bomb Nuclear Sites in Iran," *The Guardian*, September 27, 2008. "Israel gave serious thought this spring to launching a military strike on Iran's nuclear sites but was told by President George W. Bush that he would not support it."

82.   Trita Parsi, "Israel Is Bluffing: Constant War Threats against Iran Are Empty, but Still Dangerous," *Huffington Post, Alternet*, April 13, 2009. "Netanyahu's tough talk undermines the Obama administration's prospects for diplomacy. . . . [I]t fuels Iranian insecurity and closes the window for diplomacy."

83.   Sheera Frenkel, "Israel Stands Ready to Bomb Iran's Nuclear Sites," *The Times*, April 18, 2009.

84.   Thom Shanker, "Security Council Votes to Tighten Iran Sanctions," *New York Times*, March 25, 2007.

85.   Nicholas D. Kristof, "Diplomacy at Its Worst," *The New York Times*, April 29, 2007; and Nicholas D. Kristof, "Hang Up, Tehran Is Calling." *The New York Times*, January 22, 2007.

86.   Ian Black, "Mail Bonding," *The Guardian*, November 8, 2008.

87.   "The Chairman of 'the Guardian Council,' Ayatollah Ahmad Janati, Denounced Attempts to Rapprochement with the US," *The Guardian*, January 29, 2009.

88.   Roger Cohen, "From Tehran to Tel Aviv," *The New York Times*, March 23, 2009. President Obama's *No Ruz* message was preceded by Vice President Joe Biden's address at the February 7, 2009, Munich Security Conference (Ian Traynor, "Obama Administration Offers Olive Branch to Russia and Iran," *The Guardian*, February 7, 2009) and was followed by Secretary of Defense Robert Gates' April 16, 2009, speech before Marine Corps students (Paul Richter, "Gates Warns against Israeli Strike on Iran's Nuclear Facilities," *Los Angeles Times*, April 16, 2009).

89.   Obama's message was received with relief by virtually the entire world media. See *The Financial Times, The Guardian, The New York Times, The Washington Post, Le Monde,* and *Frankfurter Allgemeine Zeitung* of March 21 and 22, 2009. *The Jerusalem Post* was cautious, and *The Weekly Standard* of March 20 was dismissive.

90.   Associated Press, "Khamenei Responds to Obama with Tough Talk," *International Herald Tribune*, March 23, 2009.

AFTERWORD

1.   As former Secretary of Defense Robert McNamara found years later ("Apocalypse Soon," *Foreign Policy*, May–June 2005), the commanders of the four Soviet nuclear submarines then trailing the U.S. fleet had authorization to fire their nuclear-armed torpedoes without recourse to Moscow. Being out of touch with their headquarters, they continued to

patrol for four days after Khrushchev had announced the withdrawal and the crisis had ended. None of us in the American government knew that at the time.

2. He was not overthrown, but after his death he was "downgraded" and not buried at the Kremlin Wall as were other leaders.

3. Charles W. Nass and Henry Precht, "Shining a Light into the Darkness of Iranian-U.S. Relations," *The Washington Report on Middle Eastern Affairs,* April 2003. Nass was the State Department country director for Iran from 1975 to 1978 and chargé at the American embassy in Tehran during the revolution; Precht served in the embassy before the revolution and then was the country director at the State Department.

4. Roger Cohen, "Iran Is Job One," *International Herald Tribune,* October 23, 2008.

5. Julian Borger, "Iran Opens New Naval Base at Mouth of Persian Gulf," *The Guardian,* October 29, 2008. "Iranian naval doctrine is focused on asymmetric attacks against western navies using swarms of small high-speed fibreglass boats armed with anti-ship missiles . . . [relying] on strength in numbers and surprise, calling it a 'presence everywhere and nowhere doctrine.'" And according to Seymour Hersh ("Last Stand," *The New Yorker,* July 10 and 17, 2006), American Naval Intelligence found that "Iran has more than seven hundred undeclared dock and port facilities along its Persian Gulf coast." The Japanese kamikazes killed about five thousand Americans.

6. Arnaud de Borchgrave, "Gulf War Jitters," UPI, April 15, 2009. Even Israel's moderate President Shimon Peres was quoted as saying that if forthcoming talks with Iran didn't yield results, "we'll strike."

7. William J. Broad and David E. Sanger, "Meeting on Arms Data Reignites Iran Nuclear Debate," *The New York Times,* March 3, 2008.

8. International Institute for Strategic Studies, "Nuclear Iran: How Close Is It?" vol. 13, no. 7, September 2007. Gary Milhollin (*International Herald Tribune,* September 29, 2008) believes that Iran could already have produced (by January 2009) enough weapons-grade uranium, 35 pounds, for its first bomb and two more by February 2020. Thom Shanker ("Iran One Step Closer to Bomb, U.S. Says," *International Herald Tribune,* March 2, 2009) quotes the chairman of the Joint Chiefs of Staff as reporting that "Iran has amassed enough fissile material to build an atomic bomb," but Secretary of Defense Gates told NBC News that "[t]hey're not close to a weapon at this point."

9. Trita Parsi, "Reading Solana in Tehran," *IPS,* July 7, 2008. "Conciliatory noises from Tehran over the nuclear issue have left Washington and Brussels baffled." Also see Scott Ritter, *Target Iran* (New York: Nation Books, 2006); David Sanger, "Is Tehran Ready to Talk?" *International Herald Tribune,* February 10, 2009; editorial, "Iran's Scientists Are Working Aggressively to Master Nuclear Fuel Production—the Hardest Part of Building a Weapon," *International Herald Tribune,* February 11, 2009. But, as the director of national intelligence and head of the Defense Intelligence Agency testified before the Senate Arms Services Committee on March 11, 2009, "Iran does not have any highly enriched uranium, the fuel used to power a nuclear warhead." *The New York Times,* March 11, 2009.

10. It was apparently after George Bush labeled North Korea a part of the Axis of Evil that it moved to turn its uranium into a usable bomb.

11. Christoph Bertram, "For a New Iran Policy," *Center for European Reform Bulletin,* April–May 2008. "Sanctions will not work." Bertram was director of the International Institute for Strategic Studies and the German Institute for International Security Affairs.

12. Seymour Hersh, "Last Stand," *The New Yorker,* July 10 and 17, 2006, quoting Major Generals Paul Eaton and Charles Swannack Jr.

13.   Department of Defense, "The National Defense Strategy of the United States of America," March 2005. Another version came out the following year. The June 2008 version was signed by the current Secretary of Defense, Robert Gates. It reaffirmed that "the United States will, if necessary, act preemptively in exercising its right of self-defense to forestall or prevent hostile acts by our adversaries," among which it listed Iran.

14.   William J. Broad and David E. Sanger, "Eye on Iran, Rivals Pursuing Nuclear Power," *The New York Times*, April 15, 2007. "Two year ago, the leaders of Saudi Arabia told international atomic regulators that they could foresee no need for the kingdom to develop nuclear power. Today, they are scrambling to hire atomic contractors, buy nuclear hardware and build support a regional system or reactors."

15.   For example, see the proposal of William Luers, Thomas Pickering, and Jim Walsh in "A Solution for the US-Iran Nuclear Standoff," *New York Review of Books*, March 20, 2008. "We propose that Iran's efforts to produce enriched uranium and other related nuclear activities be conducted on a multilateral basis, that is to say jointly managed and operated on Iranian soil by a consortium including Iran and other governments." Also see their subsequent article in the February 12, 2009, issue of the same journal.

16.   Karim Sadjadpour, *Reading Khamanei: The World View of Iran's Most Powerful Leader* (Washington, DC: The Carnegie Endowment for International Peace, 2008), 11.

17.   Tariq Ali, "Why Has US Manufactured a Crisis over Iran?" *The Guardian*, May 4, 2006; and Shayerah Ilias, "Iran's Economic Conditions: U.S. Policy Issues," Congressional Research Service, January 15, 2009.

18.   Associated Press, "Iranian President Welcomes 'Honest' Talks with U.S.," *The New York Times*, April 8, 2009.

19.   Roger Cohen, "A U.S.-Iranian Conversation," *The International Herald Tribune*, December 11, 2008. In the article, Cohen describes Iranian and American cooperation in the Organization for the Prohibition of Chemical Weapons.

INDEX